Godot 4 Best Practices

Practical techniques and strategies for efficient, scalable game development

Robert Henning

<packt>

Godot 4 Best Practices

Portfolio Director: Rohit Rajkumar
Relationship Lead: Neha Pande
Program Manager: Sandip Tadge
Content Engineer: Shreya Sarkar
Technical Editor: Sumant Jadhav, Tejas Mhasvekar
Indexer: Pratik Shirodkar
Proofreader: Shreya Sarkar
Production Designer: Shankar Kalbhor
Growth Lead: Namita Velgekar

First published: June 2026

Production reference: 1240626

Published by Packt Publishing Ltd.
Grosvenor House
11 St Paul's Square
Birmingham
B3 1RB, UK.

ISBN 978-1-83546-511-0
www.packtpub.com

This book is for the Godot community. Dedicated to the indie developers, the tinkerers, and the creators driving the future of open-source game development. Let's keep building, sharing, and growing together.

– Robert Henning

Foreword

It's never been easier to make games.

The Godot game engine is going from strength to strength, and new game developers are starting their journey with it every day. The barrier to entry has never been lower. The tools are free, the community is generous, and the first prototype can come together in an afternoon. That accessibility is a wonderful thing, but the gap between starting projects and finishing projects is where most games quietly disappear.

It's rarely a lack of ideas that sinks a project. More often, it's the slow accumulation of tangled code where a single change in one place breaks things somewhere else. Before you know it, the codebase becomes so fragile that you're afraid to touch anything. Building on a foundation of good architecture means you're less likely to hit a wall along the way. The patterns in this book are more than just academic exercises. They're the practical habits that let a project keep growing without collapsing under its own weight. Behind most of your favourite games, you'll find the same principles mentioned in this book, quietly doing their work where players will never see them.

What I appreciate most about Robert is that he never loses sight of the goal, and his lessons are useful to both newcomers and veterans alike. He shares clear ways of thinking that help you make informed choices rather than rigid rules that slow you down. The right structure is ultimately the one that you understand, and that lets you finish your game.

When mentoring other software engineers, I always tell them that a clean structure is an act of kindness towards their future self. The version of you who returns to this part of the project in six months will either praise you or curse you, depending on the decisions you make today. This book will help you make decisions your future self will thank you for.

So, enjoy the journey, and I look forward to playing your shipped games.

Nathan Hoad

Founder of Little Nebula and Creator of the Godot Dialogue Manager

Contributors

About the author

Robert Henning brings over two decades of computer science education experience to his writing, with a specialized focus on game development. A consistent advocate for the Godot engine since its early iterations, he has taught programming and game design using a wide array of tools and languages. Robert also runs the educational YouTube channel **GameDev Journey** and its companion website, providing accessible tutorials for developers of all skill levels. Building on the foundation of *Godot 4 for Beginners*, his latest work, *Godot 4 Best Practices*, shifts the focus toward robust architecture, scalable data management, and professional workflows.

Thank you to my family for your endless inspiration and support. That makes two books complete—dare we aim for a third?

About the reviewers

Luca Leonardi, known online as LuxeL, is a game developer with a background in both game and web development, specializing in gameplay programming, UX/UI design, and independent game production. He has developed and published projects across web and mobile platforms, including *Zook Adventure* and *Sbaloon*, primarily using the Godot Engine.

With experience spanning programming, design, visual art, and music, he approaches development from an interdisciplinary perspective. His work focuses on understanding how requirements, game design, user experience, and technical implementation connect throughout the development process, from early concept and planning to production and release.

Passionate about technology, creativity, and the natural world, he enjoys experimenting with new tools, workflows, and ideas. His broad cross-disciplinary experience enables him to bridge creative vision and practical execution, helping transform complex requirements into cohesive and engaging interactive experiences.

Jakob Herlitz is the lead developer and co-founder of a two-person Seattle-based indie game development studio, **autotroph games**. At the time of writing, the studio's debut game, *Haunted Heist*, has been in development for under a year and has landed a spot within Steam's top 1000 most-wishlisted games. What began as a project by two best friends to build an entertaining game for Jakob, his three brothers, and co-founder Dominic Giardini to play during weekly gaming sessions has become Jakob's full-time job. After 6 years of professional experience in the software engineering industry, working for big tech companies and startups alike, Jakob quit his job to work full-time on *Haunted Heist*. The game is, of course, built using the Godot Engine.

Thank you to the team at Packt for trusting me as a technical reviewer. Working with this team has helped uplevel my own knowledge, and it is my genuine hope that the book reaches the eyes of other developers interested in building games in the Godot Engine.

Table of Contents

Chapter 4: When Not to Use Nodes 87

Chapter 6: Applying Event-Driven Patterns 137

Chapter 7: Implementing State and Strategy Patterns 169

Preface

Game development in Godot is incredibly accessible, making it easy to rapidly build fun, functional prototypes. However, every scalable game starts with a rock-solid foundation. Moving from a hobbyist experiment to a commercial release requires more than just good gameplay; it requires tackling the core architectural decisions that separate messy prototypes from professional codebases.

As a computer science educator and developer, I have seen countless projects collapse under the weight of their own spaghetti code. As systems grow, adding a simple new feature can suddenly break three others. This book, *Godot 4 Best Practices,* is designed to stop project rot before it begins. We will start by demystifying the SOLID principles within the specific context of Godot and explore the engine's unique structural philosophies. You will discover the best practices for organizing scenes, determining the exact right moments to use scripts over nodes, and learning when to step outside Godot's node system entirely for maximum performance.

Once the foundation is set, we will dive deeply into industry-standard design patterns translated specifically for Godot's idiomatic architecture. We will focus on untangling messy dependencies and creating flexible, modular gameplay mechanics. Finally, the book shifts focus toward how your game generates objects and handles complex information under the hood. We will explore advanced creational patterns, data management using custom Godot Resources, and how to take your project outside the engine by building secure modding pipelines.

In writing this book, my goal is to share practical, road-tested strategies that will give you the confidence to architect complex, future-proof projects without tangling your codebase.

Who this book is for

This book is for intermediate and advanced Godot developers, indie studio teams, technical leads, educators, advanced students, and hobbyists looking to make the jump to commercial software development. If you know how to make a player move and shoot, but struggle with organizing your project as it scales, or have ever struggled with messy prototypes, monolithic scripts, or an unscalable Scene Tree, this book is for you. A basic understanding of the Godot 4 editor and GDScript fundamentals is required to get the most out of these architectural lessons.

What this book covers

Chapter 1, Applying SOLID Principles in Godot, demystifies the SOLID principles within the specific context of Godot to establish a professional mindset.

Chapter 2, Deciding Between Scenes and Scripts, explores the engine's unique structural philosophies, teaching you the exact right moments to use scripts over nodes.

Chapter 3, Organizing Scenes for Scalability, details the best practices for organizing scenes so you can architect complex, future-proof projects.

Chapter 4, When Not to Use Nodes, teaches you when to step outside Godot's node system entirely for maximum performance.

Chapter 5, Using Autoloads and Singletons, demonstrates how to implement global orchestration using Autoloads to safely untangle messy dependencies.

Chapter 6, Applying Event-Driven Patterns, explains how to establish asynchronous event-driven communications with signals for modular gameplay mechanics.

Chapter 7, Implementing State and Strategy Patterns, provides the exact design patterns needed to build robust state machines for complex entity behaviors.

Chapter 8, Creating Component-Based Systems, explores how to construct modular, component-based actor systems to turn rigid prototypes into fluid, maintainable games.

Chapter 9, Using Factory and Builder Patterns, explores advanced creational patterns to automate complex scene instancing.

Chapter 10, Applying Command and Service Patterns, shows how to configure gameplay systems dynamically at runtime.

Chapter 11, Adopting Data-Driven Design, details how to separate configuration data from execution logic using custom Godot Resources.

Chapter 12, Structuring Gameplay Logic, teaches you how to build a secure, zero-trust modding pipeline capable of safely validating and parsing external data files.

To get the most out of this book

To successfully follow along with the architectural patterns in this book, you will need to have **Godot Engine 4** installed on your computer (preferably version 4.7). You should already be comfortable navigating the Godot editor, creating basic scenes, and writing standard GDScript logic (variables, functions, loops, and signals).

While no advanced math is required, a foundational understanding of Object-Oriented Programming concepts will be highly beneficial.

Software/hardware covered in the book	OS requirements
Godot Engine 4.7	Windows, macOS, or Linux

If you are using the digital version of this book, we advise you to type the code yourself or access the code via the GitHub repository (see the next section for access instructions). Doing so will help you avoid any potential errors related to the copying and pasting of code.

Note that the author acknowledges the use of cutting-edge AI, such as ChatGPT, with the sole aim of enhancing the language and clarity within the book, thereby ensuring a smooth reading experience for readers. It's important to note that the content itself has been crafted by the author and edited by a professional publishing team. Packt does not accept AI-generated content that replaces expert authorship.

Download the example code files

This book includes a complete downloadable code bundle containing all the example projects and files used throughout the chapters. We recommend downloading the bundle so you can follow along smoothly and experiment with the examples.

Use the bundle as a practical starting point. Modify it, extend it, and apply what you learn by creating your own variations as you progress through the chapters.

Get the code bundle

If you bought the book directly from Packt:

1. Go to `packtpub.com`.
2. Click your profile picture and select **Your Orders**.
3. Find this book and click **Download Code**.

If you bought this book from Amazon or any other channel partner:

1. Go to `packtpub.com/unlock` or scan the following QR code:
2. Search for this book.
3. Sign up or log in to your free Packt account.
4. Upload your proof of purchase and download the code bundle locally.

Usage note: You're free to use and modify this code for personal learning and non-commercial projects. The GitHub repository is organized by chapter, with each chapter's code contained in its own folder.

We also have other code bundles from our rich catalog of books and videos available at `https://github.com/PacktPublishing/`. Check them out!

Download the color images

Your purchase includes a color, DRM-free PDF copy of this book, ideal for viewing color images, screenshots, and diagrams. Refer to the *Free benefits with your book* section at the end of the *Preface* to unlock your PDF copy.

Conventions used

There are a number of text conventions used throughout this book.

`CodeInText`: Indicates code words in text, database table names, folder names, filenames, file extensions, pathnames, dummy URLs, user input, and Twitter handles. For example: "Attach a script to it named `hitbox_component.gd`:"

A block of code is set as follows:

```
class_name HitboxComponent extends Area2D

signal hit_received(damage_amount: float)

func damage(amount: float) -> void:
    hit_received.emit(amount)
```

Bold: Indicates a new term, an important word, or words that you see onscreen. For example, words in menus or dialog boxes appear in the text like this. Here is an example: "This is a powerful Godot feature: it means you can now open the **Add Node** menu in any scene, search for your new class by name, and add it just like a built-in node (such as a **Timer** or **Sprite2D**)."

> **Note**
>
> Warnings or important notes appear like this.

> **Tip**
>
> Tips and tricks appear like this.

Get in touch

Feedback from our readers is always welcome.

General feedback: If you have questions about any aspect of this book or have any general feedback, please email us at `customercare@packt.com` and mention the book's title in the subject of your message.

Errata: Although we have taken every care to ensure the accuracy of our content, mistakes do happen. If you have found a mistake in this book, we would be grateful if you reported this to us. Please visit `http://www.packt.com/submit-errata`, click **Submit Errata**, and fill in the form.

Piracy: If you come across any illegal copies of our works in any form on the internet, we would be grateful if you would provide us with the location address or website name. Please contact us at `copyright@packt.com` with a link to the material.

If you are interested in becoming an author: If there is a topic that you have expertise in and you are interested in either writing or contributing to a book, please visit `http://authors.packt.com/`.

Subscribe to Game Dev Assembly Newsletter!

We are excited to introduce **Game Dev Assembly**, our brand-new newsletter dedicated to everything game development. Whether you're a programmer, designer, artist, animator, or studio lead, you'll get exclusive insights, industry trends, and expert tips to help you build better games and grow your skills. Sign up today and become part of a growing community of creators, innovators, and game changers.

Scan the QR code to join instantly!

https://packt.link/gamedev-newsletter

Free benefits with your book

This book includes free benefits designed to support your learning and help you apply what you learn effectively. Activate them now for instant access (see the *How to unlock* section for instructions).

Here's a quick overview of what you can instantly unlock with your purchase:

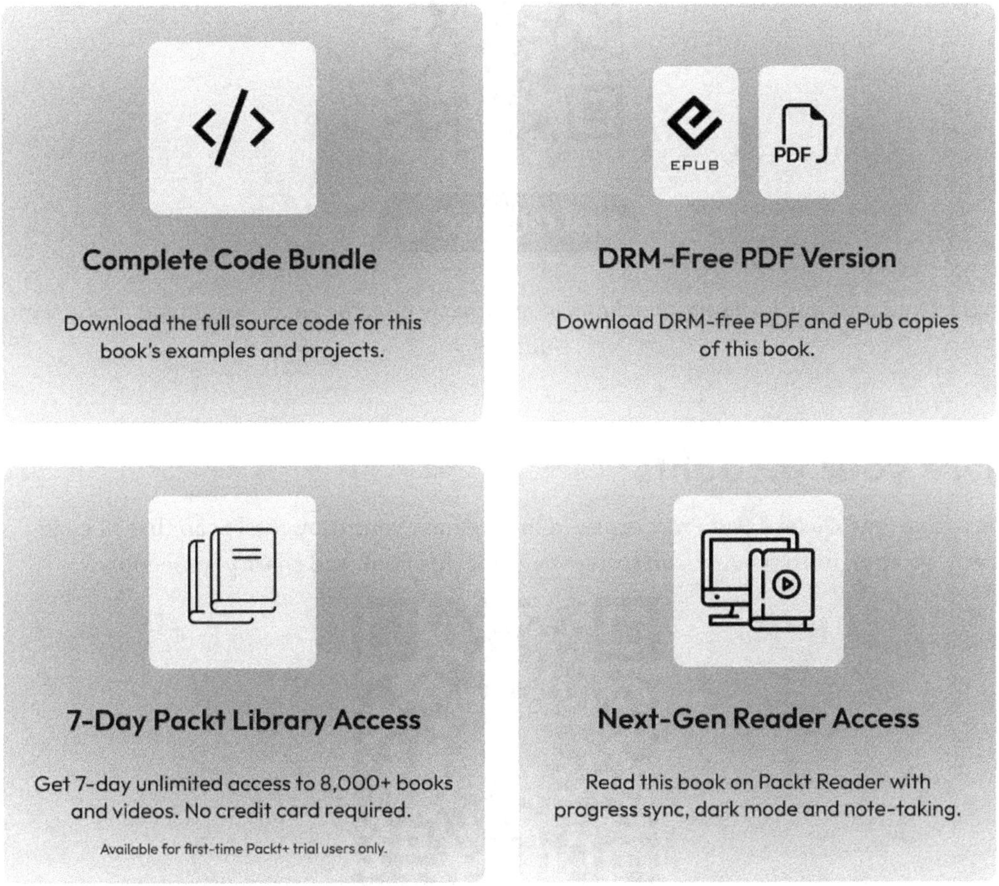

How to unlock

Scan the QR code (or go to `packtpub.com/unlock`). Search for this book by name, confirm the edition, and then follow the steps on the page.

UNLOCK NOW

Note: Have your invoice handy. Purchases made directly from the Packt website don't require an invoice.

Share your thoughts

Once you've read *Godot 4 Best Practices*, we'd love to hear your thoughts! Scan the QR code below to go straight to the Amazon review page for this book and share your feedback.

https://packt.link/r/1835465110

Your review is important to us and the tech community and will help us make sure we're delivering excellent quality content.

Part 1

Professional Foundations in Godot

Every scalable game starts with a rock-solid foundation. In this opening part of the book, we will tackle the core architectural decisions that separate messy prototypes from professional codebases. We will demystify the SOLID principles within the specific context of Godot and explore the engine's unique structural philosophies. You will discover the best practices for organizing scenes, determining the exact right moments to use scripts over nodes, and learning when to step outside Godot's node system entirely for maximum performance.

By the end of these four chapters, you will have the confidence to architect complex, future-proof projects without tangling your codebase.

This part of the book includes the following chapters:

- *Chapter 1, Applying SOLID Principles in Godot*
- *Chapter 2, Deciding Between Scenes and Scripts*
- *Chapter 3, Organizing Scenes for Scalability*
- *Chapter 4, When Not to Use Nodes*

1

Applying SOLID Principles in Godot

Welcome to *Godot 4 Best Practices*. I hope that you enjoy it and learn a lot that you can apply daily in your game development. There are many resources that will teach you the syntax of GDScript or how to navigate the editor, but fewer discuss the architecture required to build a game that lasts.

This book seeks to address the critical challenge facing intermediate developers, which is moving from a functional prototype to a scalable and production-ready project. By concentrating on proven design patterns, structural workflows, and Godot-specific strategies, we will explore how to write code that is not just functional, but also clean, modular, and maintainable. This will ensure that your project doesn't collapse under its own weight as it grows.

This chapter introduces how the five **SOLID principles** of object-oriented design, which are Single Responsibility, Open-Closed, Liskov Substitution, Interface Segregation, and Dependency Inversion, can be applied in the context of the Godot Engine. While many factors contribute to a game's commercial success, countless Godot projects are abandoned mid-development, not because of a lack of ideas, but because of a lack of structural discipline, which makes the codebase impossible to maintain. By mastering SOLID principles first, you develop the mental model for organizing nodes, scripts, and resources. These principles are not just abstract rules; they are the antidote to the "spaghetti code" that infects growing projects. Understanding them now provides the foundation for every specific pattern, workflow, and optimization strategy we will discuss in the rest of this book.

Godot uses a node-based scene system rather than the traditional class hierarchy, and so we will explore how the underlying principles of clean, modular, and maintainable code still apply. You will learn how to refactor common "spaghetti" code structures into clear, scalable systems by applying these five SOLID principles.

In this chapter, we're going to cover the following main topics:

- What SOLID is and why it matters in game development
- Understanding SOLID in the Godot context
- Designing extensible gameplay systems
- Moving from theory to practice
- Organizing for scalability – feature-based structure

By the end of the chapter, you will have a solid architectural foundation for building scalable Godot games. You will be able to refactor messy, monolithic scripts into clean, modular components and apply industry-standard patterns to prevent your code from becoming brittle.

You will also understand how to leverage Godot-specific features, such as signals, Resources, and Exports, to decouple your systems. This will allow you to create a codebase that is easy to test, safe to extend, and ready for team collaboration.

> Note
>
> **Your purchase includes a free PDF copy + code bundle**
>
> Your purchase includes a DRM-free PDF copy of this book, the code bundle, and additional exclusive extras. See the *Free benefits with your book* section in the *Preface* to unlock them instantly and maximize your learning.

Technical requirements

Readers should be familiar with basic Godot workflows, such as navigating the editor, creating scenes, and scripting with GDScript.

You can download the example project and code for this book by following the instructions in the *Download the example code files* section in the *Preface* of this book.

This chapter's code files are included in the downloadable code bundle.

What SOLID is and why it matters in game development

SOLID is an acronym for the following five principles of object-oriented programming:

- **S – Single Responsibility Principle (SRP)**: A script should have only one reason to change. It should do one thing and do it well.
- **O – Open/Closed Principle (OCP)**: You should be able to add new features without rewriting existing code.
- **L – Liskov Substitution Principle (LSP)**: A subclass must work anywhere its parent class is expected.
- **I – Interface Segregation Principle (ISP)**: Don't force a class to carry tools it doesn't need, keep your interfaces small and specific.
- **D – Dependency Inversion Principle (DIP)**: High-level logic should not depend on low-level details. Both should connect via abstractions or signals.

By following these principles, your code will be cleaner, more maintainable, and scalable. SOLID principles represent a paradigm shift in your development, moving from just making it work to building game systems that are flexible, professional, and ready for long-term growth. This reinforces the primary goal of SOLID, which is to create software that is more *understandable*, *flexible*, *maintainable*, *scalable*, and *testable* by reducing dependencies and making code more *modular*.

It is important to understand that these are design principles, not rigid laws. Programming is ultimately an art form, and there is no single *right* way to structure a project. The *right* way is simply the one that you understand, and that allows you to complete your game. While SOLID principles are powerful tools to help you get there, for instance, by keeping classes small and easy to debug, you must not get paralyzed by attempting to follow a perfect rule set. Use them to guide your decisions, not to dictate them.

Understanding SOLID in the Godot context

The Godot Engine has two primary ways of creating reusable objects: **scripts** and **scenes**. Although they are not technically *classes*, it helps to think of them as classes because they let you define objects with their own data and behavior. This is a key mental model because it means that the structural problems you face in Godot, such as tight coupling or bloated code, are object-oriented design problems. So, the solution is to apply OOP principles directly to your nodes and Scene Trees. By treating a scene as a class, we can apply the SOLID principles to ensure that our scenes have a single responsibility, are open for extension, and communicate through abstractions rather than rigid dependencies.

Godot foundations relevant to SOLID

To apply SOLID principles effectively in Godot, we must view the engine's core mechanics through an architectural lens. Unlike traditional object-oriented languages, where a single class file defines an object's entire data, behavior, and structure, Godot separates these concerns. Its two primary building blocks, **scripts** (*logic*) and **scenes** (*structure*), work together to provide the functional equivalents of inheritance and composition required for robust object-oriented design.

Let's gain a better understanding of this:

- **Scripts (inheritance and contracts)**: When you attach a script to a node, you are extending a built-in class and registering a new definition in the **ClassDB**. This registration creates the *contract* that allows other objects to interact with your code safely. This mechanism is the foundation of the Liskov Substitution Principle and Open/Closed Principle, which we'll cover later in the chapter. By extending `Node`, you create specialized behaviors that fulfill the contracts of their parent classes without modifying the engine's core logic.
- **Scenes (composition and encapsulation)**: If scripts handle inheritance, scenes handle composition. A scene is essentially a prefabricated object composed of multiple nodes and signals. This supports the Single Responsibility Principle by allowing you to build complex entities (like a Player) out of smaller, single-purpose scenes (like a `HealthBar`, `HitBox`, or `Inventory`). By pairing a script (*logic*) with a scene (*structure*), you achieve encapsulation, ensuring that the internal complexity of an object is hidden from the rest of your codebase.

Consequently, when we pair a scene (structure) with a script (behavior), we create a complete blueprint for instantiating objects. Because this blueprint fills the same role as a traditional class, we can directly apply object-oriented design principles to organize them.

Applying Single Responsibility in Godot nodes

A script should do one thing and do it well. Consider a kitchen tool that tries to be a knife, a spoon, a bottle opener, and a blender all at once. It does everything poorly and is dangerous to use. A professional chef prefers a dedicated knife because it is reliable and easy to sharpen. In Godot, your `Player` script should handle input and movement, but it should not be responsible for calculating the score, managing the UI, or saving the game to a file. If a script handles both "logic" and "presentation", it violates this principle.

At its core, the **Single Responsibility Principle** is about risk management. In game development, requirements change constantly. You might overhaul the inventory system or completely redesign the UI. If your code is tightly coupled, a simple change in one area can accidentally break unrelated features.

A class should encapsulate a single function, ensuring that there is only one case that would justify altering its code.

Practically, this means that a script should not be a Swiss Army knife. If your `Player.gd` script handles input, movement, health logic, and updates the HUD, you have created a script with four reasons to change. If you later decide to switch from a health bar to a health heart system, you are forced to open and modify the `Player` script. This introduces the risk that you might unintentionally break the player's movement code while trying to fix a UI glitch.

SRP guides us to separate these concerns so that the `Player` script focuses solely on being a player, and the UI script focuses only on the interface. When a game is small and in its early stages, SRP is easy to adhere to, as shown by the basic player controller in *Figure 1.1*:

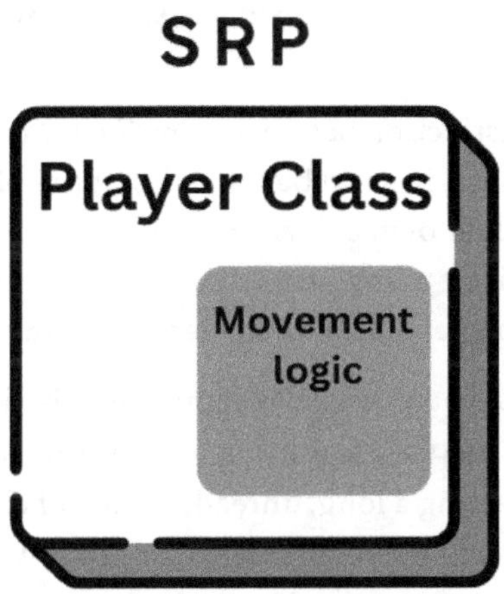

Figure 1.1 – Visual concept of SRP in action

As shown in *Figure 1.1*, the **Player Class** handles the movement logic for the player. This is common and obeys the principle of Single Responsibility since the **Player Class** is only responsible for the movement of the player, which is expected.

However, as the game grows in scale and more features are added, the class can quickly become responsible for too many things, as shown in *Figure 1.2*:

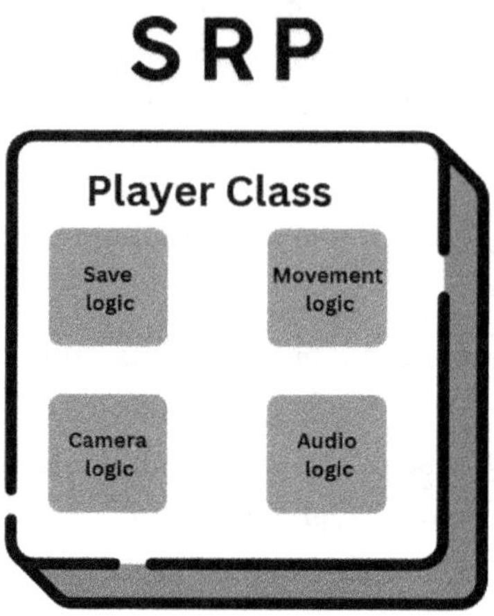

Figure 1.2 – Player taking on too many responsibilities, starting to break SRP

Figure 1.2 shows that the **Player Class** is starting to fill up with functions for different aspects of the game. As the class takes on more responsibilities, the **pure Single Responsibility Principle** starts to break down.

The reason that I now make a distinction between *pure Single Responsibility* and *Single Responsibility* is that in small games, it could be argued that the player is still technically only managing one responsibility – their own behaviors. However, the complexity is growing, and soon the game will be more difficult to maintain, debug, optimize, and work on as a team. Essentially, the class is getting bigger and is in danger of becoming too big to fail.

One of the most common places where Single Responsibility is violated in Godot is the `_process` or `_physics_process` loop. It's tempting to dump all your frame-by-frame logic directly into these functions, creating a long, unreadable list of checks and updates. A better practice is to treat `_process` as a high-level manager that simply delegates tasks to other, single-purpose functions. Instead of writing fifty lines of input code inside the loop, call a dedicated function like `handle_input()`. Instead of calculating velocity and applying gravity inline, call `apply_gravity()` and `move_character()`. This keeps your main loop clean and ensures that each specific behavior lives in its own focused function.

To illustrate this, let's look at a typical spaghetti code movement loop and then refactor it using the SRP. In this monolithic `_physics_process`, the function tries to do everything at once, which makes it hard to read and modify:

```
func _physics_process(delta: float) -> void:
    # 1. Input handling mixed with mechanics
    var direction: Vector2 = Input.get_vector(
```

```
        "ui_left", "ui_right", "ui_up", "ui_down"
    )

    if direction:
        velocity.x = direction.x * SPEED
    else:
        velocity.x = move_toward(velocity.x, 0,
        SPEED)

    # 2. Gravity logic mixed in
    if not is_on_floor():
        velocity.y += gravity * delta

    # 3. Jump logic mixed in
    if Input.is_action_just_pressed("ui_accept") and
    is_on_floor():
        velocity.y = JUMP_VELOCITY

    # 4. Actual movement
    move_and_slide()
```

The better approach is to delegate. This way, the loop acts only as a manager who delegates tasks to dedicated functions, making the logic clear and the loop easy to read.

```
func _physics_process(delta: float) -> void:
    _apply_gravity(delta)
    _handle_movement_input()
    _handle_jump_input()
    move_and_slide()

func _apply_gravity(delta: float) -> void:
    if not is_on_floor():
        velocity.y += gravity * delta

func _handle_movement_input() -> void:
    var direction: Vector2 = Input.get_vector(
        "ui_left", "ui_right", "ui_up", "ui_down"
    )
    if direction:
        velocity.x = direction.x * SPEED
    else:
```

```
        velocity.x = move_toward(velocity.x, 0, SPEED)

func _handle_jump_input() -> void:
    if Input.is_action_just_pressed("ui_accept") and
    is_on_floor():
        velocity.y = JUMP_VELOCITY
```

Another typical example of a bloated and monolithic class responsible for too many things is the **GameManager Class**, as shown in *Figure 1.3*. For small games, a class that manages player data, changes in game state, and even updates to the UI is often a quick solution. But as the game grows and more features are added, this class can become bloated and unmanageable.

Using SRP to split the **GameManager** into smaller classes with individual responsibilities for **Player Data**, **Game State**, and **UI** (or user interface) reduces the size of each class so they are easier to read, debug, and optimize and together they do the same thing as one unwieldy and bloated game manager.

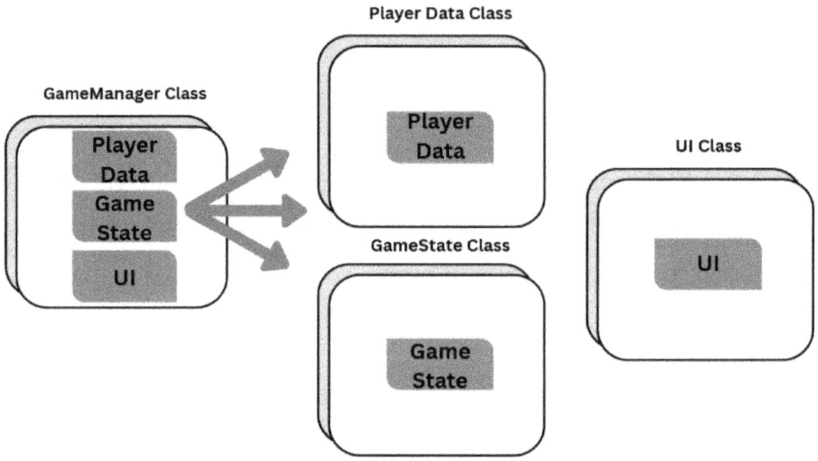

Figure 1.3 – SRP in action

As shown in *Figure 1.3*, when a class starts to get too big, you can **refactor** it. This means you restructure your code to improve its design without changing its external behavior. SRP is highly effective here, as it allows you to separate responsibilities, making the project scalable and the code modular for use in different parts of the game or entirely new projects.

To see this in action, let's look at a common "Godot Spaghetti" scenario: a Player controller that tries to do everything.

The anti-pattern – a monolithic Player script

In the following code snippet, the `Player.gd` is responsible for movement, input, managing health, updating the UI, and playing sound effects. Basically, it has *too many reasons to change.*

```
# Player.gd (Violating SRP)
extends CharacterBody2D
@onready var health_label = $UI/HealthLabel
@onready var audio_player = $AudioStreamPlayer2D
func _physics_process(delta):
     # Responsibility 1: Input & Movement
    var input = Input.get_vector("ui_left", "ui_right",     "ui_up", "ui_down")
    velocity = input * 300.0
    move_and_slide()
func take_damage(amount):
    # Responsibility 2: Health Logic
    health -= amount

    # Responsibility 3: UI Updates (Coupling)
    health_label.text = "HP: " + str(health)

    # Responsibility 4: Audio (Coupling)
    audio_player.play()
```

This script is brittle. If you decide to move the `HealthLabel` in the Scene Tree, this script crashes. If you want to reuse this movement logic for an NPC, you can't, because the NPC doesn't have a UI or audio player configured exactly this way.

The refactor – applying SRP

We can refactor this by stripping away the UI and Audio responsibilities. The `Player` script should only care about being a Player. We use Godot's **Signal** system to delegate the rest. Let's understand how:

```
# Player.gd (Refactored for SRP)
extends CharacterBody2D

# We define a signal so we don't need to know about the UI or Audio
signal health_changed(new_value)
signal player_damaged

var health = 100
```

```
func _physics_process(delta):
    # Focused purely on physics and input
    var input = Input.get_vector(
        "ui_left", "ui_right",
        "ui_up", "ui_down"
    )

    velocity = input * 300.0
    move_and_slide()

func take_damage(amount):
    health -= amount

    # Emit signals: "I am hurt, whoever cares should react."
    health_changed.emit(health)
    player_damaged.emit()
```

By replacing direct references with signals, we have decoupled the systems. A separate UI script can listen for `health_changed`, and a sound manager can listen for `player_damaged`. The Player script is now smaller, cleaner, and strictly focused on its single responsibility.

Single responsibility applies to *functions*, too, so you will want to break functions that are doing *more than one thing* into *multiple functions*. Similarly, you will break a class that is doing too many things into multiple classes, each responsible for one thing, as shown in *Figure 1.4*:

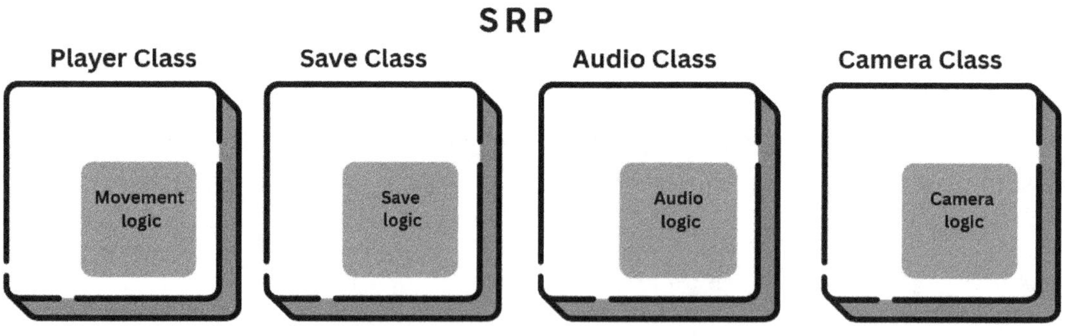

Figure 1.4 – Moving responsibilities into their own classes

In Figure 1.4, we can see that the **Player Class** has been refactored and decomposed into several classes, each with its own responsibilities. To maintain functionality of the **Player Class**, we can use dependency injection to allow our **Player Class** to access all the other classes it needs to function instead of creating them itself. In simple terms, **dependency injection (DI)** means that a script does not create the tools it needs; instead, those tools are given to it (injected) from the outside. Think of it like a remote control: it doesn't build its own batteries; you insert the batteries into it. This makes the remote versatile because it works with any brand of battery you provide.

To apply dependency injection in Godot, we move away from the `Player` script initializing its own dependencies (using `new()` or `load()`), and instead define them as variables that must be provided from the outside. The simplest form of this in Godot is using exported variables to "inject" nodes via the **Inspector**:

```
#Player.gd
@tool # We add @tool so the warning code runs in the Editor
extends CharacterBody2D

# The Player declares what it needs but does not create them
# We use explicit typing (AudioComponent) instead of a
# generic Node to ensure that we get autocomplete and
# type safety.
@export var audio_component: AudioComponent
@export var save_component: SaveComponent

func take_damage(amount: int) -> void:
    # We rely on the injected component to handle the logic
    if audio_component:
        audio_component.play_sfx("hurt")

# Solves the "Forgotten Assignment" problem
func _get_configuration_warnings() -> PackedStringArray:
    var warnings: PackedStringArray = []

    if audio_component == null:
        warnings.append("Audio Component is missing! Check Inspector.")

    return warnings
```

There is a *flexibility versus safety* trade-off in the preceding code. You will notice that we typed the variable as `AudioComponent` rather than a generic `Node`. The benefit is that by being specific, Godot's editor can provide autocomplete suggestions for the `play_sfx()` function, which prevents typos and bugs. The cost is that the variable is now less flexible; it will only accept nodes that inherit from `AudioComponent`.

Dependency injection via the Inspector also introduces a new risk: you might forget to drag the node into the slot! To solve this, the code above uses `_get_configuration_warnings()`. If you forget to assign the dependency, a yellow warning triangle will appear next to the **Player** node in the **Scene** dock, alerting you to the mistake before you even run the game.

A visual representation of the concept of dependency injection is shown in *Figure 1.5*:

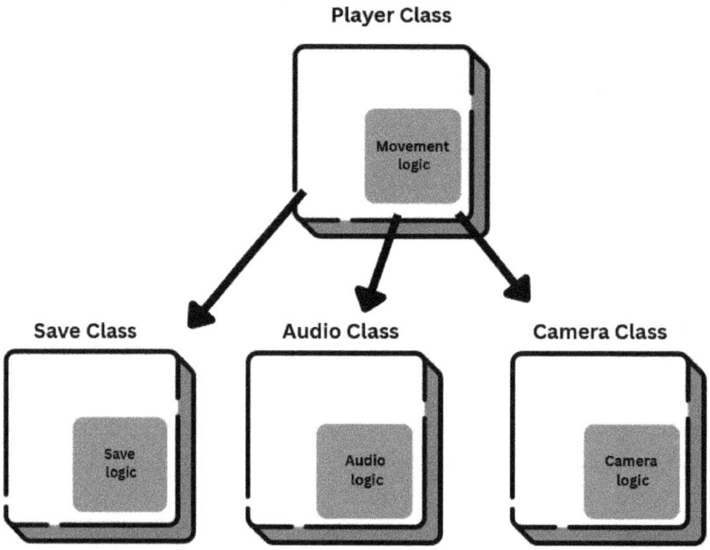

Figure 1.5 – Maintaining SRP through dependency injection

Now that our **Player Class** can rely on other classes for different functionalities, our code is easier to maintain, and this is illustrated in *Figure 1.5*. To know when to use the Single Responsibility Principle while making a class, keep these points in consideration:

- Be very clear on what the purpose of that class is.
- If the class is becoming too big to manage, it should be broken up.
- If multiple team members need to work on the game, avoid monolithic scripts. In a version control system like Git, monolithic scripts are a nightmare. If two developers edit a massive `Player.gd` file simultaneously, you will face constant merge conflicts. By splitting responsibilities into separate files (for example, `PlayerMovement.gd` and `PlayerHealth.gd`), teammates can work on different features in parallel without their commits colliding.

How this fits into Godot projects

In Godot, the Scene Tree is your primary tool for enforcing Single Responsibility. If you find yourself writing a script that handles movement, health, and audio, the engine is practically begging you to break the script apart. You can enforce Single Responsibility in the following ways:

- **Use Child nodes**: Simply adding an **AudioStreamPlayer** isn't enough if your `Player` script still manages the logic (like randomizing pitch or choosing between footstep sounds). To truly enforce SRP, attach a dedicated script to the audio node (for example, `AudioManager.gd`). Now your `Player` script simply calls `play_footstep()`, and the child node handles the specific details of how that sound is played.
- **Use Components**: Instead of writing health logic in the `Player` script, create a `HealthComponent` node (a **Node** or **Node2D**) and attach it to the Player. By pushing responsibilities out of the root script and into child nodes, you leverage Godot's natural strength: composition.

Now that we have established the fundamentals of the Single Responsibility Principle, we need a way to build upon these focused classes without constantly rewriting them. This leads us to the Open/Closed Principle, which teaches us how to safely extend our base classes for specific use cases.

The Open/Closed Principle (OCP)

You should be able to add new features without rewriting old code. Think of a smartphone. When you want a new functionality, you install an app. You don't need to unscrew the back of the phone and solder new wires to the circuit board. The phone is closed to hardware modification but open to software extension.

In Godot, instead of writing a giant `match` statement in your `Player` script to handle every type of enemy, you should use inheritance. You create a base `Enemy` script, and new enemies extend it. The `Player` script stays closed, but the enemy system stays open.

The **Open/Closed Principle** aims to help you design your classes so that you can extend their behavior with new features but never need to rewrite the original code to do so. This means that you can specialize the behavior of a class by creating a *subclass* (*child*) without modifying the *superclass* (*parent*). GDScript naturally supports this workflow through its **extends** keyword. By extending a base script, you inherit all its functionality for free while adding new, specific logic in the child script. This effectively keeps the original file *closed* to modification while keeping the system *open* to new possibilities.

The advantages of the Open/Closed Principle are easier to see when looking at an example. Let's say that we have started making a game, and at first, we only have one enemy type, but as the game develops, more enemies are added.

We might start with type checking inside a big `if/elif` statement inside the `Player` script. Each time the player encounters a new enemy, we must check what type of enemy it is and then call each enemy's specialized attack logic.

This is shown in the following code snippet:

```
# Anti-pattern inside player.gd
func _on_body_entered(body: Node2D) -> void:
    if body.is_in_group("enemies"):
        if body.name == "Archer":
            # Archer-specific logic
            body.shoot_arrow(self)
        elif body.name == "Knight":
            # Knight-specific logic
            body.slash(self)
        elif body.name == "Boss":
            # Boss-specific logic
            body.special_attack(self)
        # ...and so on.
```

The problem with this is that every time a new enemy type is added, the `player` class must be edited, and the `if` statement becomes larger and more unwieldy. This creates the exact maintenance bottleneck that the Open/Closed Principle is designed to prevent. By tightly coupling the player to the specific names of each enemy, we lose the opportunity to simply drop in new content without breaking existing code.

Instead, we should create a single `Enemy` class with abstract methods. Each different enemy type can then inherit from this class and override the functions for its own specialized behavior. We can also rely on Godot's signals to ensure that our code is neatly decoupled. This is demonstrated in the code that follows:

```
# Enemy Super (Parent) Class

class_name Enemy extends CharacterBody2D

@export var damage: int = 10
```

```
func _ready() -> void:
    add_to_group("enemies")

func attack(target: Node) -> void:
    print("Default (abstract) attack behavior")
```

With the base `Enemy` class established to handle common logic like group registration, we can now create specific variations. Here is how an `Archer` script inherits from that base class and overrides the `attack` function to define its own unique behavior:

```
# Sub (child) class - The Archer

class_name Archer extends Enemy

# Registers class globally

@export var attack_cooldown: float = 1.0

funcattack(target:Node)-> void:
    if target and target.has_method("take_damage"):
        target.take_damage(damage)
    print("%s shoots an arrow at %s"
    % [name, target.name])
```

As can be seen in the preceding code, since the `Archer` extends the `Enemy` class, it is automatically a part of the `"enemies"` group, and it has a specialized attack function that shoots arrows at the target. This simplifies the `Player` class as it has an **Area2D** to detect the enemy, and instead of multiple checks to determine the type of enemy and call enemy-specific code, we only need to call the `attack` method.

This is shown in the following `Player` code snippet:

```
func _on_enemy_detector_body_entered(body: Node2D) -> void:
    if body.is_in_group("enemies"):
        if body.has_method("attack"):
            body.attack(self)
```

This simple example is easily extensible into larger projects and demonstrates OCP nicely. The `Enemy` class is open for extension (we can add new Archers or Goblins) but closed for modification (we don't need to rewrite the base class to add them). As a direct result, the

`Player` script also remains unchanged, as it no longer needs to know exactly which type of enemy it has hit, only that it has an `attack` method. Since enemies are open for extension, new enemies could be added, each implementing their own attack differently. The `Player` is closed for modification, as there is no need to change the `Player` class when we add new enemy types. Responsibilities have also been separated; the enemies own the attack behavior and the player owns its health and the way it responds to damage.

When applying the Dependency Inversion Principle (DIP), which is discussed in detail later in this chapter, you often have a choice between Duck Typing and Explicit Typing. In the simple example above, we used `body.has_method("attack")`, which is known as **Duck Typing** (if it walks like a duck and quacks like a duck, we treat it as a duck). This is flexible because the body doesn't need to inherit from a specific class; it just needs that one method.

However, as projects scale, you might prefer **Explicit Typing** for the safety and autocomplete benefits. By checking `if body is Enemy` instead, you gain the benefit of strict type safety, ensuring you are interacting exactly with the class you expect.

The trade-off is that you sacrifice the flexibility of Duck Typing. For instance, if you later added a `SpikeTrap` that could attack the player but did not inherit from the `Enemy` class, the explicit type check would reject it. Duck typing, however, would blindly accept it simply because it has an `attack()` method.

It is again important to emphasize here that these are design patterns and, as such, they are flexible for use in your own project. In the above example, we could have implemented the OCP by making the enemies detect the player, and this would also have been a valid approach. The implementation will depend on the context and design decisions agreed upon by the team.

How this fits into Godot projects

Godot offers two powerful features that align with the Open/Closed Principle: Inheritance and Resources:

- **Inheritance**: As shown in the enemy example, using `extends` allows you to create variations of scenes (like `Goblin.gd` inheriting from `Enemy.gd`) without modifying the base script logic.
- **Resources**: This is Godot's superpower for OCP. By defining a custom `Resource` script (for example, `class_name extends WeaponStats extends Resource`), with exported variables for damage and cooldown, you can create hundreds of different weapons (like `Dagger.tres` or `Axe.tres`) just by creating new files and tweaking numbers in the **Inspector**. You are extending the game's content significantly without ever modifying the source code.

Now that our class is open for extension but closed for modification, let's ensure that every subclass still satisfies the contract of the parent script. This brings us to the Liskov Substitution Principle (LSP).

The Liskov Substitution Principle (LSP)

A replacement part must work exactly like the original. If you unscrew a burnt-out lightbulb and replace it with a new LED bulb, you expect it to fit the socket and turn on. You shouldn't have to rewire the house just because the bulb is a different type. If the new bulb makes the switch explode, it violates this principle. In Godot, if your game code expects an `Enemy` class, it should be able to work with a `Goblin` or a `Dragon` without crashing. If `Dragon.take_damage()` requires different arguments than `Enemy.take_damage()`, you have broken the "socket", and your game will crash at runtime.

The LSP states that objects of a subclass must be usable anywhere that their parent class is expected, without breaking anything. Essentially, this means that all subtypes must be usable wherever the base type is expected without changing the program. What this means in practice is that method signatures and return values should be the same in the subclass as they are in the superclass.

Here is a simple example to illustrate this: in the `Enemy` class, we add a health variable and a function to return the health of the enemy.

```
# Enemy Super (Parent) Class

class_name Enemy extends CharacterBody2D

@export var damage: int = 10

var health: int = 50

funcget_health()-> int:
    return health
```

Now we add a new enemy type to the game, a Goblin. Inside the `Goblin` class, we make a bad override of the function, returning a `String` instead of an `int`:

```
extends Enemy
func get_health():
    return("My health")
```

For testing purposes in the `Player` class, we use a call to the enemy's `get_health` function to calculate the percentage health remaining of the current enemy:

```
# Player Class
func _on_enemy_detector_body_entered(body: Node2D) -> void:
    if body.is_in_group("enemies"):
        if body.has_method("attack"):
            body.attack(self)
            print("Percentage health remaining: "
            +str(body.get_health() / 50 * 100)+"%")
```

This works perfectly on the Archer enemy, which has not overridden and changed the function, but breaks immediately when we encounter the Goblin.

The *correct* approach is to preserve the contract and keep the `get_health()` signature and semantics the same. If extra information is needed in some classes, new methods should be added rather than changing the original contract:

```
# Goblin Class
extends Enemy
var max_health: int = 100

func get_health():
    return health

func get_max_health() -> int:
    return max_health
```

Now that we have repaired the `Goblin` class to honor the original contract, the `Player` script can safely interact with it. The player can rely on the standard `get_health()` method without crashing, while optionally checking for the new `get_max_health()` capability. The following code demonstrates this robust interaction:

```
# Player Class
func _on_enemy_detector_body_entered(body: Node2D) -> void:
    if body.is_in_group("enemies"):
        if body.has_method("attack"):
            body.attack(self)

            print(
                "Percentage health remaining: "
```

```
            + str(body.get_health() / 50 * 100)
            + "%"
        )

    if body.has_method("get_max_health"):
        print(
            "Maximum health of enemy: "
            + str(body.get_max_health())
        )
```

In this corrected version of the code, the `Goblin` class now honors the contract established by the parent `Enemy` class: `get_health()` returns an `int`. This ensures that the calculation in the `Player` script (`body.get_health() / 50`) executes without crashing, regardless of whether the enemy is a base Enemy or a Goblin.

Also, the Goblin extends functionality by adding `get_max_health()`. Notice how the `Player` script uses `body.has_method("get_max_health")` before calling it. This pattern allows subclasses to introduce new features without breaking existing logic that relies on the base class, perfectly demonstrating the flexibility of Liskov Substitution.

Now `get_health` always returns an int for every subtype; any code relying on that contract continues to work. Extra information is provided by additional methods, and calling methods can optionally check for them.

How this fits into Godot projects

Because GDScript is dynamically typed (unless you use strict Static Typing, which I recommend), the Liskov Substitution Principle is your safety net against runtime crashes. Godot relies heavily on Duck Typing, which assumes that if an object has a method like `take_damage()`, then it can be used. Remember the following:

- **Runtime safety**: If you create a special enemy that removes the `take_damage()` function or changes its arguments, the editor won't warn you. The game will simply crash when the player hits that specific enemy.
- **The Rule**: If you inherit from a class in Godot, you must ensure that the child class can handle every signal and method call the parent could handle, preventing the *Game Over* crash that happens when the engine tries to call a method that doesn't exist or has the wrong arguments.

Now that we have ensured every subclass fulfils the contract of its parent class (LSP), let's ensure we write lightweight and generic parent classes to begin with. This brings us to the Interface Segregation Principle (ISP).

The Interface Segregation Principle (ISP)

Don't force a script to carry tools it does not need. Imagine a restaurant menu that forced you to order and pay for an appetizer, soup, salad, main course, and a dessert – even if you only wanted a sandwich! It's wasteful and frustrating. In Godot, you should not create a massive `Entity` class with `fly()`, `swim()`, and `cast_magic()` functions if your Zombies can only walk. If you do, your `Zombie` script inherits empty, useless code. Instead, break these abilities into small components (or small interfaces) so the `Zombie` only inherits what it uses.

The **Interface Segregation Principle** (**ISP**) states that a client should never be forced to implement an interface that they themselves do not require, and they shouldn't be forced to rely on methods they don't use either.

To put it simply, don't force classes to implement functions that they do not need. Rather than classes all using one large interface, make many small and specific components so that classes only depend on what they use.

To illustrate this principle, we could add a method for each type of enemy weapon behavior in the `Enemy` class. Then our Archer would inherit from `Enemy` so that it could use the `shoot` method to shoot the bow. However, the `Enemy` class would include methods to swing a spear and throw a flaming torch, too, even though it doesn't use them!

But the problem with this approach is that the `Enemy` class now exposes methods irrelevant to many subclasses, creating a bloated API. Method callers or tools might also assume that all enemies can shoot or swing spears, which will create confusion. Subclasses now contain dead or stubbed methods, making them longer to read and harder to maintain.

Most importantly, adding new attack types requires us to modify the base class, which can cause changes to ripple through code. This violates the Open/Closed Principle and is illustrated in *Figure 1.6*:

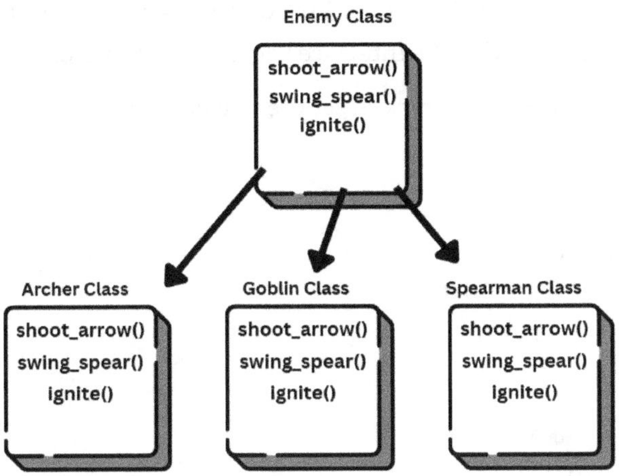

Figure 1.6 – Breaking the ISP

A better approach is to make the base class *minimal*. Let it contain only *shared state* (*properties*) and *truly common behavior* (*methods*).

For example, almost every entity needs a `health` property and methods to handle logic like `take_damage()` or `die()`. Each subclass can then define its own specific attack methods, and callers can trigger these attacks polymorphically by calling a common method name if present or by connecting signals.

This approach is shown in the following code snippet:

```
# Shared behaviour added to Enemy Class
func take_damage(amount: int) -> void:
    health -= amount
    print("%s took %d damage (HP=%d)" % [name, amount, health])

    if health <= 0:
        _die()

func _die() -> void:
    print("%s died" % name)
    queue_free()
```

This code establishes the baseline contract for all enemies. By including only universal logic, like taking damage and dying, we avoid forcing subclasses to inherit methods they do not need. A generic `Enemy` class shouldn't know about shooting arrows or swinging swords; that specific behavior belongs in the `Archer` or `Goblin` subclasses, keeping our inheritance hierarchy clean and compliant with the Interface Segregation Principle.

Now give the `Goblin` class a special attack to set the player on fire for a short time:

```
extends Enemy

@export var burn_damage: int = 2
@export var burn_duration: float = 3.0

var max_health: int = 100

func attack(target: Node) -> void:
    # Goblin's melee attack
    if target and target.has_method("take_damage"):
        target.take_damage(damage)
        _ignite_target(target)
        print("%s slashes %s" % [name, target.name])

func _ignite_target(target: Node) -> void:
    # simple immediate burn – could be improved to DOT
    if target and target.has_method("take_damage"):
        target.take_damage(burn_damage)
        print(
            "%s set %s on fire for %ds"
            % [name, target.name, burn_duration]
        )

func get_health():
    return health

func get_max_health() -> int:
    return max_health
```

In this subclass, we see the benefits of keeping the base class minimal. Because the `Enemy` class didn't enforce a generic `shoot()` or `swing_spear()` method, we were free to implement a completely custom `attack()` for the Goblin that includes a unique `_ignite_target` behavior. The Goblin adheres to the contracts of the parent (it still has health and takes damage) but encapsulates its own specific logic for burning the player. This structure prevents **method**

pollution in the base class, ensuring that other enemies like an Archer or Slime are not burdened with irrelevant fire-logic they can't use.

Refactoring the code in this way has created a minimal base API and maintains SRP, OCP and ISP. The code is easier to read and maintain, and new contributors can see where attack logic belongs (in the subclass).

How this fits into Godot projects

Godot does not have strict `interface` keywords like C# or Java. However, we apply ISP in Godot through signals and components:

- **Focused signals**: Instead of a massive signal passing a Dictionary of data (`player_updated(data_dict)`), use specific, segregated signals like `health_depleted` or `ammo_changed`. This ensures listeners only react to the specific data they care about.
- **Node composition**: Instead of a monolithic `Entity` or `GameManager` class that forces every object to have `fly()`, `swim()`, and `climb()` methods, Godot encourages you to attach specific nodes. If an enemy can fly, attach a `FlyComponent`. If it can't, don't attach it. This way, the enemy object isn't bloated with empty methods for behaviors it doesn't have.

Now that we have eliminated bloat from our classes using ISP, let's ensure that our class only knows what it needs to know and isn't tightly coupled to other systems. This brings us to the Dependency Inversion Principle (DIP).

The Dependency Inversion Principle (DIP)

Connect to the "socket", not the device. When you plug a lamp into the wall, the lamp doesn't care if the electricity comes from a solar panel or a coal plant. It just relies on the standard shape of the socket. In Godot, your `Player` script should not type `get_node("UI/HealthBar")`. That is like hard-wiring the lamp to the coal plant; if you move the `HealthBar`, the code breaks. Instead, the `Player` should emit a `signal health_changed`. The `Player` (the lamp) just provides the connection point, and the UI (the power grid) decides how to connect it.

The **Dependency Inversion Principle** (**DIP**) requires decoupling high-level systems from low-level details. Rather than linking directly to one another, both should connect to a shared abstraction. This ensures that the concrete details depend on the architectural rules rather than the architecture depending on the details.

In the context of Godot, high-level modules could be the player controller or game manager, and these should not depend on low-level or specific modules, such as different enemy types. Both should depend on abstractions, and specialized concrete classes should implement those abstractions.

To understand this better, look at the anti-pattern that leads to the typical mistakes made when developing games. Often, enemies will fetch the player via a hard-coded path and directly make changes to player variables such as `health`. This is shown in the following code snippet:

```
# Archer.gd (anti-pattern)
extends Enemy # Inherits from the base class

func attack():
    # hard-coded lookup – brittle
    var player = get_node("../Player")
    # directly touching internals – breaking DIP
    player.health -= 10
    # update HUD directly – couples enemy to UI
    var hud = get_node ("../HUD")
    hud.update_health(player.health)
```

As can be seen in the preceding code snippet, the `Archer` depends on the concrete `Player` node location and internal `health` variable. The game's HUD (Heads-Up Display) is also tightly coupled to the enemy. This is a mixing of concerns, as the enemy should not update the UI. If we were to add a new player type or refactor the `health`, this would break the `Archer` and most likely all other enemies if they were implemented in the same way.

Instead of introducing this type of bad practice, we should stick with what we already have, which is that the `Player` has a `take_damage` function, which is called by the enemy's `attack` function. We could also add a signal that triggers when the `Player` has taken damage, to which the UI manager can respond to update the health bar.

The DIP ensures that all the goals of SOLID are met, and its advantages for large, usually team-based, projects are listed as follows:

- **Reduces tight coupling**: High-level systems like a `Player` class or `GameManager` don't depend on the inner details of low-level systems, such as specific enemy types or weapons. Now your project is less brittle and changing one part of the code doesn't break anything else.
- **Makes code reusable**: Since classes now depend on small reusable abstractions such as `take_damage()` or `attack(target)` they can be easily reused in other projects without bringing unrelated dependencies with them.
- **Makes code more testable**: Classes now rely on simple contracts, not concrete implementations, so you can test them in isolation.

- **Code is more extensible and maintainable**: The game can be expanded by adding new classes that meet the rules of your abstraction. For example, adding new enemy types or weapons doesn't mean you have to change the existing code base.
- **Code is cleaner**: Following DIP makes code more modular and designs are more layered. It ensures that logic, interface, and data are separated, which prevents monolithic classes and keeps scripts short, focused and easier to read.
- **Promotes collaboration**: Multiple developers can work on different parts of the game at the same time without getting in each other's way since modularity defines clear boundaries.
- **Dovetails with Godot's Node and signal system**: Scripts can communicate through signals and share method names rather than deep node references. Now, game logic is more flexible and decoupled.

How this fits into Godot projects

The most common violation of DIP in Godot is the use of `get_node()` with hard-coded paths (for example, `get_node("../Player")`). This tightly couples your script to the specific structure of the Scene Tree. Consider the following best practices:

- **Export variables**: Instead of searching for a node, use `@export var target: Node2D`. This allows you to *inject* the dependency via the **Inspector**. The script no longer cares where the node is in the tree, only that it has a reference to it.
- **Signals**: Instead of a child node calling a specific function on a parent (which assumes the parent's class type), the child should emit a signal. The parent depends on the child (listening to the signal), rather than the child depending on the concrete implementation of the parent.

Next, we'll look at using Dependency Inversion with Autoloads.

Using Dependency Inversion with Autoloads

While `@export` variables work well for local dependencies (like a Player needing a specific audio component), large-scale systems often require global access. In Godot, we use **Autoloads** (**Singletons**) to handle this. However, accessing an Autoload directly (for example, `AudioManager.play_sound()`) creates a tight coupling to that specific implementation.

To apply Dependency Inversion with Autoloads, we should treat the Autoload as a Service Locator or an Event Bus (an abstraction) rather than a concrete manager. One of the most effective ways to implement this abstraction in Godot is by using a pattern that decouples the sender from the receiver entirely.

The Signal Bus Pattern

Instead of the `Player` tightly coupling to a specific UI scene to update health, or a specific Audio Manager to play sounds, the `Player` relies on a global **Signal Bus**. This could be achieved by creating a script called `Events.gd` and adding it as an Autoload. Then we could define the abstraction (the signals) as follows:

```
# Events.gd (Autoload)
extends Node

signal player_damaged(amount)
signal game_over
```

Then the high-level `Player` class would depend only on the abstraction:

```
# Player.gd
func take_damage(amount):
    Events.player_damaged.emit(amount)
```

The low-level details, such as UI and Audio, can also depend on the abstraction:

```
# HealthBar.gd
func _ready():
    Events.player_damaged.connect(_on_player_damaged)
```

By using an Autoload as a central hub for signals, we invert the dependency. The `Player` doesn't know the `UI` exists; it only knows that an event occurred. This allows you to completely replace the `UI` or `Audio` systems without breaking the Player logic.

With the theory of SOLID now fully established, we are ready to shift our focus from understanding the rules in isolation to applying them in combination.

Designing extensible gameplay systems

Now that we have explored the individual principles, let's look at how they combine to create **extensible gameplay systems**. A common requirement in Godot is an Interaction System that allows a Player to open doors, pick up items, or talk to NPCs.

If we do not follow SOLID, we might write a `Player` script that checks the name of the object it collides with:

```
# Bad: Tight Coupling (Violating OCP)
if collider.name == "Door":
    collider.open()
elif collider.name == "Chest":
    collider.loot()
```

To make this extensible, we combine the Open/Closed Principle and Interface Segregation. Follow these steps:

1. **Define the contract (ISP)**: We don't need complex inheritance; we just need a way to interact. In Godot, we can use a **Component approach** by defining a class name:

    ```
    # Interactable.gd
    class_name Interactable extends Area2D
    func interact(user: Node):
        push_warning("Interact not implemented")
    ```

2. **Implement specifics (SRP/OCP)**: Specific items extend this class as follows:

    ```
    # Chest.gd
    extends Interactable
    func interact(user: Node):
        print("You found gold!")
        queue_free()
    ```

3. **The extensible player**: The Player logic is now closed for modification, but handles any new interaction type we add in the future:

    ```
    #Player.gd
    extends CharacterBody2D
    # We inject the area responsible for detecting
    # objects
    @export var interaction_area: Area2D

    func _unhandled_input(event):
        if event.is_action_pressed("interact"):
            # We check for the class (Abstraction), not the object name
            var overlapping = interaction_area.get_overlapping_areas()
    ```

```
        for area in overlapping:
            if area is Interactable:
                area.interact(self)
                return
```

By designing the system this way, you can add Doors, NPCs, Levers, and Save Points (Extensions) without ever opening the `Player` script again – it is closed for modification.

Moving from theory to practice

By now, you should have a solid mental model of how to map these industry-standard principles onto Godot's unique node-based architecture. We have seen how separating responsibilities, strictly defining interfaces, and inverting dependencies can transform a brittle prototype into a scalable system.

However, architecture is a means to an end, not the game itself. There is a danger in adhering to these rules too rigidly, which can lead to paralysis. In the next section, we will discuss how to balance this architectural purity with the pragmatic reality of game development.

Using SOLID principles wisely

While the SOLID principles provide a powerful foundation for writing clean, maintainable code, they should never become rigid rules that slow you down or complicate development. These ideas are tools, not laws. Their real value appears in larger, long-term projects or in team environments where multiple developers work on the same systems. In those situations, principles, such as Single Responsibility and Dependency Inversion, make collaboration smoother, debugging easier, and scaling safer.

However, for small prototypes, game jams, or early experiments, it's often better to focus on getting something playable before worrying about perfect architecture. Over-engineering too early can be just as harmful as messy code. The key is to apply these principles where they add clarity, flexibility, and structure—not for their own sake.

Remember: players don't care how your game was coded. They care about how it feels to play. These design principles exist to help you, the developer, build, and maintain that experience more effectively. Use them thoughtfully, adapt them to your workflow, and let practicality guide your design decisions.

Good code serves the game, not the other way around. So, use these principles when they make your work easier, not harder.

Organizing for scalability – feature-based structure

Applying SOLID principles isn't limited to code; it applies to your project structure, too. Beginners often organize their files by *type*:

- `res: //Scripts/`
- `res://Scenes/`
- `res://Sprites/`

While this looks tidy initially, it violates the spirit of Single Responsibility. To work on the "Player," you must jump between three different folders. As the project grows to hundreds of files, this becomes unmanageable.

A scalable alternative is a **feature-based organization**. You group files by what they are, not by what file format they use:

- `res://Player/`: Contains `Player.gd`, `Player.tscn`, `PlayerIcon.png`
- `res://Enemies/Goblin`: Contains `Goblin.gd`, `Goblin.tscn`, `GoblinSkins.png`
- `res://UI/HUD/`: Contains `HUD.gd`, `HUD.tscn`, `HealthBar.png`

This approach keeps your systems self-contained (encapsulated). If you want to reuse your Player in a sequel, you can simply drag the `Player/` folder into a new project, and you know that you have every dependency included.

Summary

This chapter looked at the five SOLID principles in detail within the context of Godot. The goal is to write clean, scalable, and maintainable code. Each principle addresses a common problem in game development, from bloated scripts to brittle dependencies and illustrates how careful design can transform messy prototypes into more professional systems.

While the Single Responsibility Principle keeps scripts focused on one purpose, the Open/Closed Principle provides a way to introduce new behaviors through inheritance or composition without modifying existing code. The Liskov Substitution Principle enforces strict contracts, guaranteeing that subclasses can be safely swapped for their parent classes without crashing the game.

Next, the Interface Segregation Principle showed the value of creating small, focused interfaces or components so that classes only depend on the functionality that they use. Finally, the Dependency Inversion Principle demonstrated how to decouple systems by programming against abstractions rather than concrete implementations.

Together, these principles encourage developers to write Godot projects that are not only functional but flexible, reusable, and easy to extend. By adhering to SOLID design, your scripts remain organized, your game systems evolve gracefully, and your codebase becomes easier to maintain as projects grow in scope and complexity.

The next chapter will help you decide when to use a scene or a script and why it matters.

Get this book's PDF copy, code bundle, and more

Scan the QR code (or go to `packtpub.com/unlock`). Search for this book by name, confirm the edition, and then follow the steps on the page.

UNLOCK NOW

Note: Have your invoice handy. Purchases made directly from the Packt website don't require an invoice.

2

Deciding Between Scenes and Scripts

In the previous chapter, we established the foundational SOLID principles for writing clean, maintainable code. However, knowing *how* to design a class is only half the battle; you also need to know *where* to implement that logic within Godot's unique architecture. Before we can fully apply patterns like Single Responsibility or Open/Closed, we must first answer a fundamental question that arises in every project: *Should this feature be a scene, a script, or a combination of both?* Making the right choice here is the first step in turning abstract architectural theory into a concrete, scalable game.

This chapter will look at when to use each approach, what trade-offs they bring, and how to balance them effectively using composition and modularity. This decision is rarely straightforward because Godot is an unopinionated engine; it grants you the freedom to solve problems in many ways without strictly enforcing one architectural pattern over another. You might struggle to decide if an inventory item should be a full scene with visual nodes or just a lightweight data object. Any wrong choice early on can lead to performance bottlenecks or inflexible code that is painful to refactor later.

In this chapter, we're going to cover the following main topics:

- When to use scenes
- When to use scripts
- Balancing composition and inheritance
- Hybrid approaches in complex systems

By the end of this chapter, you will have developed the architectural intuition required to make these foundational decisions with confidence, ensuring your project is built on a structure that supports growth rather than hindering it.

Technical requirements

Readers should be familiar with basic Godot workflows, such as navigating the editor, creating scenes, and scripting with GDScript.

You can download the example project and code for this book by following the instructions in the *Download the example code files* section in the *Preface* of this book.

This chapter's code files are included in the downloadable code bundle.

When to use scenes

Scenes are core to Godot's design philosophy. A **Scene** can represent anything from a single object, such as a static background (**TextureRect**), to a complex system, such as a character (**CharacterBody2D**, **CollisionShape2D**, and **AnimatedSprite2D**), a main menu, or even a complete level.

Each scene will define its own hierarchy of nodes known as the **Scene Tree**, which describes how these nodes are organized, what data they hold, and how they interact. This is illustrated in *Figure 2.1* as follows:

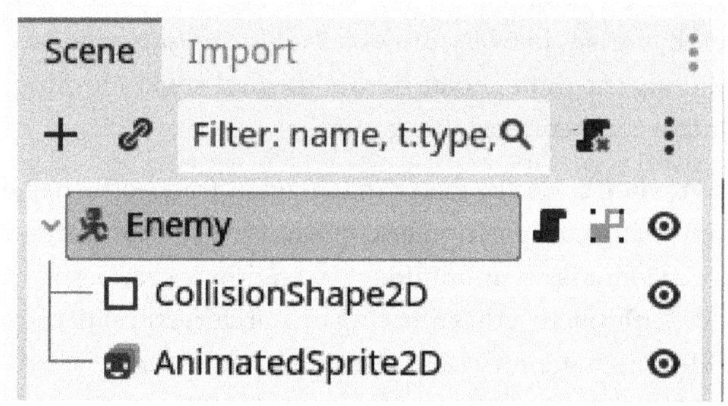

Figure 2.1 – Different scenes representing the hierarchy of nodes

This organizational power is not just for your benefit as a developer; it also provides critical information to the engine itself. Since a scene defines a strict, predictable arrangement of data, Godot can optimize how it loads and manages these objects in memory far more effectively than it can for raw code.

Declarative structure versus imperative behavior

Scenes provide the blueprint for your game objects, representing nodes, their hierarchy, properties, and resources. Because they are declarative, meaning they describe *what* exists rather than *how* it behaves, they are essentially just structured data. This data-driven approach is highly optimized by Godot. When you instantiate a scene file, Godot's backend rapidly parses this structured data and constructs the entire node tree in one highly efficient motion.

While you could achieve this exact same result imperatively, by writing dozens of lines of GDScript to manually `Node.new()`, set properties, and `add_child()` one by one during `_ready()`, it would not only be a nightmare to maintain, but it would also be slower for the engine to execute line by line. By letting declarative scenes handle the heavy lifting of your structure, your imperative scripts are free to focus entirely on your game's behavior.

The step-by-step logic describing the actions of scenes or nodes in a scene belongs to a script. By contrast, scripts are *imperative*, and so we define the behavior of game objects through code. This tells the engine what to do and when to do it.

By separating scenes (*structure*) and scripts (*behavior*), we mirror the core principles of object-oriented programming (OOP). In OOP, a class defines both the data an object holds (*state*) and the functions that define how it behaves (*methods*). In Godot, scenes play a similar role to state and composition, while scripts define behavior and logic.

Consequently, you should strive to define as much of your object's static structure as possible within the **Scene** dock. Avoid writing scripts that manually instantiate nodes, set textures, or position elements in `_ready()` if those values are constant. Doing so ignores the engine's strengths. Instead, let the scene handle the setup declaratively, so your script remains clean, focused purely on the action, and free of clutter.

By combining a scene with a script, you are creating a self-contained object:

- The scene describes the object's components (nodes, hierarchy, properties)
- The script defines how the object behaves and interacts with other objects

This structure encourages **encapsulation** in which each scene and script pair manages its own data and functionality. It also supports composition over inheritance because complex systems can be built by combining smaller, reusable scenes rather than relying on long inheritance chains.

It's important to note that scenes are saved as `.tscn` files, which are lightweight, serializable, and easy for the engine to load efficiently. The extension stands for `text scene` and is a file format that represents a single Scene Tree inside Godot. Since it is text, it has the advantage of being mostly human-readable and is easy for version control systems to manage.

However, this comes with a caveat for our decision-making process: scene files are verbose. If you embed too much complex logic or frequently changing data directly into scene properties (rather than a script), your version control diffs can become cluttered and difficult to review, making a pure script the better choice for volatile systems.

How Godot stores scene structures

In Godot, a `.tscn` file stores information such as:

- Which nodes exist in the scene
- Hierarchy (the parent-child relationships)
- Properties (position, scale, rotation, etc.)
- Connections (references, resources, and signals)

This combines to form a declaration of the object structure, which is a static description of what the scene contains. It does not have imperative instructions for how the scene should behave. *Figure 2.2* shows the structure of the scene for the paddle for Player 1. Note the script attached, as annotated in the figure:

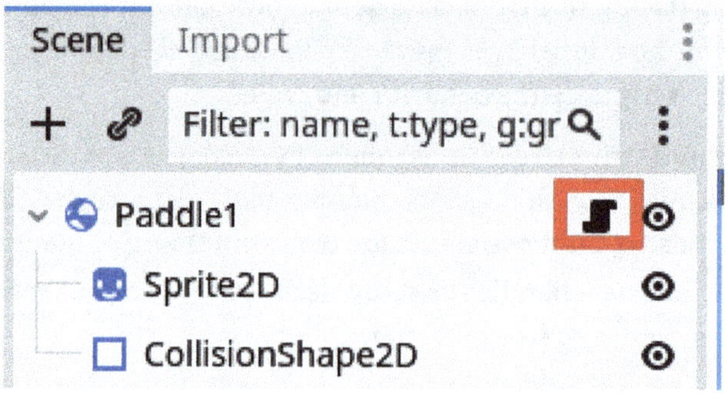

Figure 2.2 – Scene structure for Paddle1 in Godot

If we open the `.tscn` file for this scene, you can see how Godot stores the structure, as shown here:

```
[gd_scene load_steps=4 format=3 uid="uid://5njrw47swna7"]

[ext_resource type="Texture2D" uid="uid://ckk6tg4h3sjx3" path="res://Assets/
Paddle_1.png" id="1_msuwi"]
[ext_resource type="Script" uid="uid://dp7ywuwo6k654" path="res://Scripts/
paddle_1.gd" id="1_q4l7w"]

[sub_resource type="RectangleShape2D" id="RectangleShape2D_q4l7w"]
size = Vector2(16, 106)

[node name="Paddle1" type="RigidBody2D"]
gravity_scale = 0.0
lock_rotation = true
```

```
script = ExtResource("1_q417w")

[node name="Sprite2D" type="Sprite2D" parent="."]
texture = ExtResource("1_msuwi")

[node name="CollisionShape2D" type="CollisionShape2D" parent="."]
position = Vector2(0, 1)
shape = SubResource("RectangleShape2D_q417w")
```

Unlike some other game engines that use unreadable binary files, Godot scenes are simple, declarative text files. We can easily break this file down into three main sections:

- **The Header (**`[gd_scene...]`**):** This tells the engine that this file is a scene and assigns it a unique ID so it can be referenced safely anywhere in your project.
- **The Resources (**`[ext_resource]` **and** `[sub_resource]`**):** This acts as the scene's inventory. Before building anything, Godot lists all the external files it needs to load (like your paddle image and script) and internal data it needs to define (like the specific dimensions of your collision box). It gives each of these an ID, like `1_msuwi`.
- **The Node Tree (**`[node...]`**):** This is the actual hierarchy of your objects. It defines the root **RigidBody2D** node and sets its properties (`gravity_scale = 0.0`). For the child nodes, you can see `parent="."`, which tells the engine to attach them to the root. Finally, it links the resources from the inventory directly to the nodes, such as assigning `ExtResource("1_msuwi")` to the Sprite's texture.

Because this structure is just plain text, it makes collaborating with other developers easy, as you can track exactly what changed in a scene using version control systems like Git.

The preceding snippet essentially declares that there is a **Paddle1** node with **Sprite2D** and a **CollisionShape2D** as children. If we investigate the script attached to the **Paddle1** node, we can see the instructions for how this paddle behaves:

```
extends RigidBody2D

@export var speed = 500

func _physics_process(delta):
    var movement = Vector2.ZERO

    if Input.is_action_pressed("paddle_1_down"):
        movement = Vector2.DOWN
```

```
    elif Input.is_action_pressed("paddle_1_up"):
        movement = Vector2.UP

    linear_velocity = movement * speed
```

To put it succinctly, scenes are declarative and describe the structure, whereas scripts are imperative and define the behavior of the object.

Practical implications of using scenes

Scenes offer several practical advantages in day-to-day development:

- **Visual composition**: Scenes provide an intuitive, visual approach to building game objects. Instead of mentally mapping out how objects relate to one another, you can construct your node tree directly in the editor, getting immediate visual feedback on the spatial relationships and hierarchy of your components.
- **Rapid prototyping and modularity**: Scenes are highly modular and can be easily instanced multiple times across different contexts. Because they exist visually in the editor, you can preview, tweak, and perfect your game objects without having to run the game to see the results.
- **Team collaboration**: For larger projects, scenes are an invaluable collaborative tool. They allow non-programmers, such as level designers, UI artists, and sound engineers, to work independently on Levels and prefabs without ever needing to touch the underlying codebase.

However, these advantages come with important performance considerations that become especially relevant as projects scale.

Performance considerations

Scenes are efficient to store because they are declarative data but bringing them into the live game world requires processing power. The main performance cost associated with scenes is their *instantiation*. When you spawn a complex scene, Godot must allocate memory, set properties, and register callbacks for every single node in that tree simultaneously. If this hierarchy is too deep, that split-second calculation can cause a visible frame drop (stutter) during gameplay.

The cost of instantiation is *performance*. While scenes are highly efficient to work with, bringing them into the game world takes computing power. Loading and instantiating a large Scene Tree is a synchronous operation. If you call `load("res://Level1.tscn").instantiate()` in the middle of gameplay, say, right when a player fires a complex weapon, the game will briefly freeze (dropping frames) while Godot parses the text file and allocates memory for every node.

The best practice solution for this is preloading. To prevent this mid-gameplay stutter, the go-to approach in Godot is to use the `preload()` function. Let's have a look at this example:

```
# Bad: Parses the file at the exact moment the button is pressed, causing stutter
func fire_laser():
    var laser = load("res://laser.tscn").instantiate()
    add_child(laser)

# Good: Parses the file upfront when the script first initializes
const LASER_SCENE = preload("res://laser.tscn")

func fire_laser():
    var laser = LASER_SCENE.instantiate()
    add_child(laser)
```

When you use `preload()`, Godot loads the scene data into memory the moment the script itself is parsed by the engine (typically during a loading screen). By the time the player acts in the game, the heavy lifting of reading the file is already finished; the engine simply must stamp out a copy of the preloaded data.

While `preload()` is fantastic, it cannot be used for absolutely everything. You will still need to rely on standard `load()` in a few specific situations:

- **Dynamic paths**: `preload()` requires a static, hard-coded string. If you need to figure out which scene to load dynamically via code (for example, `load("res://levels/" + next_level_name + ".tscn")`), you must use `load()`.
- **Memory conservation**: Preloading forces the scene into memory immediately. If you have a massive asset, like a secret boss or a late-game cutscene that the player might not ever see, preloading it upfront wastes valuable RAM. In those cases, it is better to load it only when needed.

However, for small-scale games or prototypes, this complexity is often unnecessary. If your scenes are lightweight – containing only a few dozen nodes – instantiation will likely happen in a fraction of a frame, making the stutter imperceptible. In these cases, you should prefer the simplicity of *synchronous loading*. As a rule, only reach for threaded loading when you can feel the game freeze during transition.

For extremely large scenes (like an entire new Level or a dense 3D city), even `preload()` isn't enough, as it will still cause your game to freeze during the initial loading screen. The professional standard is to load these massive assets asynchronously in the background.

This is a three-step process using Godot's `ResourceLoader`:

1. **Request the load**: You tell the engine to start loading the file on a separate CPU thread using `ResourceLoader.load_threaded_request()`.
2. **Check the status:** During your `_process()` loop, you monitor the progress using `ResourceLoader.load_threaded_get_status()`. This allows you to update a visual loading bar for the player.
3. **Retrieve the resource**: Once the status reports that it is finished, you physically grab the loaded data using `ResourceLoader.load_threaded_get()` and instantiate it.

Here is how that looks in practice:

```
var next_level_path = "res://Levels/Level_2.tscn"

func _ready() -> void:
    # Step 1: Start loading the scene in the background
    ResourceLoader.load_threaded_request(next_level_path)

func _process(_delta: float) -> void:
    # We use an array to catch the progress percentage (0.0 to 1.0)
    var progress = []

    # Step 2: Check the current status of the requested file
    var status = ResourceLoader.load_threaded_get_status(
        next_level_path,
        progress
    )

    match status:
        ResourceLoader.THREAD_LOAD_IN_PROGRESS:
            # Update your UI loading bar here!
```

```
            print("Loading: ", progress[0] * 100, "%")

        ResourceLoader.THREAD_LOAD_LOADED:
            # Step 3: The file is ready! Grab it and instantiate it.
            var level_scene =
                ResourceLoader.load_threaded_get(next_level_path)

            var level_instance = level_scene.instantiate()
            get_tree().current_scene.add_child(level_instance)

            # Stop the _process loop so we don't keep checking
            set_process(false)

        ResourceLoader.THREAD_LOAD_FAILED, \
        ResourceLoader.THREAD_LOAD_INVALID_RESOURCE:
            push_error("Background load failed.")
            set_process(false)
```

By utilizing this threaded approach, your game's main loop never stops running. Animations keep playing, loading spinners keep spinning, and you maintain a perfectly smooth framerate while Godot handles the heavy lifting out of sight.

When to use scripts

While scripts are the engine that drives behavior *inside* almost every scene, this section refers to using **stand-alone scripts** that do not require a corresponding `.tscn` file.

When you have a pure logic system – like a damage calculator or a save manager – that requires no visual representation or Scene Tree hierarchy, a **script** file alone is the superior choice. Unlike scenes, these scripts can extend lightweight non-node classes to save processing power. Two of the most common examples are:

- **RefCounted**: The most basic, lightweight object in Godot. It exists entirely in memory and automatically deletes itself (preventing memory leaks) the exact moment your game is done using it. It is perfect for temporary logic, like a complex math calculator or our `MenuBuilder`.
- **Resource**: A data container that can be saved directly to your hard drive (as a `.tres` file). It is ideal for defining passive game data, such as enemy stats, inventory items, or configuration settings, without ever needing a physical node in the game world.

By relying on these classes, you can define your logic and store your data through pure imperative code, completely bypassing the performance overhead of the Scene Tree.

Scripts are limited only to imperative composition; they are very useful as reusable building blocks for game systems, which are implemented as lightweight classes. Examples include:

- Data handling (save systems, scoring systems)
- Logic controllers (spawning enemies, enemy logic)
- Tool scripts (procedural generation, editor plugins)

Using scripts for shared and reusable logic

A good example of when to use a script instead of a scene is with a *save and load utility*. *Figure 2.3* shows the structure of an example **Scene** that could represent a Level or a UI.

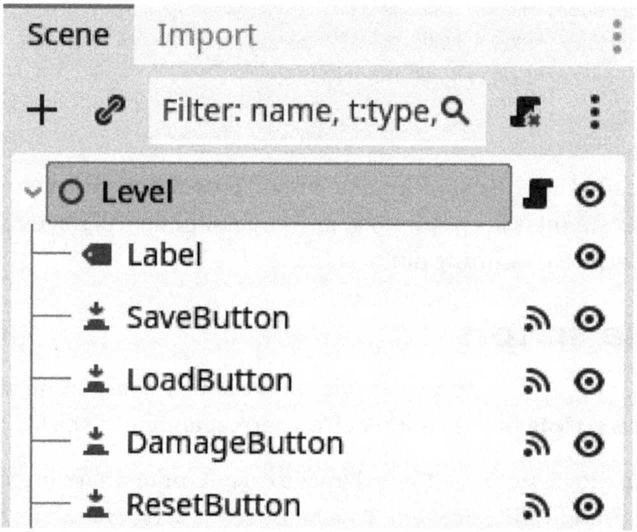

Figure 2.3 – Structure of the example Scene

The **Scene** in *Figure 2.3* is for demonstration purposes only. When running, it shows the value of the **Player Health** variable with buttons to reduce the health by taking damage, reset the health to full, save the current state of the health, and load the saved state. The interface is shown in *Figure 2.4* as follows:

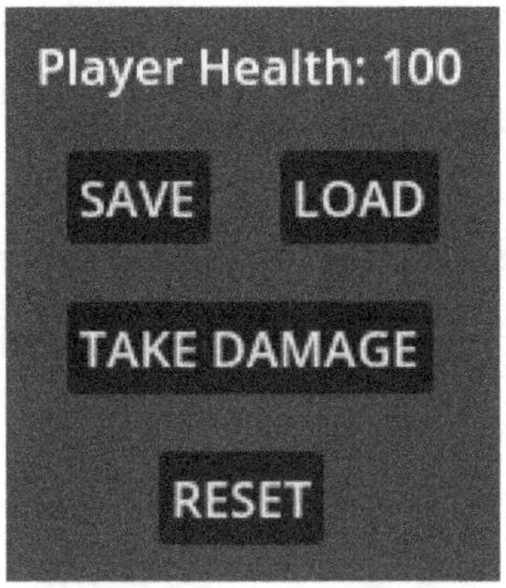

Figure 2.4 – Output of the Level Scene

The interface in *Figure 2.4* is made in the typical way with a hierarchy of nodes combining to produce the output shown. However, the save and load facility will not be created using nodes; instead, we will write a script and make the `SaverLoader`, a class that can be instantiated or used as needed. The `SaverLoader` script is shown as follows; note that this is a script only, with no nodes attached:

```
class_name SaverLoader extends RefCounted

static func save_game(player_health: int) -> void:
    var file = FileAccess.open("user://savegame.data", FileAccess.WRITE)
    file.store_var(player_health)
    file.close()

static func load_game() -> int:
    var file = FileAccess.open("user://savegame.data", FileAccess.READ)
    var player_health: int = file.get_var()
    file.close()
    return player_health
```

The preceding code represents the simplest possible save and load system. The class `SaverLoader` is now available for use by other classes in the project, and because its methods are static, they can be called without creating an instance of the `SaverLoader` class.

Essentially, the `save_game` function receives the `player_health` variable and writes it to a file, whereas the `load_game` function reads the variable from the file and returns it to the calling method.

This illustrates why a script is the superior architectural choice for this specific feature. Since saving and loading are pure logic operations that require no visual representation or physical presence in the game world, wrapping them in a scene would introduce unnecessary memory overhead. By using a static script, we create a lightweight, globally accessible tool without cluttering the Scene Tree with invisible nodes that serve no structural purpose.

This functionality can be seen in action in the `Level` script, which is as follows:

```
extends Node2D

@onready var label: Label = $Label

var _player_health: int = 100
var player_health: int = 100:
    set(value):
        _player_health = value
        label.text = "Player Health: " + str(_player_health)
    get():
        return _player_health

func _ready() -> void:
    player_health = _player_health

func take_damage(amount: int = 10) -> void:
    player_health = max(0, player_health - amount)

func _on_damage_button_pressed() -> void:
    take_damage()

func _on_save_button_pressed() -> void:
    SaverLoader.save_game(player_health)

func _on_load_button_pressed() -> void:
    player_health = SaverLoader.load_game()

func _on_reset_button_pressed() -> void:
    player_health = 100
```

As can be seen in the above script for the simple Level, when the `save` button is pressed, the `save_game` function of the `SaverLoader` class is run, and when the `load` button is pressed, the `load_game` function of the `SaverLoader` class is run.

Extending scripts into the editor

It's also worth noting that scripts can become full citizens of the Godot editor through the `class_name` keyword. When you define a script with `class_name MyCustomNode`, Godot registers it globally. This doesn't just allow you to use the type in your code; it adds your script to the **Create New Node** dialog in the Godot editor. This bridges the gap between scripts and scenes, allowing you to create lightweight, script-only nodes that you can drop into your Scene Tree just like Godot's built-in nodes.

However, simply appearing in the **Create New Node** menu is only half of the integration story. To create a true **hybrid workflow** where your script doesn't just run for the player but also actively assists you, the developer, during the design process, we need to unlock its ability to execute code directly inside the editor.

In this regard, a powerful feature often overlooked is the `@tool` annotation. Placing this at the top of your script allows it to run inside the Godot editor, not just during the game!

This opens two new possibilities:

- **Visual debugging**: If you have an `AttackComponent` with a `range` variable, a `@tool` script can draw a circle in the editor Viewport to show that range visually. This helps level designers place enemies correctly without guessing.
- **Data validation**: A tool script can issue configuration warnings (`_get_configuration_warnings`) if a required node (like a **Sprite**) is missing from the scene, preventing bugs before the game is even run.

If we wanted to implement the range tool script for level designers, we could create a new scene with a **Node2D** as the root and rename it to `RangeTool`. Then we could attach the following script to it:

```
@tool
extends Node2D
@export var radius: float = 100.0:
    set(value):
        radius = value
        queue_redraw()
func _draw() -> void:
    if Engine.is_editor_hint():
        # Draws a red circle with 0.3 (30%) opacity
        draw_circle(Vector2.ZERO, radius, Color(1, 0, 0, 0.3))
```

Now instance the range tool scene in the main Level scene, and you have an opaque *red* circle indicating the currently selected range in the **Inspector**. This can be updated live in-engine! This is shown in *Figure 2.5* as follows:

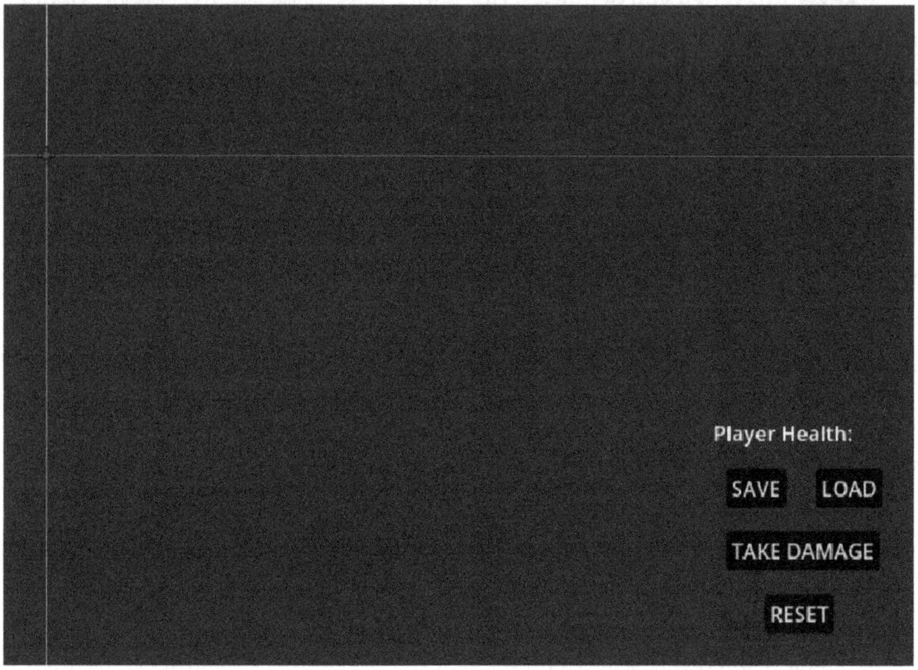

Figure 2.5 – The range tool

As seen in *Figure 2.5*, the radius of the *red* circle can represent the range of a spell or weapon, and it can be adjusted in the engine by changing the value of the exported `Radius` variable in the **Inspector**.

At this point, we've examined both approaches in detail. *Table 2.1* summarizes the key differences between scenes and scripts to help you make quick, informed decisions when designing new systems:

Feature	**Scene (.tscn)**	**Script (.gd)**
Primary role	Structure and visuals	Behavior and logic
Mental model	Declarative (what things are)	Imperative (what things do)
Best for	UI layouts, game objects (Player, Enemy), Levels	Data handling, calculations, save systems, state machines, tooling

Feature	Scene (.tscn)	Script (.gd)
Inheritance	Visual inheritance (changes propagate to children)	Logical inheritance (shared functions/variables)
Performance	Higher memory overhead (tracks transforms, visibility)	Lightweight (`Object`/`RefCounted`) or standard overhead (`Node`).
Key advantage	Visual composition in the editor; easy for non-programmers	Modular, reusable logic; cleaner version control diffs.

Table 2.1 – Choosing between scenes and scripts

Once the scene-versus-script decision is clear, the next challenge is choosing between inheritance and composition.

Balancing composition and inheritance

While we often debate between **Script Inheritance** (*code reuse*) and **Composition** (*node reuse*), Godot offers a middle ground: Inherited Scenes.

An **Inherited Scene** allows you to create a new scene based on an existing one. This creates a dependency link and changes made to the base scene (like moving a collision shape) automatically propagate to all Inherited Scenes. However, you can modify specific properties in the Inherited Scene (like the **Sprite** texture or stats).

This capability creates a powerful third option in your decision-making process: **Visual Inheritance**. While pure composition allows for maximum flexibility, it suffers from maintenance overhead; if you build 50 different enemies by manually adding components to empty scenes, changing the collision layer for all of them requires editing 50 separate files.

By using Inherited Scenes, you solve this problem. You can enforce a shared *Base Structure* (an *Is-A* relationship) that updates globally, while still retaining the freedom to configure unique stats and textures for each variant of a specific entity – like Goblins, Orcs, and Trolls – that share a fundamental identity.

When to use Inherited Scenes

Inherited Scenes are the ideal architectural choice when your goal is to create distinct variations of a single archetype. Rather than rebuilding the common elements (like collision shapes) for every new iteration, you treat the base scene as a master template. This approach ensures consistency across your project while significantly reducing the workload when generating content.

You should prioritize this workflow in the following scenarios:

- **Visual variations**: You have a `BaseEnemy.tscn`. You want a `Goblin.tscn` and an `Orc.tscn`. They share the exact same node structure and scripts but have different sprites and scales.
- **UI skinning**: You have a `BaseButton.tscn` with complex animations and sounds. You create `ConfirmButton.tscn` and `CancelButton.tscn` that inherit the logic but change the color and text.

In each of these cases, the inheritance is being used primarily for **visual specialization**—tweaking the appearance or configuration of an object without fundamentally changing its logic. This observation leads us to a guiding principle for balancing your architecture:

The best practice is to use Inherited Scenes for visual specialization; Script Inheritance for logic specialization; and Composition (Components) for functional additions.

While Godot gives you the flexibility to achieve the same result through either composition or inheritance, composition generally scales better, especially in large or complex projects. This is because it keeps systems modular and easier to maintain. The power of breaking your game logic into smaller, reusable components cannot be overstated.

Use inheritance when a class truly extends the behavior of its superclass, adding or overriding functionality in a meaningful way. If a class only reuses the superclass behavior without modifying it, it's usually a sign that it should be implemented as a component instead.

In Godot, this often means designing smaller, self-contained scenes or scripts that can be attached, instanced, or reused across multiple objects rather than relying on deep inheritance chains. For example, instead of creating separate subclasses for each enemy type, give enemies modular behavior components such as `Health`, `Attack`, or `Patrol` scripts that can be mixed and matched as needed.

Implementing behavior with Resource-based components

This can be shown in practice with a simple example. A `base attack` script is created and saved as `attack_component.gd`, which contains the instructions for the default enemy attack:

```
class_name AttackComponent extends Resource

func attack():
    print("Default attack")
```

This script will be saved as a `Resource` that we can access for each different enemy type. To do that, right-click in the **FileSystem** and choose **Create New** | **Resource** as shown in *Figure 2.6*:

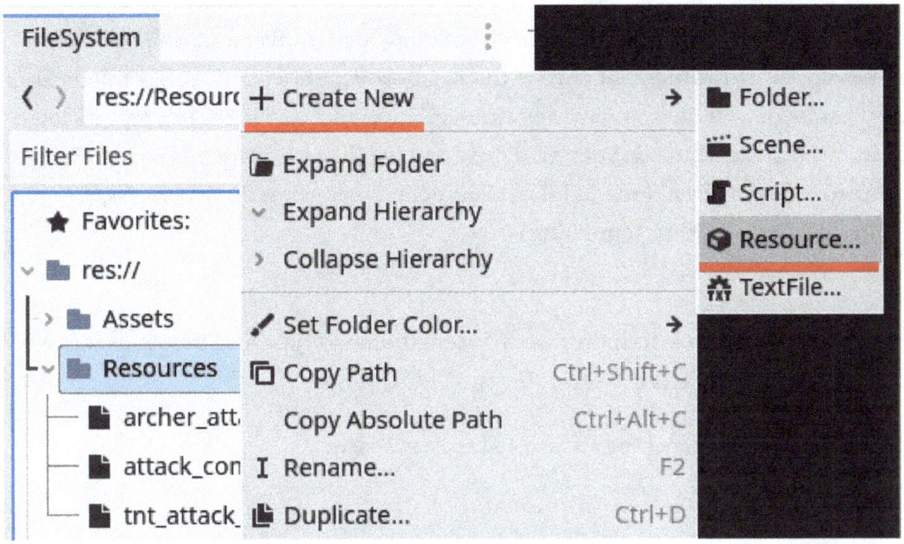

Figure 2.6 – Creating a New Resource in the FileSystem

As shown in *Figure 2.6*, clicking on the **Create New Resource** button will take you to another pop-up, as shown in *Figure 2.7*, which will give you the chance to select the type of resource. Choose the **AttackComponent** resource, click **Create**, and save it as `attack_component.tres`.

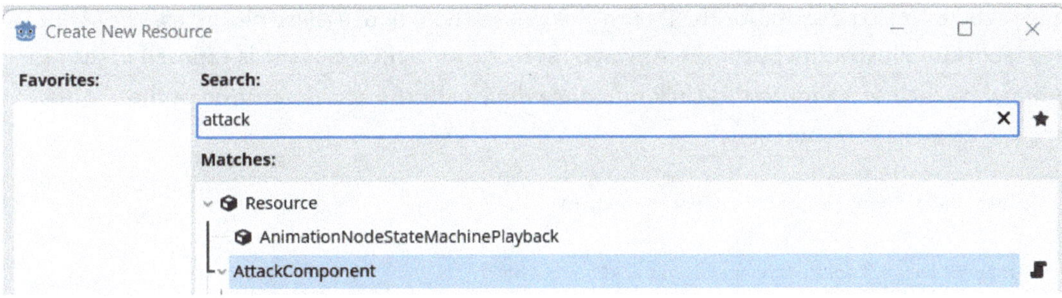

Figure 2.7 – The Create New Resource pop-up

> Note
>
> **What is a Resource?**
>
> If Nodes are the machinery of your game – handling logic, movement, and collisions – then Resources are the fuel that powers them. A **Resource** is a passive object that exists solely to store data. It doesn't have a position in the world, and it doesn't process logic each frame. Instead, it sits on your hard drive as a file (like a texture or a sound clip), waiting to be loaded by a Node. While a Node defines *how* something behaves, a Resource defines *what* that something is.

Now we can write an `attack` script for each different enemy type and save it as its own Resource. For example, here is the script for the TNT Goblin:

```
class_name TntAttackComponent extends AttackComponent

func attack():
    print("Throws dynamite")
```

The script is saved as `tnt_attack.gd`. As you can see, it extends the general `attack_component` class, but it overrides the default `attack` function and implements its own behavior. The class is saved as `tnt_attack_component.tres`, which is the resource.

If we head over to the script for the Enemy, we can see how to use these resources. The script is kept short for illustration purposes. As can be seen, an `AttackComponent` is exposed in the editor, and there is a `perform_attack` function which calls the attack function of the `attack_component` resource:

```
class_name Enemy extends CharacterBody2D

@export var attack_component: AttackComponent

func perform_attack():
    attack_component.attack()

func _ready() -> void:
    perform_attack()
```

Each **Enemy** that has the `Enemy` script attached to it will have an area in the editor where an attack component can be loaded. This is shown in *Figure 2.8* as follows:

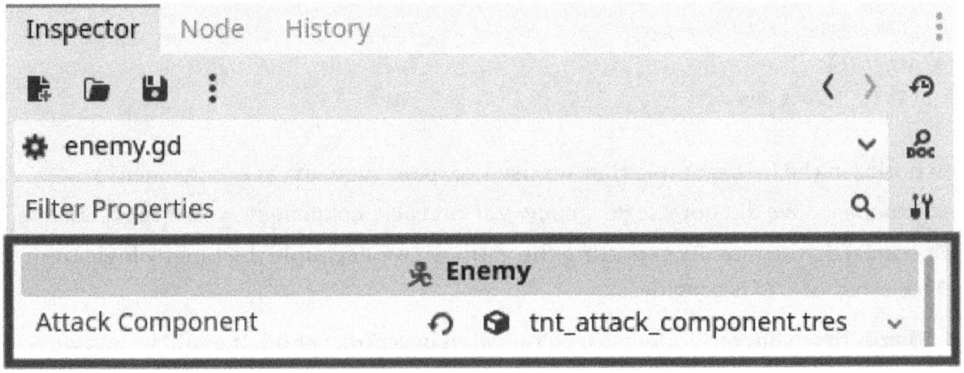

Figure 2.8 – Adding the attack component through the Inspector

There are two common ways to assign these components: through the Godot editor or directly in code.

Assigning components via code vs the Godot editor

If you prefer not to add resources via the Godot editor, they can just as easily be added through code, as shown in the following script:

```
class_name Enemy extends CharacterBody2D

#@export var attack_component: AttackComponent

var attack_component

func_ready()-> void:
    attack_component = tnt_attack_component.new()
    perform_attack()

func perform_attack():
    attack_component.attack()
```

If we wanted to create a new specialized attack, perhaps for an Archer enemy, we can write the `Archer Attack` script and save the `archer_attack` Resource as shown here:

```
class_name ArcherAttackComponent extends AttackComponent
func attack():
    print("Shoots Arrow")
```

Did you notice in the first example that we used `@export var attack_component: AttackComponent`? We did not use `@onready var attack_component = $AttackComponent`. This is a crucial distinction. By exporting the variable, we decouple the Enemy logic from the Scene Tree structure. This provides:

- **Flexibility**: The component doesn't need to be a direct child. It could be anywhere in the tree, or even a resource file, and we can simply drag and drop it in.
- **Safety**: If a designer renames the component node, a `$Path` reference breaks. An export reference remains linked.

Now you will have a different output depending on which attack resource you attach to the enemy. If you attach the `tnt_attack`, the output will be: **Throws dynamite**. Similarly, if you attach the `archer_attack`, the output will be: **Shoots Arrow**.

Pitfalls, tooling, and scaling trade-offs

There is one major pitfall you must be aware of when using Resources for gameplay components. By default, Resources in Godot are shared by reference to save memory. This means if you have a `HealthComponent` resource with `current_hp = 100`, and you give it to ten different Goblin enemies, they are all sharing the exact same resource instance. If one Goblin takes damage, all of them will take damage because they are reading from the same data container. To fix this for mutable (changeable) data, you have two primary solutions:

- **Solution 1 – The Editor Approach (**`Local to Scene`**)**: If you are building your Goblins directly in the Godot editor, you can click on the resource in the **Inspector** and check the **Local to Scene** property. This tells Godot, "Whenever you load this scene, automatically make a unique copy of this resource just for this specific instance."
- **Solution 2 – The Code Approach (**`duplicate()`**)**: Often, you will want to keep a base resource shared (like a "Goblin Template" that defines their max health and speed) but make unique copies of the volatile data (like their current health) when spawning them via code. You can achieve this using the built-in `duplicate()` function:

```
@export var base_stats: Resource # The shared template
var current_stats: Resource
```

```
func _ready() -> void:
    # Create a unique, runtime copy for this specific enemy
    current_stats = base_stats.duplicate()
```

By understanding how Godot shares memory, you can strategically use shared resources for static, read-only data (like a weapon's base damage) and duplicated resources for active, unique gameplay states.

This tells Godot to create a unique copy of that resource for every instance of the enemy, ensuring they each track their own separate health.

As you move more logic into scripts and expose more variables to the **Inspector**, your interface can become cluttered. To keep your *script-based* systems user-friendly, make use of Godot's annotation tools like `@export_group` and `@export_category`. These allow you to organize your exported variables into collapsible headers in the **Inspector**.

It may seem like a small detail, but properly structuring your exports is a professional necessity, even if you are working entirely alone.

In a team environment, you are effectively building a custom user interface for your level designers and artists. This ensures that as the project scales, your teammates can intuitively configure objects without needing to understand the underlying code or constantly ask you for guidance.

However, this practice is just as crucial for solo development. As your project grows in complexity and weeks or months pass, it is very easy to forget how your own systems work. By taking the time to organize and categorize your exported variables now, you are building a clean, self-documenting interface for your future self, saving you from having to constantly dig back through old scripts just to remember how to balance a specific mechanic.

The implementation of these different export options is demonstrated as follows:

```
class_name Enemy extends CharacterBody2D

# Export options demonstration
@export_group("My Properties")
@export var first_property = 1
@export_subgroup("Additional Properties")
@export var flag = false
@export_category("Primary Category")
@export_range(0,20) var i
```

The output of the preceding code snippet is shown in the **Inspector** in *Figure 2.9*:

Figure 2.9 – Organizing the Inspector with the export annotation

Benefits and trade-offs of the component/resource approach

The **component/resource approach** may seem like a hassle since there is so much upfront work; however, it pays off as projects grow larger. This is because it reduces duplication and encourages reusability. This can be seen in our Enemy example. Instead of copying and pasting nearly identical code into dozens of enemy scripts, there is a single `AttackComponent` (or several focused ones) that is reused. This reduces the complexity of code and narrows the search for bugs.

In practice, the component/resource approach offers several concrete advantages:

- **Mix-and-match flexibility**: You can mix and match resource components. Components can be combined without creating new scripts for each variant. If you want to add a fire effect after the TNT enemy attacks, create a `fire_effect` resource and include that along with the `tnt_attack`. No subclassing, no code duplication!
- **Designer-friendly workflows**: Resources are also designer-friendly since they are text-based. Designers can tweak things like damage, cooldowns, or effects in the `.tres` files without touching code, or in the **Inspector**. Separating data and logic this way can make iteration faster and give non-programmers some safety.

- **Improved maintainability and testing**: Keeping components small makes bug hunting easier and testing simpler. Small components with a single responsibility are quicker to look through than one large monolithic script. This is also in keeping with SOLID principles, which we discussed in *Chapter 1*.
- **Rapid experimentation**: Another advantage of the component/resource approach is that it allows you to quickly test different behaviors. Swap a resource in the **Inspector**, and you can instantly see the effects. There is no need to duplicate scenes or re-attach scripts. This allows for faster experimentation and rapid prototyping.

The greatest advantage of this approach is that it supports extensibility and good architecture by aligning with the SOLID framework. This makes the codebase easier to extend as new requirements appear or new features are added.

Do be sensible, though, as this approach can be overkill for a small project or a game jam where speed matters far more than long-term maintainability. Similarly, if you have a one-off boss with highly specific, non-reusable mechanics, a single per-enemy script is often simpler and faster.

An iterative approach is often best: prototype first and architect second. Even on large commercial projects, you do not need to start with perfect architecture. Take advantage of GDScript's flexibility to quickly hard-code a prototype and find the fun first.

Once you prove a mechanic works, and you realize you need to apply that exact same behavior to ten different enemies, that is your cue to pause, clean up your code, and extract that logic into a reusable component. This continuous cycle of "experimentation > refinement > code cleanup" is the secret to maintaining both rapid development momentum and a scalable, long-term architecture.

In summary, use components for anything you plan to reuse or fine-tune. Use a single, custom script only for truly unique behavior. If you invest some time in the beginning, you will save hours, particularly in debugging, later.

To wrap up this discussion, *Table 2.2* summarizes the practical trade-offs between inheritance and composition discussed in this section and can be used as a reference when making architectural decisions:

Approach	**Inheritance (extends)**	**Composition (Components/ Resources)**
Relationship	"Is-A" relationship (for example, A `Goblin` *is* an `Enemy`)	"Has-A" relationship (for example, A `Goblin` *has* a `HealthComponent`)

Approach	Inheritance (extends)	Composition (Components/ Resources)
Flexibility	Rigid. Changing the base class affects the entire chain.	Flexible. You can mix and match behaviors (swap `Attack` for `Heal`).
Complexity	Simple to start, but gets complex with deep trees (spaghetti inheritance)	More setup upfront (creating resources), but scales indefinitely.
Reusability	Limited to a specific class hierarchy.	High. A `HealthComponent` can be a Player, Enemy, or Crate.
When to use	When objects share a strict fundamental identity (`BaseEnemy` => `Orc`).	When objects share capabilities but not identity (Player and Crate both take damage).

Table 2.2 – Composition versus Inheritance

In practice, many real-world systems benefit from combining these approaches rather than choosing just one, as we'll see in the next section.

Hybrid approaches in complex systems

For the majority of Godot projects, the best solution will not be purely scene-based or solely script-based, but a combination of both. A typical hybrid system could:

- Make use of scenes for structural and visual composition, which could include characters, the environment, and the UI
- Make use of scripts for data, configuration, and logic, which could include player statistics, inventory, and even types of attack
- Scenes and scripts could be linked together using Autoloads and resources

Combining them is a win-win: you get visual organization through scenes and modular flexibility through code.

Consider a complex weapon system in a modern shooter. Trying to force this entire system into a single scene or a single script would be messy. Instead, a hybrid approach splits the responsibilities:

- **The Scene** (`assault_rifle.tscn`): This handles the physicality. It contains the **Sprite2D** for the gun, the **AudioStreamPlayer** for the gunshot sound, and a **Marker2D** to define where the bullet spawns. It cares only about presentation – the visuals.
- **The Resource** (`rifle_stats.tres`): This handles the data. It stores the fire rate, damage, and number of rounds. This allows designers to tweak the balance without touching code.
- **The Pure Script** (`ballistics.gd`): This handles the logic. This is a standalone script (not attached to a node) that contains the complex formulae for calculating bullet drop and wind resistance.

Therefore, hybrid systems enable you to utilize the strengths of each approach, resulting in architectures that scale without sacrificing clarity or maintainability.

Summary

In this chapter, we explored the critical decision-making process between using scenes, scripts, or a hybrid of both to structure your Godot projects efficiently. We established that scenes are declarative, defining the *what* (*structure and visuals*), while scripts are imperative, defining the *how* (*logic and behavior*).

We moved beyond the basics to explore advanced architectural patterns, learning that:

- **Composition** (using Components) is generally superior to deep Script Inheritance for shared logic, allowing you to mix and match behaviors like attacks or health
- **Inherited Scenes** provide the perfect middle ground for creating visual variations of objects (like different enemy types) without duplicating the underlying node structure
- **Tool scripts** (`@tool`) bridge the gap between development and runtime, allowing you to build custom visual debuggers and validation tools directly inside the Godot editor
- **Performance** considerations are vital as projects grow; techniques like threaded loading ensure that instantiating large Scene Trees does not cause frame stutters

Ultimately, the choice between scenes and scripts isn't binary. It is about using the right tool for specific problems. Scenes give you declarative structure; scripts give you flexible behavior; and tools like Inherited Scenes and Resources glue them together. By mastering this spectrum, you ensure your project remains modular, maintainable, and ready to grow without collapsing under its own complexity.

In the next chapter, we will tackle the challenge of organizing these scenes into a scalable hierarchy that can support hundreds of assets without becoming a tangled mess.

Get this book's PDF copy, code bundle, and more

Scan the QR code (or go to `packtpub.com/unlock`). Search for this book by name, confirm the edition, and then follow the steps on the page.

UNLOCK NOW

Note: Have your invoice handy. Purchases made directly from the Packt website don't require an invoice.

3

Organizing Scenes for Scalability

In Godot, scenes are your building blocks, but how you assemble them determines whether your project will remain flexible or slowly grind to a halt under the weight of its own complexity. As projects grow, poor scene organization often becomes the single greatest source of bugs, confusion, and inefficiency. Without this organization, you may find yourself afraid to touch your own code, where moving a single UI element crashes the entire game because of a broken file path!

This chapter will guide you through building shallow, modular, and scalable scene hierarchies, show you how to use groups and naming conventions to stay organized, and explain how to avoid Scene Tree bloating before it happens.

In this chapter, we'll cover the following topics:

- Creating modular scene hierarchies
- Using groups to simplify management
- Naming conventions for teams
- Avoiding Scene Tree bloat
- Implementing a scalable architecture in *Void Defenders*

By the end, you'll be able to manage large, professional Godot projects confidently—the kind that can scale to hundreds of scenes without collapsing into chaos.

Technical requirements

Readers should be familiar with basic Godot workflows, such as navigating the Godot editor, creating scenes, and scripting with GDScript.

You can download the example project and code for this book by following the instructions in the *Download the example code files* section in the *Preface* of this book.

This chapter's code files are included in the downloadable code bundle.

Project – Void Defenders

Starting now, we will build a modular space shooter called *Void Defenders*. In this chapter, we will focus on constructing ships.

Instead of building one massive `player_ship` script that handles movement, shooting, health, and audio, we will use scene composition. We will build separate, reusable scenes for the Ship and the Plasma Blaster and then snap them together to create our player ship.

This approach allows us to easily swap out a `basic_laser` for a **Blaster** without rewriting our ship code. For enemy ships, we will focus on Scene Inheritance.

Creating modular scene hierarchies

Remember when you first started using Godot, and you put everything into a single scene?

This is often normal when you are learning, as the projects and prototypes are typically small, designed to teach a single concept. So, a few nodes for the player, some enemies, and maybe a UI generally work fine. However, for larger projects, the hierarchy grows deeper and becomes more tangled and increasingly fragile.

In a real-world production environment, this leads to significant bottlenecks. Simple changes, like moving a UI element to a new container, will instantly break every script that relies on that specific node path. Furthermore, if your entire game is in one scene file, multiple team members cannot work on different features simultaneously without causing disastrous merge conflicts in version control.

Modular scenes will make your Godot project scalable. Your scenes should be self-contained units that do not depend heavily on their environment. In the context of Godot, this means you should be able to run the scene in isolation (by hitting *F6*) without it crashing because it cannot find a specific parent node.

Each scene should represent one focused idea or piece of functionality. Think of a **PlayerShip** scene, an **EnemyDrone** scene, or a **CockpitUI** scene. When someone opens the scene, they should immediately understand its purpose.

To help you self-diagnose your project, compare these two approaches:

- **Non-modular and fragile**: A Player scene that breaks if it isn't placed at a specific spot in the tree because it relies on hard-coded paths like `get_node("../Cockpit/HShieldGauge")`.
- **Modular and robust**: A Player scene that works in any level, or even a blank test chamber, because it uses signals to broadcast changes (`signal shield_changed`) rather than looking for neighbors.

To maintain this single-purpose, single-functionality characteristic for scenes, it will be helpful to create some rules to follow.

Rule number 1: Keep scenes shallow

If your Scene Tree is deeply nested, then that is a bad sign. **Deep nesting** often emerges naturally in Godot, particularly when developers use extra Nodes simply to group items together visually, or when building complex UI layouts. While this might make the Scene Tree look organized, every additional level of depth tightens coupling and makes the task of debugging more difficult.

Rather, break up large systems into smaller, composable sub-scenes. As an example, your **PlayerShip** should not directly contain every particle emitter and sound effect for the engines. Instead, the `Engine` should exist as its own scene (containing the thruster sprites and sounds), instantiated by the Ship when needed.

This separation yields immediate benefits:

- Structurally, it prevents the `player_ship` script from becoming a monolithic God class that handles unrelated logic, such as calculating particle emission rates or managing thruster audio volumes.
- In terms of efficiency and scalability, it ensures that your heavy engine assets are entirely modular. You can now instantiate this exact same **Engine** scene on different ship types, like Enemy Fighters or Allied Drones, without duplicating the underlying logic, thereby keeping your project's overall memory footprint low and reducing development time.

Does this mean that you must never nest deeply? Not necessarily. The exception to this rule is the user interface. In Godot, building complex, responsive menus often requires deeply nested chains of Containers (like `MarginContainer` => `VBoxContainer` => `Panel` => `HBoxContainer`) to handle automatic resizing correctly. This is justified because these nodes are strictly for visual positioning, not logic.

However, for gameplay objects like characters or level props, you should strictly adhere to the shallow rule to keep dependencies clean. However, this necessary depth creates a new problem: accessing a node buried five levels deep typically requires a long and brittle path that is prone to breaking.

Sometimes you need to reference a specific node in your own scene, but moving nodes around breaks the path. For example, `get_node("UI/Container/Label")` will break if you decide to move the `Label` out of the `Container`.

To solve this without over-engineering signals, you have two great options depending on your needs: *export variables* and *Scene Unique Nodes*.

Using an **export variable** (for example, `@export var shield_label: Label`) is clean because it doesn't rely on Scene Tree paths or string names at all. However, if you have a complex scene with dozens of internal components, exposing all of them as export variables can quickly clutter your **Inspector** and allow designers to accidentally clear essential internal references.

For these purely internal references, Godot introduced **Scene Unique Nodes**. By right-clicking a node in the Scene Tree and selecting **Access as Unique Name**, the node is marked with a **%** (**percent**) sign, for example, **%ShieldBar**. You can then access this node from any script in the same scene using `get_node("%ShieldBar")` or simply `%ShieldBar`.

A highly recommended practice is to store this reference at the top of your script using the `@onready` keyword: `@onready var shield_bar: ProgressBar = %ShieldBar` (you can hold *Ctrl*/*Cmd* and drag the node from the Scene Tree directly into your script to generate this line automatically.)

This creates a robust reference that will not break, even if you drag the node to a completely different location within that scene's hierarchy. Ultimately, this feature grants you the freedom to refactor your scene's visual hierarchy as often as needed without the fear of breaking your underlying code logic.

Rule number 2: Instancing is best for reuse

If you find that you are duplicating the same node structure across multiple scenes, such as a **Fuel Canister** or a **Pause Menu**, then that is a sure sign that it should become its own scene.

One of the standout features of Godot is that its **Instancing** system encourages you to easily reuse scenes. This means that you can keep one authoritative version to which changes can be made and then updated everywhere. The huge advantage of keeping your hierarchy flat and composed of reusable parts is the reduction of duplication and risk.

To understand the value of this, consider the alternative. If you manually copied and pasted a **Fuel Canister** node structure into 50 different levels and later decided to change the canister's pickup sound effect, you would have to open all 50 levels and update every single canister individually. This approach is prone to human error and creates a maintenance nightmare! By using Instancing, you simply update the original scene file once, and the change propagates to every instance across the entire project instantly.

While you can drag parts onto your ship in the editor, you cannot predict when the player will fire their weapon. This requires **Runtime Instancing**. A common example is to preload projectile scenes and then add them as children in the Scene Tree during runtime.

This is shown in the code snippet as follows:

```
extends Node2D

# Preload the bullet scene so it's ready in memory
var laser_scene = preload("res://Projectiles/Laser_Blue.tscn")

func fire_weapon():
    # Create the instance
    var new_laser = laser_scene.instantiate()

    # Critical: Add it to the main game world, NOT the ship
    # (If added to the ship, the bullet would move with the ship!)
    get_tree().root.add_child(new_laser)

    # Set the bullet's starting position to the cannon's muzzle
    new_laser.global_position = global_position
```

In the preceding script, we first load the Laser scene into memory using preload and create a new instance of it. Crucially, the laser does not actively exist in the game world until we explicitly attach it to the Scene Tree using `add_child()`.

When to use Runtime Instancing

While you can simply drag-and-drop scenes in the editor for static objects (like placing a specific door or a boss), Runtime Instancing is essential for dynamic content. You should use this method whenever you need to spawn objects on the fly, such as projectiles, loot drops, or waves of enemies. These are objects that cannot be placed beforehand.

Using Inherited Scenes for specialization

While Instancing is powerful, Godot offers another layer of reuse called **Inherited Scenes** (a concept introduced in *Chapter 2*).

You will likely have many types of enemies in *Void Defenders*: fast interceptors, heavy bombers, and stationary turrets. Instead of coding movement logic for each one, create a `BaseEnemy.tscn` that defines the collision shape, AI scripts, and a basic sprite setup. You can right-click that file and select **New Inherited Scene**. This creates a new scene (for example, `KamikazeDrone.tscn`) that is linked to the base.

Any changes you make to `BaseEnemy` will automatically propagate to `KamikazeDrone`, but you can still override specific properties in the **Drone** scene, such as changing the sprite texture or increasing the speed variable. This allows you to create libraries of object variations without duplicating the core logic nodes.

Composition versus Inheritance

Instancing and Inherited Scenes are not competing solutions for the exact same problem; rather, they are distinct tools with specific architectural purposes. Knowing what these tools do allows you to apply the correct pattern to your game elements. Use *Table 3.1* to understand how these approaches differ:

Strategy	Best used for	Reason	Example
Instancing	Composition	You need to combine distinct pieces of functionality or place multiple copies of the same object.	Placing Asteroids in a level; attaching a **Laser Cannon** scene to a **PlayerShip**.
Inherited Scenes	Specialization	You need to create a specific variation of a generic object that shares common logic.	Creating a "Fast Interceptor" and "Heavy Bomber" from a generic `BaseEnemy scene`.

Table 3.1 – Choosing between Instancing and Inherited Scenes

Rule number 3: Loose coupling between scenes

As far as possible, scenes should communicate via *signals* and not *direct references*. This is because when one scene directly calls a method on another, it creates a dependency that breaks when the hierarchy changes. Signals are anonymous by design; the emitter does not care who is listening. This decoupling makes it easy to move or reuse scenes without breaking anything.

Does this mean you should never use direct references? Not at all. Direct references are perfectly acceptable, and often preferred, when nodes are inherently dependent and exist strictly within the same encapsulated scene.

For example, a parent `player_ship` script using a direct reference to call `blaster.fire()` on its child node is correct. Since the blaster is an intrinsic part of the ship's internal structure, this tight coupling is intentional and safe. It is only when you are communicating across different, unrelated scenes (like the Player talking to the UI or a Game Manager) that direct references become a dangerous anti-pattern.

To maintain loose coupling where it matters, the Godot community adheres to a golden rule of architecture: **Call Down, Signal Up**. This mantra describes the direction of communication in your hierarchy.

To visualize this, imagine the flow of information as a loop. Parents give commands downwards, while children report status upwards. This is illustrated in *Figure 3.1*:

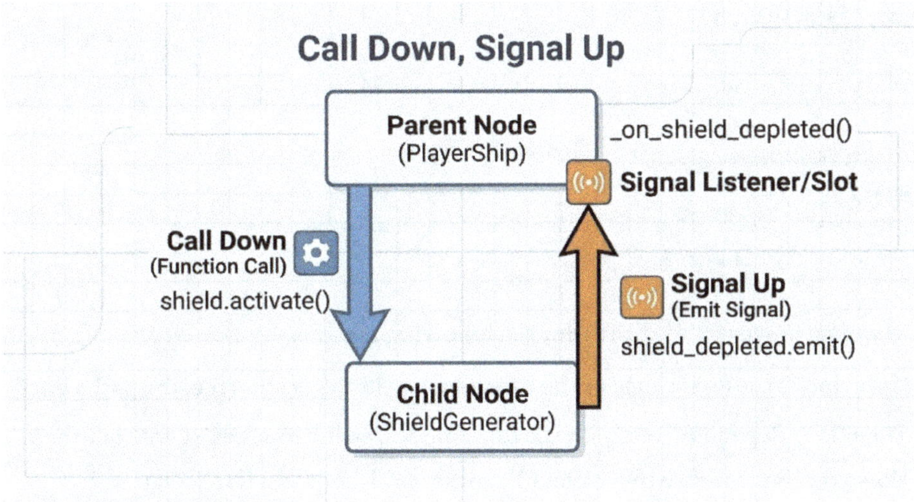

Figure 3.1 – A visual representation of Call Down, Signal Up

As illustrated in *Figure 3.1*, the **Parent Node** (**PlayerShip**) *owns* the **Child** (**ShieldGenerator**) and can safely call functions like `shield.activate()` (**Call Down**). The **Child Node**, however, is blind to its owner; it simply shouts "Shield Depleted!" (**Signal Up**), and whoever happens to be listening can respond.

A parent node calls down because it knows exactly what children it has. However, children should never call up to their parents directly, because a child shouldn't need to know who their parent is. If a button is clicked, it shouldn't try to find the **Menu** node to call a function; instead, it should **Signal Up** by emitting a pressed signal. The parent (the **Menu**) listens for that signal and decides what to do.

What about **sibling nodes**? If you have two sibling components, such as a `WeaponComponent` and a `MovementComponent`, they should never reference each other directly. If equipping a heavy weapon needs to slow the ship down, the `WeaponComponent` should *Signal Up* to the parent `PlayerShip`. The parent script listens to this update and then *Calls Down* to the `MovementComponent` to adjust the speed. The parent acts as the manager, keeping the siblings entirely decoupled.

Example: The Player Hull

In *Void Defenders*, the Player can take damage from Enemy Lasers or collide with Asteroids. Without using signals, you might write code like this:

```
# Bad Practice: Tight Coupling
extends CharacterBody2D

var health: int = 50

func take_damage(amount: int) -> void:
    health -= amount
    get_node("../CockpitUI/HealthBar").update_health(health)
    get_node("../GameManager").check_game_over()
```

This code works; however, it is brittle for the following reasons:

- If you move the `HealthBar` or the `GameManager` in the Scene Tree, the paths break
- The Player depends directly on the other nodes, so it cannot exist without them
- Now you cannot reuse the Player in another project or test it in isolation

This is a case of tight coupling, and it does not scale well at all.

If we apply the same logic using signals to demonstrate loose coupling, we get a much better result.

Therefore, in the PlayerShip script, we write:

```
class_name PlayerShip extends CharacterBody2D

signal hull_damaged(amount)
var health: int = 50

functake_damage(amount:int)-> void:
    health -= amount
    hull_damaged.emit(health)

func_physics_process(delta:float)-> void:
    # Ship movement logic…
    move_and_slide()
```

Notice the crucial difference here: we have removed the specific reference to the UI node (get_node("../UI/HealthBar"). Instead, we defined a custom signal at the top of the script (signal hull_damaged) and simply emitted it when damage occurred. This change means the Player script no longer cares if a **HealthBar** exists or not; it strictly focuses on its own status, fulfilling the goal of loose coupling.

Now the Player doesn't need to know who else needs to be aware that it took damage. It simply broadcasts an event alerting anyone listening that it took damage and provides an updated health value. The listener then decides how to respond.

In this case, I have attached a script to the health bar so that it can redraw itself based on the new health value:

```
extends ColorRect

@onready var color_rect: ColorRect = $ColorRect

func _on_player_hull_damaged(new_health: int):
    color_rect.size.x = new_health
```

For signals to work, the listener must connect to the emitter. While you can do this visually in the Godot editor, establishing connections via code in the _ready() function is the safest and most readable approach for dynamic objects.

But how does the listener find the emitter without using brittle file paths? This is where your scene structure matters.

Let's say that your **MainLevel** scene contains both your **PlayerShip** node and your **HealthUI** node. Instead of writing a fragile `get_node()` path, we define an `@export` variable inside the `HealthUI` script. This exposes an empty slot in the Godot **Inspector**.

In the editor, you simply click the **HealthUI** node, grab the **PlayerShip** node from the Scene Tree, and drag it directly into that **Inspector** slot. Now the UI has a direct, safe reference to the player, allowing us to connect the signal in code:

```
extends Control

@export var player_node: Node2D # Passed in safely via the Inspector

func _ready() -> void: # Connect signal to local listener function
    if player_node:
        player_node.hull_damaged.connect(_on_player_hull_damaged)

func _on_player_hull_damaged(new_health: int) -> void:
    # Logic to update the health bar goes here
    pass
```

In this script, the function `_on_player_hull_damaged` acts as the listener. Unlike a `_process` loop that checks variables every single frame, this function waits passively. It only runs when the `player_node` emits the signal, ensuring the UI updates exactly when needed and not a moment sooner. This reactive approach is far more efficient and keeps the UI logic strictly separated from the gameplay logic.

Since the Player's signal is connected to the health bar's function, whenever the player takes damage, the health bar is updated. This provides several advantages:

- **Decoupled**: The player doesn't need to know about the UI or a `GameManager`.
- **Extensible**: Multiple listeners can be connected to the same signal. For instance, a sound manager could also connect to `hull_damaged` and play a "Warning Alarm" sound without having to change any code inside the Player.
- **Refactor-safe**: If you reorganize your Scene Tree, nothing breaks.

Essentially, the player updates listeners regarding its state rather than directly controlling behavior, such as updating the UI itself or playing a sound effect. This keeps the game modular, maintainable, and makes it far easier to scale.

This pattern applies to interactions between environmental objects as well, not just the UI. Consider a Terminal and a Hangar Door. Instead of the terminal script searching for a specific door node to call `door.open()`, the terminal should simply emit a `toggled` signal. You can then connect any number of objects, doors, lights, or force fields to that single signal. The terminal acts as a universal trigger, oblivious to what it is actually activating.

Using groups to simplify management

As your game grows ever larger, there will be a point when you need to manage collections of nodes. Instead of a single enemy, you will have multiple enemies, collectibles, interactable objects, and so on. Godot has a built-in way to do this, and they are called **Groups**.

It is vital to distinguish Groups from the scene hierarchy. The *hierarchy* (parent-child relationship) defines spatial ownership – if you move a parent node, its children move with it. *Groups*, on the other hand, act as logical tags. They allow you to categorize and manipulate a set of nodes (like all `"enemies"`) regardless of where they physically exist in the Scene Tree. You should use hierarchy to build objects, but use groups to organize them logically.

Groups let you tag nodes with descriptive names to categorize them. This allows you to retrieve them or broadcast to them without keeping explicit references.

Example: Managing destructible targets with groups

Let's go back to our example of the *Void Defenders*. In *Void Defenders*, the player's laser might hit an Enemy Ship, an Asteroid, or a Fuel Tank. To manage these different objects, we can group them under a common label: `Destructible`. We don't want the laser to check for three different class types. Instead, we can tag all these objects in the `"Destructible"` group:

```
# Asteroid.gd - Adds itself to the group "Destructible"
func _ready() -> void:
    add_to_group("Destructible")

# Asteroids have a take_hit function
func take_hit(amount: int) -> void:
    health -= amount
    print("Asteroid took: " + str(amount) + " damage")
```

In this script, the `_ready()` function acts as a registration step: as soon as the asteroid spawns, it tags itself with the label `"Destructible"`. It is important to note that these nodes are not actively "listening"; they simply possess a tag that allows the engine to look them up easily. We also define the `take_hit` function here. This is crucial because when we later broadcast a command to the group, Godot will look for a function with this exact name on every member of that group to execute.

Now that the targets are properly registered and listening, we need a trigger. In the `Player` script, we can detect a key press and broadcast the damage command to the entire group at once (for example, a "Smart Bomb" weapon):

```
# Player script calls group attack function from a key press
if Input.is_action_just_pressed("fire_smart_bomb"):
    fire_smart_bomb()
func fire_smart_bomb() -> void:
    get_tree().call_group("Destructible", "take_hit", 100)
```

In the preceding code, the function `get_tree.call_group()` does the heavy lifting. It requires three arguments: the group name (`"Destructible"`), the method name to execute (`"take_hit"`), and the value to pass (`100`).

Risks of using call_group

While `call_group` is convenient for executing a big broadcast without worrying about signal setup, it carries significant architectural risks:

- **Manual setup**: It relies entirely on you, properly adding your nodes to groups either from the **Inspector** or in the `_ready` function.
- **Dangerous assumptions**: You are making a blind assumption that every single node in that group possesses a function named exactly `take_hit` that receives exactly one integer parameter.
- **No IDE tracing**: Because `call_group` relies on a "magic string" (`"take_hit"`) instead of a direct reference, your IDE cannot trace the function, making refactoring difficult and error-prone.

For these reasons, in most cases, a broadcast is better handled with a global `EventBus`. Nodes that should receive such broadcasts can set up a strict, type-safe signal connection in their `_ready` function.

When naming your groups, the best practice is to keep group names semantic and non-technical. Use `Collectibles` or `Destructible` rather than `Group1`. Keep to the principle of singular purpose per group. Even though a node can belong to more than one group, each group should still represent a single concept.

Also, avoid using groups as a substitute for good scene structure. Groups are for logic-level relationships, not hierarchies.

In large-scale systems, groups really shine in management roles for things such as:

- Keeping multiplayer entity updates synchronized
- Ensuring that environmental triggers all respond to the same event
- Showing or hiding UI elements during scene transitions
- Grouping all sound-emitting nodes allows you to update the volume of every active sound source in the game when the player drags a slider without a direct reference to every audio player

However, even the most powerful organizational tools like Groups won't help if your team cannot agree on what to call them.

Naming conventions for teams

As soon as there is more than one person working on a game, **naming conventions** become critical. Consistent names make it possible to understand the structure instantly – whether you are onboarding a new junior developer who has never seen the code or simply returning to your own project after a six-month break. This is why careful consideration needs to be put into the names that the team will assign to everything in the game.

Some best practices for naming are:

- **Prefix nodes by role**: Prefix node names based on their role in the scene, such as `UI_`, `Enemy_`, `Menu_`, `Btn_`, `Lbl`. This allows you to differentiate between nodes that might have similar names (like a health variable versus a `HealthLbl` label) briefly in the script editor.
- **Apply consistent file naming conventions**: Use `snake_case` for all files in your file system, including scenes (`main_menu.tscn`) and scripts (`enemy_controller.gd`). However, ensure the root node inside the scene remains `PascalCase` (`MainMenu`), so it matches Godot's native class naming conventions.
- **Keep file names and class names aligned**: A script file called `enemy_controller.gd` should define `class_name EnemyController`. This ensures that global search and **Quick Load** tools work predictably – typing the class name will always find the correct file.

While clear naming helps you identify individual nodes and files, a well-organized folder structure helps you manage the project as a whole.

Project folder organization

A clean project structure is the backbone of a scalable game. Without a strict folder hierarchy, your `res://` directory will quickly become a dumping ground, making it impossible to find specific assets as the file count rises into the hundreds.

While there are many ways to organize a project, the structure illustrated later in *Figure 3.2* follows a **Type-Based Organization strategy**. This is widely recommended for teams because it mimics the separation of concerns we use in our code:

- **Assets**: This folder contains raw, imported data, such as `.png` sprites, `.wav` audio files, and fonts. These are the building blocks of your game but contain no logic.
- **Scenes**: This folder holds your assembled `.tscn` files. By keeping scenes separate from the raw assets, you create a clear distinction between what you imported and what you built. Subfolders should be organized by category (for example, Levels, UI, Characters).
- **Scripts**: This folder contains your `.gd` logic files. Isolating scripts in their own directory (mirroring the structure of your `Scenes` folder) makes it easier to navigate your codebase using external editors like VS Code, which often treat the project as a file system.

This structure works because the organization reduces cognitive load. When you are looking for a specific goblin sprite, you know immediately to look in `Assets/Sprites/Enemies`. You don't have to wade through scripts, save files, or scene files to find it.

Consistency is the key here. Whether you choose to organize by Type or by Feature (grouping all "Goblin"-related files in one folder), the most critical rule is that every team member follows the same pattern. This reduces friction during collaboration and ensures that anyone can jump into the project and locate a file easily.

Use a clear folder organization that you decide on as a team. It could be as shown in *Figure 3.2*:

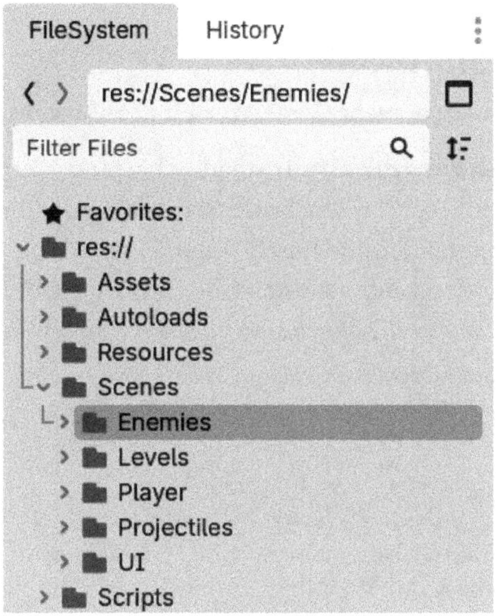

Figure 3.2 – Example of folder structure

The design principle guiding this structure is *Predictability over Preference*. In the long run, a folder structure's primary role is to reduce cognitive load for everyone. No one on the team should expend mental energy deciding where to put a file or where to find one. Through organization, you create a workflow that scales safely. This will prevent the *cluttered-drawer effect*, ensuring that artists can update sprites without wading through code and programmers can refactor scripts without accidentally deleting source assets.

Maintaining consistency will reduce friction for everyone, particularly when debugging or merging scenes across a team.

Avoiding Scene Tree bloat

There are some proven strategies for improving performance – one of them is to target Scene Tree bloat. When too many nodes are active at once, you might encounter **Scene Tree bloat**. Godot handles thousands of nodes efficiently; however, unnecessary complexity can slow down both development and runtime performance.

Some of the symptoms of bloat are:

- Nodes with dozens of child nodes that serve as "containers"
- Complex scenes that are reloaded every frame instead of using sub-scenes
- Deeply nested signals or hard-coded dependencies between siblings

Let's learn how to address these issues in the next section.

Strategies to prevent bloat

The following practices can help prevent Scene Tree bloat as your project grows:

- **Load and free scenes dynamically**: Instead of keeping every object active in the Scene Tree at once, you should rely on **Dynamic Instancing**, loading scenes only when needed and removing them immediately when finished.
  For example, a Scrap Metal collectible should destroy itself the moment it is used. The script below demonstrates this by calling `queue_free()` to remove the item from memory as the player collects it:

  ```
  extends Area2D
  func_on_body_entered(body:Node2D)-> void:
      if body.is_in_group("player"):
          body.collect_scrap(1)
          queue_free()
  ```

- **Use signals and groups to decouple dependencies:** Avoid maintaining hard references to every specific node (for example, `get_node("Player")`). As shown in the preceding code, checking if a body is in the player group is safer than checking its name. By leaning on *groups* for categorization and *signals* for communication, you prevent your Scene Tree from becoming a tangled web of dependencies that break whenever you move a node.
  Note that while `call_group` is convenient for simple states (like pausing all enemies), an `EventBus` is fundamentally safer for complex broadcasts. IDEs can trace standard signals, but they cannot trace string names passed into a `call_group`.

- **Move static or configuration data in Resources**: Don't use Node objects just to store data like RPG stats, inventory lists, or game settings. Instead, convert this static data into Resources (`.tres` files). Resources are lighter on memory and don't clutter the Scene Tree, leaving the tree free to handle only visual and logic objects.
  Note the use of groups in the preceding code snippet. The Player has been added to the player group, and we check to see if the body, which entered the area of the scrap metal pickup, is in that group before acting. The scrap metal itself is an **Area2D** node and relies on a signal to know when a body has entered its space. This is another strategy for dealing with scene overloading – lean heavily on groups and signals instead of maintaining references to every node.

- **Refactor regularly to keep the focus**: If a single node starts handling too many tasks (for example, a Player node handling input, movement, and inventory UI), it is a sign of bloat. Extract logic into child scenes or separate scripts. Remember, the goal isn't necessarily to have the fewest nodes possible, but to ensure that every node has a clear, singular purpose. This makes debugging easier and navigation more intuitive.

Take, for example, the construction of the simple UI for *Void Defenders*. On the left is the score; in the middle is the weapon and ammo; and on the right are the lives remaining. The UI scene structure could look like that shown in *Figure 3.3*:

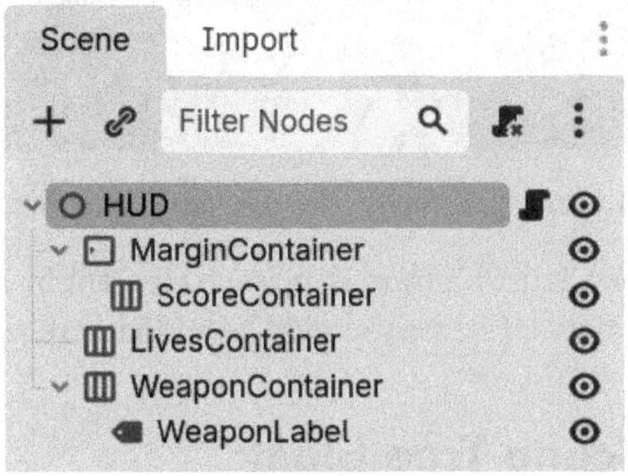

Figure 3.3 – UI Scene structure

Since this UI is composed as its own scene, we can instance it in any class that would benefit from it, such as the main level, as shown in *Figure 3.4*:

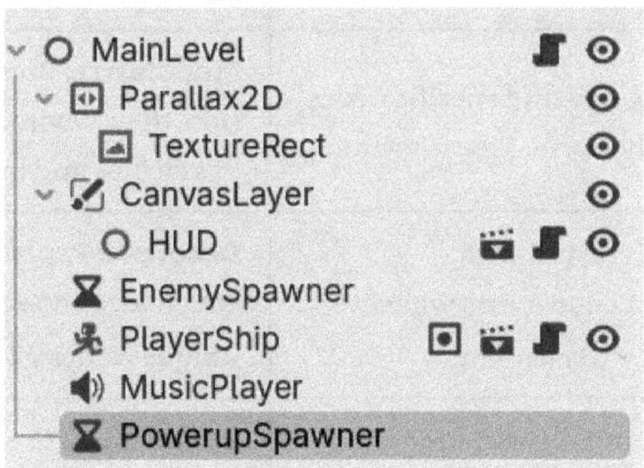

Figure 3.4 – Instancing the UI scene in the Player scene

The outcome of combining these two scenes would be a pleasing information overlay that moves with the player around the level, as shown in *Figure 3.5*:

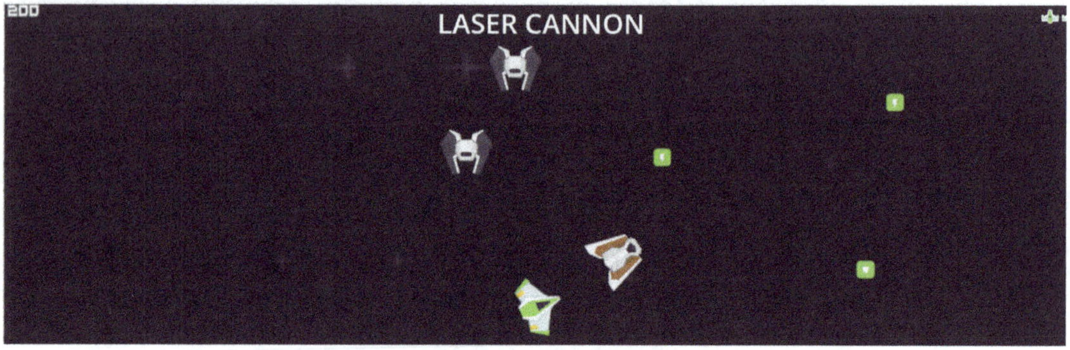

Figure 3.5 – The result of combining the Player scene and UI scene

The whole idea can be extended further by making each element in the UI its own scene. This structure would ensure that new UI elements could be added or removed without having any impact on existing ones.

Troubleshooting Scene Tree bloat

If you suspect that your project is suffering from poor structure, use *Table 3.2* to identify the problem and apply the correct architectural fix:

Symptom	**Diagnosis**	**Solution**
Endless scrolling	You struggle to find specific nodes because the Scene Tree is too long	**Modularize**: Break distinct branches (like UI or environment) into their own `.tscn` files and instance them back in.
Broken paths	Your code crashes with `null instance` errors whenever you move a UI element.	**Decouple**: Replace hard-coded paths like `get_node("root/UI/Bar")` with Scene Unique Nodes (`%Bar`) or use signals.
Copy-paste fatigue	You are manually updating the same property on 50 different copies of an object.	**Inheritance**: Create a `Base` scene with the common logic and make your objects Inherited Scenes.

Symptom	Diagnosis	Solution
Slow load times	The game freezes briefly when loading a level because thousands of objects are spawning at once.	**Runtime Instancing**: Don't place every object in the editor. Use code to `instantiate()` heavy objects only when they are actually needed.

Table 3.2 – Common Scene Tree scaling issues and their architectural solutions

Now that we understand what we want to achieve, we can start putting *Void Defenders* together in the next section.

Implementing a scalable architecture in Void Defenders

All the assets for *Void Defenders* can be found at the link below, generously provided for free under the Creative Commons CC0 license by **Kenney**: `https://kenney.nl/assets/space-shooter-remastered`.

First, we will create our Autoload Singleton, which will act as the postman and receive and deliver the signals in the game.

In the **FileSystem**, create a new script called `event_bus.gd`. Code it as shown to be ready to receive the signals created in other parts of the game:

```
# ==========================================
# EVENT BUS (Autoload / Singleton)
# ==========================================
# This script acts as the central communication switchboard for Void
# Defenders.
# By registering this script as an Autoload in the Project Settings, it
# becomes globally accessible.
# Instead of the Player needing a direct path to the HUD to update
# health,the Player simply shouts to this EventBus. The HUD listens to the
# EventBus.
# Neither node knows the other exists. This is the purest form of Loose
# Coupling.

extends Node
# Godot's error checker will flag a warning if a signal is defined
# but never emitted from within the same script.
```

```
# Because this is an Event Bus, these signals are exclusively emitted by
# OTHER scripts (like PlayerShip.gd or Enemy.gd).
# We use @warning_ignore to suppress this false positive and keep our
# console clean.

@warning_ignore("unused_signal")
# Emitted when an enemy is destroyed, an asteroid is mined, or scrap is
# collected.
# Listeners: The HUD (to update the visual numbers) and potentially a
# GameManager.
signal score_changed(new_amount: int)

@warning_ignore("unused_signal")
# Emitted specifically when the Player's hull integrity fails and a life
# is lost.
# Listeners: The HUD (to remove a life icon) and the GameState (to trigger
# Game Over).
signal player_lives_changed(current_lives: int)

@warning_ignore("unused_signal")
# Emitted by the Blaster component whenever a weapon powerup is picked
# up,
# or when a limited-ammo weapon (like the Plasma Blaster) fires a shot.
# Listeners: The HUD (to display the name and remaining ammunition).
signal weapon_changed(weapon_name: String, ammo: int)
```

Make sure that you add the script as a Global in **Project** | **Project Settings** | **Globals** | **Autoload**.

Building modular weapon scenes

Now, we can create weapon components for the **PlayerShip**. We will start with the default weapon, the Laser Cannon. Follow these steps:

1. Create a new scene with an **Area2D** node as the root, rename it to `Laser`.
2. Add a **Sprite2D** node as a child to visualize the laser.
3. Add a **CollisionShape2D** node for the detection area.
4. Add a **VisibleOnScreenNotifier2D** node so we can delete off-screen lasers. Your Scene Tree should look like the one shown in *Figure 3.6*:

Figure 3.6 – Scene Tree for the laser cannon

5. Select **Sprite2D** and add one of the laser images as the texture. I used `laserRed01.png`. Ensure that you enclose the laser with your **CollisionShape2D**.
6. Now select the **Laser** node and attach a new script to it.
7. Instead of connecting our signals visually through the Godot editor, we will establish these connections directly in our code. Defining signal connections in the `_ready()` function is readable and makes it immediately obvious which handler is connected to what signal, keeping the connection setup exactly where the logic lives.
   Here is the code for the laser, and it is fully commented for your instruction:

```
# We use Area2D for projectiles because we only need to detect
# overlap (hitboxes)
extends Area2D

# @export exposes these variables to the Godot Inspector
@export var speed: float = 1000.0
@export var damage: int = 10

# Grab a reference to our child node as soon as the scene loads
@onready var visible_notifier: VisibleOnScreenNotifier2D =
$VisibleOnScreenNotifier2D

func _ready() -> void:
    # Connect the signals in code so the logic is completely transparent
    area_entered.connect(_on_area_entered)
    visible_notifier.screen_exited.connect
    (_on_visible_on_screen_notifier_2d_screen_exited)

# _physics_process runs at a fixed, consistent rate
func _physics_process(delta: float) -> void:
    # Vector2.UP (X: 0, Y: -1) is the default "forward" direction.
    # Rotating this vector by the current rotation means the
    # projectile will always fly straight out of the cannon
```

```
    var direction = Vector2.UP.rotated(rotation)
    # Move the laser forward.
    position += direction * speed * delta

# This function acts as our automatic garbage collector.
func _on_visible_on_screen_notifier_2d_screen_exited() -> void:
    # queue_free() safely deletes the laser at end of frame.
    queue_free()

# Function triggers when another Area2D's collision shape overlaps
func _on_area_entered(area: Area2D) -> void:
    # Classic example of "Duck Typing" and Loose Coupling.
    # Ask the engine: "Does it have a take_damage function?"
    if area.has_method("take_damage"):
        # If it does, we pass our damage value to it.
        area.take_damage(damage)
        # Finally, the laser destroys itself upon impact
        queue_free()
```

Since all weapons fundamentally do the same thing, move a projectile away from the player's ship, we can create the second weapon (Plasma Blaster) by inheriting the **Laser** scene:

1. Click on the **Scene** menu and select **New Inherited Scene** (or press *Ctrl* + *Shift* + *N*), then select `laser.tscn`.
2. You can now rename the root node to `PlasmaBlaster` and save the scene with its own name, like `plasma_blaster.tscn`. You will notice that all the children of Plasma Blaster are in *orange* text; this is a visual hint that you are working with an Inherited Scene.
3. Now we can simply set what makes the plasma blaster different from the laser cannon. I changed the speed to `1250.0` and the damage to `50`. I also set the texture of **Sprite2D** to `laserGreen14.png`.
4. While modifying these exported variables directly on the Inherited Scene works perfectly for a small arsenal, a highly recommended architectural step for larger games is to use Resource files for the configuration of variables defined by the base class. Instead of manually typing `1250.0` and `50` into the **Inspector** of the new scene, you could create a custom `WeaponStats` Resource. You would then save a `plasma_stats.tres` file and plug that directly into the blaster. This completely separates your raw statistical data from your visual Scene Tree—a powerful data-driven pattern we will explore fully in *Chapter 4*!

This is illustrated in *Figure 3.7*, as follows:

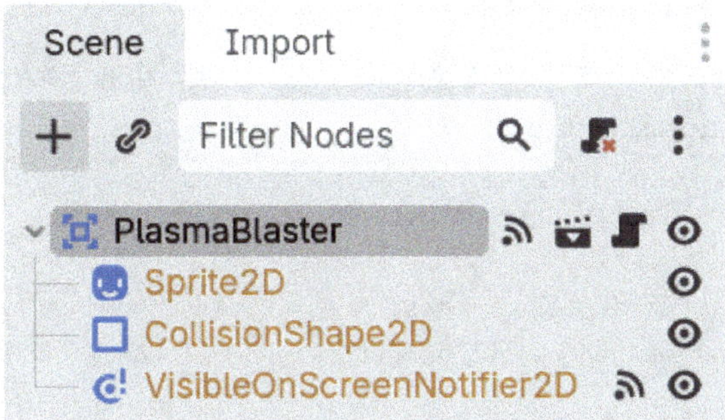

Figure 3.7 – Orange denotes that this is an Inherited Scene

With our weapon components now defined, it's time to assemble them into a functional **PlayerShip**.

Assembling the PlayerShip with components

Now that we have weapons to fire, we need something to fire them from. For this, we will create the **Blaster** scene as a component and later attach it to the ship. Follow these steps:

1. Create a new scene with **Node2D** as the root, rename it to `Blaster`.
2. Add a **Marker2D** node as a child and rename this to `Muzzle`.
3. Add a **Timer** and rename it to `CooldownTimer`.
4. Add an **AudioStreamPlayer2D** and rename it to `FireSound`.

Your Scene Tree should look as shown in *Figure 3.8*:

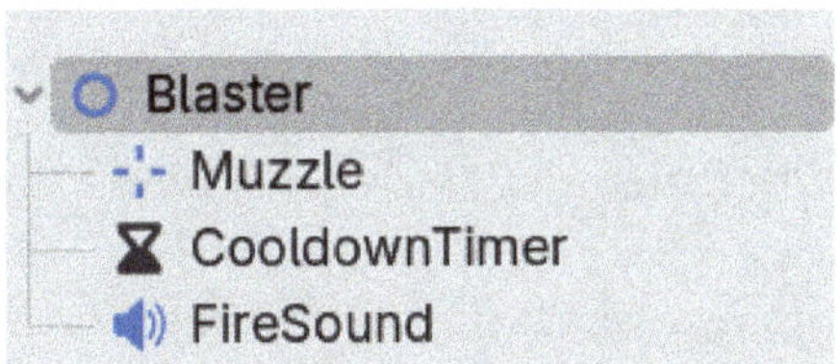

Figure 3.8 – Scene Tree for the blaster

Next, configure the nodes to define the **Blaster**'s behavior:

1. Select the **Muzzle** and position it slightly higher on the *Y*-axis, perhaps at `-25px`.

2. The **CooldownTimer** will prevent spamming the fire button, set the **Wait Time** to `0.5s`, and set **One Shot** to **On**.
3. For the **FireSound**, set the **Stream** to `sfx_laser1.ogg`. Now select the **Blaster** node and attach a new script to it:

```
class_name Blaster extends Node2D

@export var projectile_scenes: Array[PackedScene]
@export var weapon_names: Array[String] = ["LASER CANNON", "PLASMA
BLASTER"]

@onready var muzzle: Marker2D = $Muzzle
@onready var cooldown_timer: Timer = $CooldownTimer
@onready var fire_sound: AudioStreamPlayer2D = $FireSound

# TRACKER: This variable remembers which gun we are using.
# 0 = Normal Laser (Index 0), 1 = Laser Level 2 (Index 1)
var current_weapon_index: int = 0
var special_ammo: int = 0

func fire() -> void:
    if not cooldown_timer.is_stopped():
        return

    # Safety Check: prevent crashing if the list is empty
    if projectile_scenes.is_empty():
        return

    # 3. SELECT SCENE: Pick the laser based on our current index
    var current_scene = projectile_scenes[current_weapon_index]
    var shot = current_scene.instantiate()

    get_tree().root.add_child(shot)
    shot.global_position = muzzle.global_position
    shot.rotation = global_rotation

    fire_sound.play()
    cooldown_timer.start()

    if current_weapon_index > 0:
```

```
            special_ammo -= 1

            if special_ammo <= 0:
                current_weapon_index = 0
                EventBus.weapon_changed.emit(
                    weapon_names[current_weapon_index], -1
                )
            else:
                EventBus.weapon_changed.emit(
                    weapon_names[current_weapon_index],
                    special_ammo
                )

# 4. UPGRADE: This function switches us to the next laser in the list
func upgrade_weapon() -> void:
    # If we are at Index 0 (Level 1), this moves us to Index 1 (Level 2)
    if current_weapon_index < projectile_scenes.size() - 1:
        current_weapon_index += 1

        special_ammo = 5
        var new_weapon_name = weapon_names[current_weapon_index]

        EventBus.weapon_changed.emit(
            new_weapon_name,
            special_ammo
        )

        print("Blaster switched to weapon index: ", current_weapon_index)
```

This is the gun that we will attach to **PlayerShip**, so let us make that ship now. Follow these steps:

1. Create a new scene with **CharacterBody2D** as the root.
2. Rename this node to `PlayerShip`.
3. Add a **Sprite2D** as a child for the visual of the ship.
4. Add a **CollisionPolygon2D** for the hitbox.
5. Instance the **Blaster** scene we created earlier.
6. Add a **Camera2D** to follow the ship through space.

7. Add a **Sprite2D** for the shield, rename it to `ShieldSprite`, and hide it for now.
8. Add two **AudioStreamPlayer2D** nodes for shield-up and shield-down sounds.

Your Scene Tree should look as shown in *Figure 3.9*:

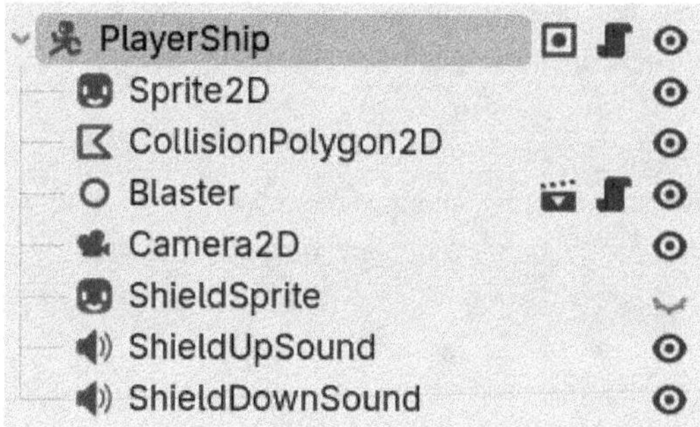

Figure 3.9 – The PlayerShip Scene Tree

Now configure the nodes to complete the **PlayerShip** setup:

1. Select the **PlayerShip** node and tag it as part of the **Player** group to make things easier when we are detecting collisions between objects and deciding what functions to call.
2. Select the **Sprite2D** and assign a ship texture; I used `playerShip2_green.png`.
3. Select your **CollisionPolygon2D** and trace the shape of your chosen ship with points.
4. For the **ShieldSprite** node, assign the `shield3.png` texture.
5. For the **ShieldUpSound** and **ShieldDownSound** nodes, assign the corresponding sound effects.

Adding Player movement, lives, and power-ups

Now attach a script to the main node and code it as shown (note that standard movement code has been omitted for clarity):

```
extends CharacterBody2D

# NODE REFERENCES
@onready var shield_sprite: Sprite2D = $ShieldSprite
@onready var shield_down_sound: AudioStreamPlayer2D = $ShieldDownSound
@onready var blaster: Node2D = $Blaster

@export var max_lives: int = 3
var current_lives: int
var current_health: int = 100
var has_shield: bool = false
```

```
func _ready() -> void:
    current_lives = max_lives
    # SIGNAL UP: Broadcast state to the UI via our EventBus Autoload
    EventBus.player_lives_changed.emit(current_lives)

func _physics_process(delta: float) -> void:
    # (Movement and Rotation math omitted for brevity...)

    if Input.is_action_pressed("fire_weapon"):
        # CALL DOWN: Safely command the child component
        blaster.fire()

func take_damage(amount: int) -> void:
    if has_shield:
        has_shield = false
        shield_sprite.visible = false
        shield_down_sound.play()
        return # Shield absorbed the hit

    current_health -= amount
    if current_health <= 0:
        lose_life()

func lose_life() -> void:
    current_lives -= 1
    EventBus.player_lives_changed.emit(current_lives)
    if current_lives <= 0:
        get_tree().call_deferred("reload_current_scene")
```

By stripping out the explicit references to UI nodes and `GameManager` scripts, the `PlayerShip` is now completely self-contained. It handles its own health, receives input to fire its component blaster, and simply broadcasts changes to its lives via the `EventBus`. This structure proves the power of the "Call Down, Signal Up" architecture. You can now drop this exact `PlayerShip.tscn` into a completely empty test level, and it will fly, shoot, and take damage without throwing a single null reference error.

Summary

One of the strongest indicators of a professional Godot project is a well-organized scene hierarchy. By designing modular scenes that are loosely coupled, the codebase is easier to debug, extend, optimize, and collaborate on. This chapter focused on keeping hierarchies shallow and modular using Instancing. Emphasis was placed on groups to manage collections of nodes efficiently. The importance of naming conventions was highlighted for clarity.

Finally, techniques like dynamic loading and regular refactoring were shown to combat scene bloating. Clarity is the most important thing, not minimalism. Each scene should exist for a reason and should function independently as far as possible. Communication should be done cleanly using signals or dependency injection. Using this mental model, projects will scale gracefully from small prototypes to commercially ready games.

With a solid architectural foundation in place, we are now ready to tackle a counterintuitive truth: while Godot encourages nodes for everything, sometimes the best node is no node at all! In the next chapter, *When Not to Use Nodes*, we will explore how to move data and logic out of the Scene Tree entirely. You will learn to use Resources and data-driven patterns to build scalable systems like inventories and AI, ensuring your game logic remains completely decoupled from your visual hierarchy.

Get this book's PDF copy, code bundle, and more

Scan the QR code (or go to `packtpub.com/unlock`). Search for this book by name, confirm the edition, and then follow the steps on the page.

UNLOCK NOW

Note: Have your invoice handy. Purchases made directly from the Packt website don't require an invoice.

4

When Not to Use Nodes

If you ask many developers how to build an inventory system in Godot, a common answer is to create an "item" node and add it as a child of an "inventory" node. While this approach works well for a quick prototype, it is the architectural equivalent of using a hammer to drive in a screw.

Godot's philosophy is "Everything is a Node", but that slogan refers specifically to the Scene Tree, not your entire codebase. Nodes are heavyweight objects specifically designed for simulation, rendering, and Scene Tree processing. They carry the overhead of transforms, pause modes, physics callbacks, and signal connections.

When you use nodes to store abstract data, like ship hull stats, a cargo hold's contents, or a pilot skill tree, you are paying a massive performance cost for functionality you are not actually using. More importantly, overusing nodes creates a system that is difficult to save, hard to debug, and tightly coupled to the Scene Tree, which will severely damage your project's long-term maintainability.

In this chapter, we will learn to identify when a system should leave the Scene Tree entirely and how to rebuild it using Resources and RefCounted scripts.

In this chapter, we'll cover the following topics:

- Recognizing node overuse
- The hierarchy of lightweight objects
- Using Resources for data
- Separating logic from presentation
- Data-driven patterns in Godot
- Void Defenders – designing enemy systems with Inheritance

By the end of this chapter, you will be able to architect robust, data-driven systems that can scale to thousands of objects without dropping a single frame.

Technical requirements

Readers should be familiar with basic Godot workflows, such as navigating the Godot editor, creating scenes, and scripting with GDScript.

You can download the example project and code for this book by following the instructions in the *Download the example code files* section in the *Preface* of this book.

This chapter's code files are included in the downloadable code bundle.

Recognizing node overuse

The most common symptom of node overuse is using the Scene Tree as a database. This usually manifests as **container nodes**: nodes that exist solely to hold other nodes, which in turn exist only to hold variable data. To understand why this structure becomes a massive liability as your game scales, let's examine one of the most frequent traps developers fall into: the Inventory Node anti-pattern.

The Inventory Node anti-pattern

An **anti-pattern** is a common but fundamentally flawed solution to a recurring problem. In Godot, the **Inventory Node anti-pattern** occurs when developers use actual Scene Tree nodes to represent abstract data, like items in a Player's inventory or cargo hold, rather than using lightweight data structures.

While it feels intuitive to build an inventory by adding child nodes for every sword, potion, or laser battery, this approach is highly counterproductive. It forces the engine to process physics, transforms, and manage drawing logic for abstract concepts that only exist in a menu. Ultimately, this wastes memory, tightly couples your game logic to the UI, and makes saving the Player's progress a complex nightmare.

To see this in action, consider how someone might initially construct a Cargo Hold system for *Void Defenders*. A common mistake is to structure it visually with a parent node holding individual item nodes, as shown in *Figure 4.1*. Notice how every single piece of cargo, such as a Scrap Metal or Plasma Blaster, exists as a physical child node directly attached to the **ShipCargo** parent in the Scene Tree:

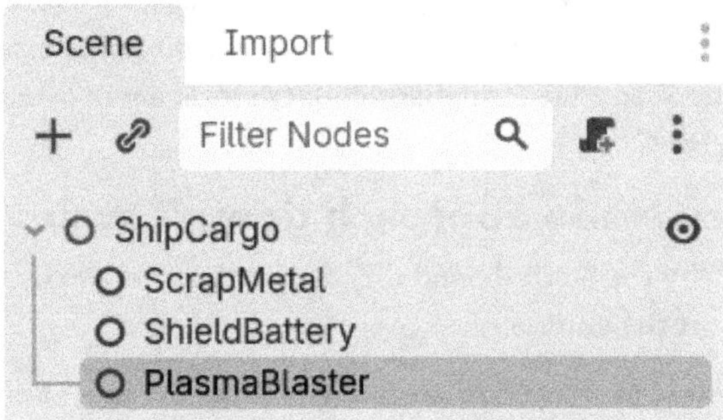

Figure 4.1 – Memory-heavy Inventory System Structure

When developers build the visual structure shown in *Figure 4.1*, their underlying code inevitably mirrors it. To make items appear in that list, the script attached to the `ShipCargo` parent node must load and instantiate entire sub-scenes just to track basic data.

The anti-pattern occurs explicitly when you use Godot's Scene Tree manipulation functions, like calling `add_child()` to store an item and `get_children()` to read your inventory, as a substitute for a proper data array or dictionary.

In code, this flawed logic typically looks like this:

```
# CargoHold.gd (The Anti-Pattern)

extends Node2D

func add_item(item_scene: PackedScene):
    var new_item = item_scene.instantiate()
    add_child(new_item)
    print("Added " + new_item.item_name)

func get_items():
    return get_children()
```

The fundamental mistake in this code is conflating data storage with scene instantiation. By calling `instantiate()` and `add_child()`, the developer is forcing the engine to construct a heavyweight node, calculate its spatial transform, and hook it into the active game loop, all just to remember that the player picked up a piece of Scrap Metal.

While this visual, node-based approach might feel comfortable and intuitive during early prototyping, it creates severe architectural bottlenecks as your game grows. Let's break down exactly why relying on the Scene Tree for abstract data storage will eventually crush your project under its own weight.

Why the Inventory Node approach doesn't scale

It is easy to understand why the Node-based cargo approach feels so intuitive, especially when you are first learning about the engine.

Godot's entire design philosophy revolves around the Scene Tree, making it tempting to treat the editor's hierarchy panel as a visual database. This pattern almost always appears early in development because it allows for rapid prototyping; you can literally see your Scrap Metal and Plasma Blaster nodes stacked neatly inside the editor, and you can instantly retrieve that list using a simple `get_children()` command.

Many developers think this is a great idea because it provides immediate visual feedback without requiring them to code custom data structures.

The upside of this approach is undoubtedly its visual simplicity, but it introduces significant architectural debt:

- **Memory overhead**: Every item in the inventory is a node. It must track its position in the tree, check for `_process`, and listen for input, even though it is just data sitting in a virtual satchel.
- **Save system complexity**: To save this inventory, you cannot simply save the data. You must iterate through the children, read their properties, serialize them to JSON, and then re-instantiate the distinct scenes when loading.
- **Tangled dependencies**: To check if the player has a certain item, you must use `get_node()` or iterate through children. If the game logic runs before the node enters the tree, the inventory will fail.
- **Rendering versus Data:** If the inventory is hidden (the UI is closed), these nodes are still in memory. If you delete the node, the data is lost. This forces you to keep the UI loaded just to preserve the player's items.

To prevent this kind of architectural debt from infecting other systems in *Void Defenders*, we need to step back and ask a fundamental question: *what actually belongs to the Scene Tree?*

Deciding what belongs in the Scene Tree

So how should we determine if a system belongs in the Scene Tree? Generally, we should ask ourselves three questions:

- Does the object need to draw something on the screen?
- Does this object need to collide physically with something?
- Does this object need to exist in the spatial hierarchy (parent/child transforms)?

If the answer to all three questions is "No," it likely does not belong in a node. The rare exceptions to this rule are utility nodes that rely heavily on the Scene Tree's internal systems to function properly. For example, a **Timer** node needs the scene's internal clock to count down, an **AudioStreamPlayer** needs the engine's audio bus to play the *Void Defenders* background track, and an **AnimationPlayer** needs the frame-by-frame loop to drive properties over time.

However, if you are strictly dealing with pure data, math, or abstract logic, it absolutely belongs in a Resource or a plain Object. To understand why, let's shift our focus away from the visual Scene Tree and explore how utilizing these lightweight data containers can drastically optimize your game's architecture.

The hierarchy of lightweight objects

While Nodes are powerful, they are expensive. A Node carries the weight of the notification system, the Scene Tree logic, pause behaviors, and physics callbacks. If you have tens of thousands of objects, like bullets in a hell-shooter or items in a massive database, using Nodes for each one will crush your performance.

Godot provides a **hierarchy of lightweight objects** that acts as a lighter alternative. At its core, this hierarchy is the object-oriented inheritance tree that underpins the entire engine. Every complex tool in Godot is built on top of simpler, foundational classes. Moving down this inheritance tree, away from the heavy Node class and towards the foundational Object class, you strip away rendering and physics overhead, leaving only the pure data and logic capabilities you need.

Understanding the difference between these specific class tiers allows you to choose the exact level of complexity you need without paying for features you don't use.

Object – The ultra-lightweight foundation

At the very bottom of the chain is the **Object**. This is the lowest form of class in Godot. It is fast and memory efficient, but it comes with a cost: manual memory management.

When you create an Object, it stays in memory until you explicitly delete it using `free()`. Godot will not clean it up for you. This poses an inherent risk that if you store a reference to an

Object in a variable, and that object is deleted elsewhere, your variable becomes a dangling pointer. Accessing it will cause a crash or an error state immediately.

Godot itself relies on lightweight Objects for performance in its own engine tools. A perfect example is the **Tree** node, a specific UI **Control** node used to build complex lists, which should not be confused with the global game Scene Tree. Because a complex UI list might contain thousands of rows, the **Tree** node uses lightweight `TreeItem` objects for its rows rather than full-blown Nodes, saving massive amounts of memory and processing power. These are not Nodes; they are raw Objects managed by the **Tree**. This allows the **Tree** to display thousands of rows without the overhead of thousands of Nodes.

Object should be used only when you need the absolute maximum performance for temporary data structures and you are comfortable managing memory manually.

RefCounted – for memory safety

One step up the ladder from Object is **RefCounted**. This used to be known as `Reference` in Godot 3 and is the default class for any script that doesn't use the `extends` keyword.

RefCounted functions just like an Object, but with one big difference – it counts how many variables are holding a reference to it. When that count reaches *zero*, it automatically deletes itself.

The obvious benefit is that you do not need to call `free()`. This prevents memory leaks and dangling pointers in most cases.

An example of this is the `FileAccess` class. This is a RefCounted object. When you open a file, read it, and when your variable goes out of scope, the file is closed automatically. This is proven if we look at the entry for `FileAccess` in the Godot Docs shown in *Figure 4.2*:

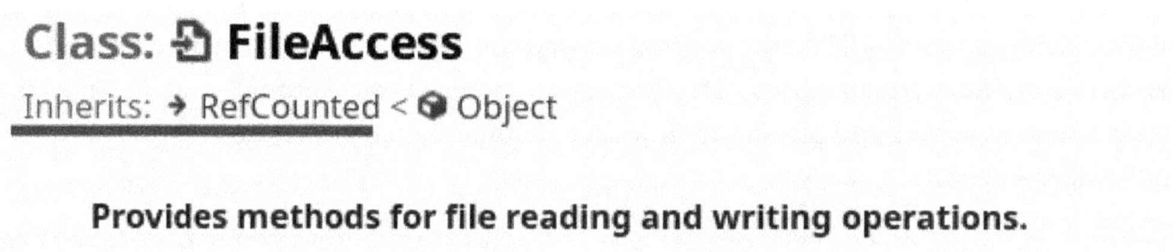

Figure 4.2 – FileAccess inherits from RefCounted

Figure 4.2 clearly shows that **FileAccess** is inherited from **RefCounted**. This is useful because it means **FileAccess** will automatically close its file stream and free itself from memory the moment it goes out of scope.

What does out of scope mean? Because this object is RefCounted, the Godot engine keeps a running tally of how many variables are actively referencing it. The moment that count hits zero, for example, when the specific function that created the `FileAccess` variable finishes running, the object instantly deletes itself. You do not have to manually call a `free()` or `delete` command; the engine handles the cleanup for you safely and automatically.

RefCounted, therefore, is your workhorse for pure logic systems, state machines, and data processors that don't need to be saved to disk.

Resource – for persistence and Inspector support

Resource extends RefCounted, so it keeps the memory safety, but adds the ability to serialize (save/load) and display in the **Inspector**. Resources can save their properties to `.tres` or `.res` files. They are also uniquely integrated into the Godot editor, allowing you to export them as properties using the `@export` annotation: `@export var my_data: Resource`.

To visualize this, imagine defining the different spaceships for *Void Defenders*. Instead of attaching a heavy script full of hardcoded variables to every enemy node, you create a lightweight `ShipStats` Resource that holds just `max_health`, `turn_speed`, and `shield_capacity`. You can then save a `HeavyBomber.tres` file and a `ScoutFighter.tres` file directly to your project folder.

The benefit of this is that, although Resources are slightly more complex than a basic RefCounted object, they bridge the gap between code and the Godot editor. They allow you to build data structures that act like sub-nodes in the **Inspector** without the performance costs of actual Nodes.

This establishes an efficient game design workflow. Programmers must only write the Resource blueprint once to establish the rules. From that point on, game designers can take over, creating, duplicating, and fine-tuning dozens of unique items, stats, or abilities purely through the visual **Inspector** without ever needing to read or edit a single line of GDScript.

Therefore, Resources are ideal for any data that needs to be configured by a designer, saved to a file, or shared between multiple objects (like inventory items or RPG stats).

To help decide which object to use, have a look at *Table 4.1*:

Class type	**Use case**	**Memory management**	**Inspector support**	**Serializable**
Object	Extreme performance, temporary data	Manual, `free()`	No	No
RefCounted	Math calculators, logic managers, state machines	Automatic	No	No
Resource	Items, stats, configurable data, save files	Automatic	Yes	Yes
Node	Rendering, Physics, Scene Hierarchy	Automatic `queue_free()`	Yes	Partial

Table 4.1 – Comparing object types

By moving down the hierarchy, you can simplify your API. Rather than working with the entire Node library, you create an abbreviated set of objects from which a node can generate and manage the appropriate sub-nodes only when necessary.

With this hierarchy of lightweight objects in mind, we can now focus on the most practical and powerful tier for your *Void Defenders* project: how Resources are best used to store, share, and manage your persistent gameplay data.

Using Resources for data

Godot's **Resource system** is arguably its most powerful and underutilized feature. While most users know Resources as things like textures or audio streams, you can define your own Custom Resources to store gameplay data.

Resources offer three big advantages over Nodes for data storage:

- **They are serializable:** Godot knows how to save and load them natively as `.tres` files
- **They are shared:** Multiple objects can reference the same resource in memory, reducing overhead
- **They are integrated into the Inspector:** They can be edited directly in the **Inspector** and can be dragged and dropped between objects

With these three powerful advantages in mind, we can now revisit our problematic Cargo Hold from earlier and refactor it the right way, using lightweight Resources instead of heavy Scene Tree Nodes.

Refactoring the cargo system

Let's replace the flawed Node-based cargo system from the previous section with a robust Resource-based system.

First, we define the data structure for a single item. Instead of extending `Node`, we extend `Resource`. This script acts as a blueprint:

```
# ItemData.gd
class_name ItemData extends Resource

@export var name: String = "Ship Item"
@export_multiline var description: String = ""
@export var icon: Texture2D
@export var stackable: bool = false
@export var trade_value: int = 10
```

By extending `Resource` instead of `Node`, we guarantee that this script acts as a pure, lightweight data container with absolutely no Scene Tree overhead. The `class_name` keyword registers `ItemData` as a native Godot type within your project, allowing the engine to recognize it globally.

Most importantly, using the `@export` annotation exposes these specific properties directly to the Godot **Inspector**. This establishes a robust, data-driven pipeline: as a programmer, you must only define this blueprint once. After that, your game designers can create hundreds of unique items, setting their names, tweaking their trade values, and assigning icons, entirely within the visual editor, without ever needing to touch or duplicate the code.

Because we registered the `ItemData` script with `class_name`, we can now right-click in the **FileSystem**, select **New Resource**, and search for `ItemData`. We can create files like `PlasmaBlaster.tres`, `ShieldBattery.tres`, and `ScrapMetal.tres` directly in the editor and fill out their specific stats.

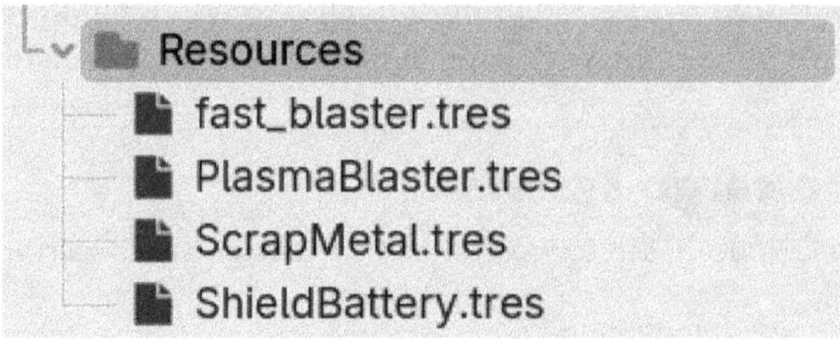

Figure 4.3 – Resource files created in the FileSystem

The next step is to create the actual Cargo Hold as a Resource, not a Node:

```
# CargoData.gd
class_name CargoData extends Resource

# We store an array of our custom ItemData resources!
@export var items: Array[ItemData] = []

func add_item(new_item: ItemData):
    items.append(new_item)
    emit_changed() # Built-in function to notify listeners that data
    # changed


func remove_item(index: int):
    items.remove_at(index)
    emit_changed()
```

Notice two key features in this script. First, we use a typed array, `Array[ItemData]`, to ensure only valid cargo items can be added to this resource. Second, we use `emit_changed()`, which is a built-in function for Resources that automatically broadcasts a signal whenever the data is modified. This allows other systems to listen for updates without needing to constantly check the array manually.

Now that our data exists purely as lightweight Resources, the Scene Tree only needs to handle *Presentation*. The UI does not hold the data; it simply displays it.

To connect these data and presentation layers, we will write a script for our UI that receives the `CargoData` resource and listens for that changed signal to redraw the inventory slots automatically, using the **Model-View-Controller (MVC) Pattern**.

As a quick refresher, MVC is an architectural concept that separates your game into three distinct parts:

- **The Model (Data)**: Our pure `CargoData` resource. It knows how many items the player has but knows absolutely nothing about the screen.
- **The View (Presentation)**: Our Scene Tree UI nodes (like **GridContainer** and **TextureRect**). They know how to draw pixels but know nothing about the player's inventory.
- **The Controller (Logic)**: Our new UI script. It acts as the middleman, listening to the Model's signals and telling the View exactly what to draw.

By strictly enforcing this separation, we guarantee that a bug in our drag-and-drop UI will never accidentally delete a Player's hard-earned cargo data.

While you could export the `CargoData` to the **Inspector** for quick testing, in a production game, you want to assign this volatile Player data dynamically at runtime. This prevents accidental data bleed between save files and allows you to load inventories on the fly. Here is how we set up our `Controller` script to accept injected data:

```
# cargo_ui.gd
extends Control

# The Data (Model) - Injected at runtime, NOT exported!
var cargo_data: CargoData

# The Visual Prefab (View) - The scene used to draw a single slot
@export var slot_scene: PackedScene

# Called by whatever manager creates the UI (Dependency Injection)
func initialize(new_cargo_data: CargoData) -> void:
    cargo_data = new_cargo_data

    # Connect the UI to listen for data changes
    cargo_data.changed.connect(update_ui)

    # Force an initial draw of the inventory
    update_ui()

func update_ui() -> void:
    # 1. Clear existing UI nodes to prevent duplicates
    for child in $Grid.get_children():
```

```
            child.queue_free()

    # 2. Create visual representations strictly based on the data
    for item in cargo_data.items:
        var slot = slot_scene.instantiate()
        $Grid.add_child(slot)

        # Pass the specific item data to the visual slot
        if slot.has_method("set_icon"):
            slot.set_icon(item.icon)
```

This code perfectly demonstrates a decoupled, reactive architecture. The `CargoData` (the Model) knows absolutely nothing about the UI; it just holds items and shouts when it changes. The `CargoUI` (the View) passively listens to that shout, clears its old visual nodes, and builds fresh ones based on the current data state.

By decoupling the data into Resources and letting the UI simply react to it, we achieve massive architectural wins:

- **Reduced scene bloat**: The player ship can hold 1,000 units of Scrap Metal, and it costs almost nothing in performance because they are simple data references, not Nodes
- **Separation of concerns**: You can test the `CargoData` logic in an automated unit test without ever creating a UI
- **Persistence**: To save the player's game, simply save the `CargoData` resource directly to disk using `ResourceSaver.save()`.

By treating the Scene Tree strictly as a visual renderer rather than a clunky database, your game will run faster, save easier, and scale effortlessly. With data ownership clarified, the next step is to separate game logic from visual presentation.

Separating logic from presentation

Resources are excellent for data, but what about pure logic? Sometimes you need complex calculations, state management, or utility functions that don't fit neatly into a data container.

If a script doesn't need to be in the Scene Tree, and it doesn't need to be saved to disk, it should extend RefCounted (or Object). By offloading these invisible calculations to lightweight scripts, your game's underlying systems can run at peak efficiency without dragging down the engine's rendering or physics pipelines. Let's examine exactly why keeping this pure logic out of the Scene Tree is so critical.

The hidden cost of nodes

When you create a generic **Manager** node to handle turn-based combat logic or loot generation, you are forcing the engine to track that object's position in the tree. If you write `extends Node`, you are inheriting a massive amount of engine code. If your logic is purely mathematical or structural, this is unnecessary.

A perfect example of not using a node applies to the screen-wrapping mechanic common in space shooters like *Asteroids* (1979) and our own *Void Defenders*. Both the Enemy drones and the Player ship need to wrap around the screen limits. Instead of repeating this calculation in every entity's script, we can create a lightweight utility script.

By creating a pure logic script with a `static func`, any entity in the game can calculate and retrieve the screen bounds instantly, without us ever needing to add a heavyweight `GameUtils` node to our Scene Tree:

```
class_name GameUtils extends RefCounted

const SCREEN_MARGIN: float = 50.0
enum Size {BIG, MEDIUM, SMALL}

static func get_screen_bounds(context_node: Node) -> Vector2:
    var viewport_rect = context_node.get_viewport().get_visible_rect()
    var world_size = viewport_rect.size
    var camera = context_node.get_viewport().get_camera_2d()

    if camera:
        world_size = world_size / camera.zoom

    var x_limit = (world_size.x / 2) + SCREEN_MARGIN
    var y_limit = (world_size.y / 2) + SCREEN_MARGIN

    return Vector2(x_limit, y_limit)
```

Notice that we explicitly declare `extends RefCounted` at the top of this script. In GDScript, if you completely omit the `extends` keyword, the engine will secretly default to extending `RefCounted` behind the scenes. However, as an architectural best practice, it is always better to be explicit. Writing it out clearly signals to any other developers (and to your future self) exactly what kind of object this is and how its memory is being managed, without requiring them to memorize engine trivia.

Instead of creating a node or even a global (Autoload), we create a script with a static function. Since this function is bound to the `GameUtils` class, rather than a specific object instance, it can be called directly on the class itself. This is perfect for operations that don't need object data, such as in this case, when we are simply calculating and returning the limits of the screen edges. This solution is performant since it has a low overhead.

However, static functions are stateless; they cannot remember information from one frame to the next. What happens when your game logic does need to track active data, like calculating complex combat damage or remembering a player's hit combo? For these scenarios, we step slightly up the hierarchy and use instantiated RefCounted objects.

Using RefCounted for logic systems

To see how RefCounted prevents Scene Tree coupling and handles its own memory, consider how we might calculate damage in *Void Defenders*.

Imagine a complex damage formula that involves base power, armor penetration, and elemental weaknesses. This doesn't belong in the **Player** node, as it would violate the Single Responsibility Principle (SRP), but it also doesn't need to be a permanent Node in the Scene Tree.

Instead, we can create a pure logic container. Notice in the following snippet how we explicitly extend `RefCounted`. We can instantiate this object exactly when a laser hits an Enemy, use it to hold our complex math, and then let it vanish:

```
class_name DamageRoll extends RefCounted

var raw_damage: int
var armor_penetration: int

# The _init function fires the moment we call DamageRoll.new()
func _init(attacker_power: int, penetration: int) -> void:
    raw_damage = attacker_power
    armor_penetration = penetration

func calculate_against(target_armor: int) -> int:
    # Pure logic, no scene tree interaction
    var effective_armor = max(0, target_armor - armor_penetration)
    var final_damage = raw_damage - (effective_armor / 2)

    return max(0, final_damage)
```

Because it is completely detached from the Scene Tree, any script can request this calculation freely. For instance, here is how the `PlayerShip` script can instantly calculate an attack's outcome:

```
# Inside PlayerShip.gd
func attack(target: Node2D) -> void:
    # 1. Create the object in memory, passing in our stats
    var roll = DamageRoll.new(stats.weapon_power, stats.armor_pen)

    # 2. Use it to get our final number against the target
    var damage = roll.calculate_against(target.stats.hull_armor)
    target.take_damage(damage)

    # 3. The function ends, the 'roll' variable goes out of scope,
    #    and Godot instantly deletes it from memory!
```

While our **DamageRoll** exists only for a split second inside a single function, you can also use `RefCounted` objects to hold persistent state over a long period of time. For example, tracking a combo multiplier for successive hits:

```
class_name ComboTracker extends RefCounted

var combo_count: int = 0
var last_hit_time: float = 0.0

func add_hit(time: float) -> void:
    if time - last_hit_time < 1.0:
        combo_count += 1
    else:
        combo_count = 1
    last_hit_time = time
```

Rather than creating this inside a function, the `Player` script creates the tracker as a class-level variable (`var combo = ComboTracker.new()`). Because it extends `RefCounted`, when the Player ship is eventually destroyed and freed, that variable loses its reference. Godot automatically deletes the `ComboTracker` from memory along with it. No call to `queue_free()` is required, keeping your memory management completely hands-off!

More importantly, this approach completely avoids Scene Tree coupling. Because we never call `add_child()`, the `ComboTracker` never enters the visual hierarchy. It exists entirely in the background as raw data attached to a variable, meaning the engine doesn't have to waste processing power updating its transform, checking its pause state, or sending it internal tree notifications.

With our static data and math logic now cleanly separated from heavy Nodes, we can take the ultimate architectural step: using lightweight Resources to define active gameplay behavior itself.

Data-driven patterns in Godot

The goal of removing logic and data from Nodes is to achieve **Data-Driven Design**. This is a pattern where gameplay behavior is defined by assets (Resources) rather than hard-coded scripts. This allows designers to create new enemies, items, and abilities without asking a programmer to write new code.

Using the Strategy Pattern with Resources

We can combine the **Strategy Pattern**, a design concept that allows you to dynamically swap out algorithms or behaviors at runtime, with Resources to create highly flexible AI systems.

Instead of writing a complex `Enemy.gd` with thousands of lines of `if/else` statements for every possible attack type, we define the attacks as modular Resources.

First, we define an abstract `Resource`. An **abstract class** serves as a blank template that defines the rules other scripts must follow, but doesn't do anything on its own:

```
@abstract class_name AttackPattern extends Resource

@export var damage: int = 10
@export var cooldown: float = 1.0

# Abstract function enforces subclasses to implement this method
@abstract func execute(user: Node2D, target: Node2D) -> void
```

Notice that we placed the `@abstract` annotation before both the `class_name` and the execute function. This provides two massive benefits for our architecture:

- **It prevents instantiation**: Because the class itself is marked as abstract, the Godot Editor knows this is purely a template. If you right-click to create a new Resource,

  `AttackPattern` will no longer clutter your menu; only the complete, usable subclasses (like `LaserAttack` or `MissileAttack`) will be available.

- **It enforces contracts**: By marking the execute function as `@abstract`, we can completely remove the empty pass body. If you create a new subclass that extends `AttackPattern` and forget to write its own specific `execute()` logic, Godot will immediately throw an error, preventing you from accidentally running broken code.

This script defines our abstract base class. Think of it as a blank template for all enemy attacks in *Void Defenders*. By extending Resource, we ensure that these attack blueprints can be saved, shared, and configured in the editor.

The most important part of this script is the `execute()` function. Notice that it contains the `pass` keyword, meaning it does absolutely nothing on its own. This acts as a virtual function. It establishes a strict architectural rule: any specific attack script (like a plasma burst or a missile strike) that inherits from this blueprint must possess an execute function that accepts a user node and a target node.

Now we create concrete behaviors, specific scripts which extend this template to perform unique actions. Here is a pattern for a plasma burst:

```
# PlasmaBurst.gd
extends AttackPattern

@export var fire_speed: float = 500.0
@export var projectile_scene: PackedScene

func execute(user: Node2D, target: Node2D) -> void:
    var plasma = projectile_scene.instantiate()
    plasma.position = user.position
    plasma.direction = (target.position - user.position).normalized()
    user.get_parent().add_child(plasma)
```

Because the behavior is isolated in the Resource, the `EnemyDrone` node becomes purely data driven. It doesn't know how to attack; it just knows when to execute whatever resource it was handed.

To see why this Strategy Pattern is so powerful, let's look at the `EnemyDrone` script. Instead of hardcoding attack logic into the drone itself, we simply expose an `attack_pattern` variable to the **Inspector**. This demonstrates the principle of composition over inheritance; the drone is granted a specific ability at runtime rather than being locked into a rigid class hierarchy, making your enemies infinitely modular.

```
class_name EnemyDrone extends CharacterBody2D

# The designer drags an AttackPattern resource here in the Inspector!
@export var attack_pattern: AttackPattern
@export var target: Node2D

func _on_attack_timer_timeout() -> void:
    if target:
        # Drone doesn't know WHAT the attack is, it just tells it to run!
        attack_pattern.execute(self, target)
```

Notice that the `EnemyDrone` script never asks if the `attack_pattern` is a laser, a missile, or a melee strike. It simply `calls .execute()` and trusts the Resource to handle the rest.

In computer science, this concept is called **polymorphism**. It means that different objects can be treated as if they were the same type if they share the same interface. Because every attack we create will inherit from our base `AttackPattern` class, the Drone can swap between entirely different behaviors on the fly without changing a single line of its own code!

The architectural win here is profound: the `EnemyDrone` script is now completely immune to feature-creep. You can design fifty distinct enemy behaviors without ever opening this script again, keeping your core codebase small, clean, and bug-free.

Because of this brilliant separation, we never have to write new scripts for each Enemy type. To make a lethal "Plasma Bomber" variant, a designer simply:

1. Creates a generic **EnemyDrone** scene.
2. Creates a new Resource file using the `PlasmaBurstAttack.gd` script.
3. Adjusts the damage and fire speed directly in the **Inspector**.
4. Drags the newly minted resource into the Drone's Attack Pattern slot.

This generates entirely new gameplay content purely through data configuration, which is the hallmark of a professional, scalable Godot project.

Void Defenders – designing enemy systems with Inheritance

Let's jump back into assembling *Void Defenders*. So far, we have a Player Ship, which can move and shoot, so now we need some enemies. We should create a base class for our enemies. Follow the steps below:

1. Create a new scene with **Area2D** as the root, rename it to **BaseEnemy**.
2. Add **Sprite2D** and **CollisionShape2D** as children.
3. Assign a texture for the base enemy sprite. I used `enemyBlack1.png`.
4. Create a new **RectangleShape2D** for the collision shape and surround the texture.
5. Add the **BaseEnemy** node to the `"Destructible"` group.
6. Finally, add a new script to the **BaseEnemy** node.

The `BaseEnemy` script acts as our foundation, containing the generic logic every Enemy needs (like `health`, `base speed`, and the `die()` function). Before we can inherit from it, let's look at what our `BaseEnemy.gd` script actually contains:

```
class_name BaseEnemy extends Area2D

@export var speed: float = 200.0
@export var health: int = 50

func _physics_process(delta: float) -> void:
    # Default behavior: fly straight down the screen
    global_position += Vector2.DOWN * speed * delta

func die() -> void:
    queue_free()
```

Now that we have a basic Enemy foundation, we can inherit it and change it to make it specialized. Right-click on the `base_enemy.tscn` file in the **FileSystem** and choose **New Inherited Scene**. When the scene opens, rename the root node to represent the Enemy you are creating. I want to make an Enemy that tries to crash into the Player Ship, so I named mine **KamikazeEnemy**. You will notice that the child nodes are orange; this is a visual clue that you are working in an Inherited Scene.

Change the value of the exported variables in the **Inspector** to set this Enemy apart from the base. I set **Health** to `20`, and **Speed** to `400.0`. Select the **Sprite2D** node and change the texture used to represent this Enemy. I used `enemyRed5.png`.

You will notice that the scene uses the same script as `BaseEnemy`. Disconnect the script from the root node. Then, attach a new script. Notice that instead of extending a standard Godot node, we use the `extends` keyword to pull from our custom class:

```
class_name KamikazeEnemy extends BaseEnemy

# We add a NEW variable specific only to this enemy type
@export var rotation_speed: float = 5.0
```

Because of inheritance, this script instantly has access to the `speed` variable and the `die()` function from `BaseEnemy`. We don't need to declare them here, keeping this file clean. We only need to add what makes this Enemy unique: a `rotation_speed` to control how fast it turns.

Next, we override the `_physics_process` to give the Kamikaze its unique ability: actively chasing the Player's ship:

```
func _physics_process(delta: float) -> void:
    # 1. Find the target safely using Groups
    var player = get_tree().get_first_node_in_group("Player")

    if player:
        # 2. Calculate the Direction Vector towards the player
        var direction = (player.global_position -
        global_position).normalized()

        # 3. Rotate smoothly to face the player
        var target_rotation = direction.angle() + PI / 2.0
        rotation = lerp_angle(rotation, target_rotation, rotation_speed *
        delta)

        # 4. Move relative to where the nose of the ship is pointing
        var velocity = Vector2.UP.rotated(rotation) * speed
        global_position += velocity * delta

    else:
        # If the player is dead/missing, revert to flying straight
```

```
        var velocity = Vector2.UP.rotated(rotation) * speed
        global_position += velocity * delta
```

You might be wondering why we calculate the angle manually instead of using Godot's built-in `look_at()` function. While `look_at()` is great, it instantly snaps an object to face its target. By calculating the angle ourselves and using `lerp_angle`, our Enemy rotates smoothly, giving the Player a fair chance to dodge!

Furthermore, we add `PI/2` (90 degrees) to our target rotation. In Godot, 0 degrees points exactly to the right (the X-axis). Because our spaceship sprite is drawn with its nose pointing straight up, this 90-degree offset ensures the nose of the ship tracks the Player rather than its right wing.

We are replacing the generic movement logic with a homing algorithm. By recalculating the Player's position every single frame, the Kamikaze continuously adjusts its trajectory to chase them down. Notice that we are still multiplying our final velocity by the `speed` variable, a variable that exists securely inside the parent `BaseEnemy` script.

Finally, we need to define what happens when the Kamikaze ship actually catches the Player. We use the `_on_body_entered` signal, combining Godot's Groups with Duck Typing (`has_method`) to ensure we only deal damage to valid targets:

```
func _on_body_entered(body: Node2D) -> void:
    # Ensure we only hit the player, ignoring asteroids or other enemies
    if body.is_in_group("Player"):
        if body.has_method("take_damage"):
            body.take_damage(50)

        # Call the generic cleanup function inherited from BaseEnemy
        die()
```

By structuring our enemies this way, we aren't just making the `KamikazeEnemy` script shorter; we are actively future-proofing the entire *Void Defenders* project. Utilizing inheritance achieves three critical architectural goals:

- **The DRY Principle (Don't Repeat Yourself)**: If you decide later that enemies should flash red when taking damage, you don't have to update 20 different enemy scripts. You write the visual effect exactly once inside `BaseEnemy.gd`, and every single specialized enemy in your entire game instantly inherits that new behavior.

- **Infinite scalability**: Creating a new enemy type now takes minutes instead of hours. If you want to create a `SniperEnemy` that runs away from the player, or a `TankEnemy` with a shield, you only have to write the unique logic. The foundation is already built and tested.
- **System trust (Polymorphism)**: Because every enemy extends `BaseEnemy`, your game's core systems (like the `EventBus`) can blindly trust them. A missile doesn't need to know if it hit a Kamikaze, a Sniper, or a Tank; it just knows it hit a `BaseEnemy` that is guaranteed to have a `take_damage()` function.

We can now add multiple different types of enemies in the same way – inherit the basic Enemy functionality, extend the script, and define what specializes it.

A good logical next step would be to create a test Level, which we could drop the Player and enemies into. Do so by following the steps below:

1. Create a new scene with **Node2D** as the root. Rename it to **MainLevel**.
2. Add a **Parallax2D** node (for a scrolling background) as a child.
3. Add a **TextureRect** as a child of **Parallax2D**.
4. Select the **Parallax2D** node and set the **Repeat Size** to the window size (Mine is `1920 x 1080`). Set **Autoscroll** to `100.0 px/s` on the `y-axis`.
5. Select the **TextureRect** node, set the texture to `darkPurple.png`, set **Stretch Mode** to **Tile**, and **Anchors Preset** to **Full Rect**. You may still need to set the size to `1920 x 1080`.
6. Instance your **PlayerShip** scene, **BaseEnemy** scene, and **KamikazeEnemy** scene.

In the future, we won't want to instance our enemies; we will want to spawn them dynamically. This is something we will do in the next chapter.

Summary

In this chapter, we learned that while Nodes are powerful, they are not the correct tool for every job. Overusing nodes for data storage leads to performance bloat and architectural spaghetti. Hence, we learned that:

- Nodes are for simulation and presentation (Sprites, Physics, UI)
- Resources are for data storage and configuration (Items, Stats, Abilities)
- RefCounted and Objects are for pure logic and utility (Calculators, State Machines)

By moving data into Resources, we gained the ability to save/load easily and edit gameplay values in the **Inspector**. By moving logic into RefCounted classes, we decoupled our systems from the Scene Tree, making them easier to test and maintain.

Finally, we explored Data-Driven Design, where we used Resources to inject behavior into our nodes, allowing us to create vast amounts of content without writing new code for every variation.

In the next chapter, we will look at Singletons and Autoloads (globals) – when to use them, and more importantly, how to avoid abusing them to keep your architecture clean.

Get this book's PDF copy, code bundle, and more

Scan the QR code (or go to `packtpub.com/unlock`). Search for this book by name, confirm the edition, and then follow the steps on the page.

UNLOCK NOW

Note: Have your invoice handy. Purchases made directly from the Packt website don't require an invoice.

Part 2

Godot Design Patterns in Depth

With a firm grasp of foundational principles, *Part 2* dives deeply into industry-standard design patterns translated specifically for Godot's idiomatic architecture. This section focuses on untangling messy dependencies and creating flexible, modular gameplay mechanics. You will learn how to safely implement global orchestration using Autoloads, establish asynchronous event-driven communications with signals, build robust state machines for complex entity behaviors, and construct modular, component-based actor systems. These chapters provide the exact design patterns needed to turn rigid prototypes into fluid, maintainable game systems.

This part of the book includes the following chapters:

5

Using Autoloads and Singletons

In *Part 1* of the book, we focused heavily on decoupling. We learned how to build modular, self-contained scenes that don't rely on brittle, hardcoded paths, and how to use Resources to pull static data out of the Scene Tree entirely.

However, this strict modularity introduces a new architectural challenge. If our scenes are completely isolated, how do we manage data that needs to persist across the entire game? When the player finishes `level_1.tscn`, and the engine transitions to `level_2.tscn`, the current Scene Tree is completely destroyed and rebuilt. If your player's score, inventory, or current health were stored in that local Level tree, they would be wiped out. Furthermore, how do we manage systems that need to run continuously in the background, like a music player or an Event Bus?

To solve this, we need to establish a global architecture.

One of the most appealing features in Godot is the **Autoload**, which is now managed in the **Globals** tab of the **Project Settings** in Godot 4. To be clear, the Autoload system does not generate a new script for you. Rather, it allows you to take any standard script you have already written and register it as a global entity.

When you register a script here, Godot asks you to give it a Node Name (which defaults to the name of the script itself). This custom name becomes the global identifier you will use to access that script from anywhere in your codebase! With just a few clicks, your standard scripts become universally accessible. For example, if you register a script and name it `GameState`, you can call `GameState.player_health` from any other file. If you register an audio script and name it `AudioManager`, you can play a sound effect anywhere using `AudioManager.play_sfx()`.

It feels like magic, but in software architecture, magic usually comes at a very heavy price. Autoloads are Godot's implementation of the **Singleton Pattern**, which we will explore in the subsequent sections.

In this chapter, we will learn how to use Autoloads strictly as Services rather than global state containers and explore cleaner alternatives for managing game data, such as utilizing custom Resources for saving player stats or passing localized data directly through the Scene Tree.

Ultimately, the goal of this chapter is to teach you how to maintain persistent game systems without sacrificing the clean, decoupled architecture you built in *Part 1*. In this chapter, we're going to cover the following main topics:

- Understanding Autoloads and the Singleton Pattern
- Creating Global Managers with Autoload
- Avoiding Global State pitfalls
- Using dependency injection with Singletons
- Injection via a Setter
- Alternatives to Singletons
- Void Defenders – implementing data-driven enemy spawning

By the end of this chapter, you will understand exactly when a global Autoload is the right tool for the job, and when it is an architectural trap. You will be able to confidently build persistent, game-spanning systems, like audio managers and event buses, that keep your codebase organized, scalable, and easy to debug.

Technical requirements

Readers should be familiar with basic Godot workflows, such as navigating the Godot editor, creating scenes, and scripting with GDScript.

You can download the example project and code for this book by following the instructions in the *Download the example code files* section in the *Preface* of this book.

This chapter's code files are included in the downloadable code bundle.

Understanding Autoloads and the Singleton Pattern

In traditional software engineering, the **Singleton Pattern** is a design rule that ensures a class only ever has exactly one instance running at any given time, providing a single, global point of access to it. Consider a game's *audio system*: you don't want five different audio players fighting to play the background music, nor do you want the music to stop completely just because the player walked through a door into a new level. You want one absolute authority, a single instance, that persists and controls the soundtrack regardless of what is happening elsewhere in the game.

Godot achieves this Singleton behavior through its **Autoload** feature. When you register a script or scene as an Autoload, Godot instantiates it at the very top of the absolute Scene Tree (specifically, as a direct child of the root window), entirely outside of your current Level. Because it sits above your active gameplay scenes, it is immune to being destroyed when you change scenes. Whether you transition Levels using `change_scene_to_file()` or swap out a loaded Resource using `change_scene_to_packed()`, the Autoload simply persists in the background, waiting to be accessed by any script, anywhere.

While these persistent Singletons are essential for certain tasks, like maintaining that background music across scene changes, saving player data, or acting as an Event Bus, overusing them is the fastest way to turn a clean codebase into unmaintainable spaghetti. When every local script constantly talks to a global "Manager" to get things done, you create a tangled web of hidden dependencies that make your game impossible to debug, test in isolation, or safely refactor.

To use Autoloads effectively without falling into these pitfalls, we first need to understand how they work in practice.

Creating Global Managers with Autoload

Technically, an Autoload is simply a standard Node or script that Godot automatically instantiates and adds to the very top of the Scene Tree (as a direct child of the root Viewport) the moment the game starts.

To understand why this makes them persistent, it helps to look at how Godot structures its absolute node paths. When your game is running, your active gameplay scene is loaded directly under the root, looking something like this: `/root/MainLevel`.

However, your Autoloads are loaded right alongside it, completely outside of the Level itself: `/root/AudioManager`.

Because the Autoload is a direct peer of the Level rather than a child of it, it remains completely untouched when you eventually destroy `/root/MainLevel` to load `/root/LevelTwo`.

Because it sits at the root, it is never deleted when you change scenes using `get_tree().change_scene_to_file()`. This permanent placement above the active gameplay Level grants Autoloads a unique set of characteristics that dictate how they should and shouldn't be used.

Architectural properties of Autoloads

Autoloads offer three key architectural benefits:

- **Persistence across scene changes**: Because Autoloads sit above your active Level, they are not destroyed when you switch scenes. This allows systems to maintain an uninterrupted state. A background music track can continue playing smoothly while the game loads a new Level, or a network connection can stay alive while the player moves between lobbies.
- **Global accessibility**: Because Godot registers Autoloads as global variables, you don't have to use `get_node()` or pass references through complex parent-child chains to access them. You can just call `AudioManager.play()` from deep within a nested UI component or a player script without any setup. This significantly reduces boilerplate code where objects are constantly asking their parents for references to managers.
- **Guaranteed single instance**: Because an Autoload acts as Godot's native Singleton, the engine handles its instantiation automatically. This guarantees that there is only ever exactly one instance of this script running at any given time. You never have to worry about accidentally spawning two Audio Managers that fight over the same sound channels.

This prevents conflicts. Now you will not have two `AudioManagers` trying to play different music tracks simultaneously, or two `NetworkManagers` trying to connect to the server. Autoloads enforce a single point of truth for all of these systems.

Let's examine the scenarios where Autoloads are architecturally appropriate.

Exploring use cases for Autoloads

As we have seen, Autoloads live at the absolute root of the Scene Tree, making them completely immune to the destructive process of `change_scene_to_file()`. When a Level is unloaded and cleared from memory, your Autoloads remain safely untouched. This makes Autoloads the perfect place for foundational systems that must persist independently of the current Level.

Here are the most common and architecturally sound use cases, along with how they might look in practice:

- **Audio Managers**: Background music shouldn't stop or stutter just because a new Level is loaded. An Autoload can keep the audio stream playing seamlessly across transitions:

  ```
  # Called from any script, anywhere in the game
  AudioManager.crossfade_music("res://audio/boss_theme.ogg")
  ```

- **Scene Loaders**: When moving between Levels, you often want to display a loading screen or a fade-to-black animation. An Autoload can handle this visual transition on a UI canvas layer that sits above the game world, orchestrating the scene swap securely in the background.

```
# Tell the global loader to handle the transition safely
SceneLoader.fade_to_scene("res://levels/level_2.tscn")
```

- **Network Managers**: In a multiplayer game, your connection to the server must remain uninterrupted. If your network script was attached to a specific lobby scene, changing to the actual gameplay Level would destroy the node and sever the connection. An Autoload keeps that network socket open globally. Here is a basic example of what a global `NetworkManager` Autoload might look like:

```
# NetworkManager.gd (Set as an Autoload)
extends Node

const PORT: int = 7000
const DEFAULT_SERVER_IP: String = "127.0.0.1"

var peer: ENetMultiplayerPeer = ENetMultiplayerPeer.new()

func host_game() -> void:
    # Start the server and assign it to the global multiplayer API
    peer.create_server(PORT)
    multiplayer.multiplayer_peer = peer
    print("Server started on port ", PORT)

func join_game(ip_address: String = DEFAULT_SERVER_IP) -> void:
    # Connect as a client
    peer.create_client(ip_address, PORT)
    multiplayer.multiplayer_peer = peer
    print("Joining game at ", ip_address)
```

Because this script is an Autoload, a player can click **Join Game** in the **Main Menu** to run `NetworkManager.join_game()`. When the game subsequently deletes the **Main Menu** to load the 3D Level, the `NetworkManager` remains perfectly untouched in the background, keeping the peer connection alive without dropping a single packet of data.

- **The Event Bus (Global Signals)**: As we built in *Chapter 3* for *Void Defenders*, an Event Bus acts as a central communication switchboard. By making the Event Bus an Autoload, any node in the game can broadcast or listen to global events without needing a direct, brittle file path to the other nodes.

```
# A collectible safely broadcasts to the global EventBus
EventBus.score_changed.emit(100)
```

Now, let's examine each of these use cases in more detail.

Audio and Persistent systems

The `AudioManager` really is the "Hello World" of Autoloads, and for good reason. If you put an `AudioStreamPlayer` in your **Level1** scene, the music stops abruptly the moment the Level ends. The solution is to Autoload an `AudioManager`, which holds the music player. Levels can then simply send signals or call functions asking the `AudioManager` to "Play Track B," and it will handle the crossfade.

Scene transitions and loading

A loading screen or a scene switcher is another good use for an Autoload. Most games have a transition between scenes. Using a `SceneManager` Autoload can act as the director. It can play a fade-out animation, show a progress bar while loading the next Resource in the background (using `ResourceLoader`), and then fade back in. Since the Autoload exists between the two scenes, it is the only Object capable of managing the transition without being deleted itself.

Event Bus/Signal Hub

Another clever use for an Autoload is an **Event Bus**, sometimes called a **Signal Bus** or **Signal Hub**. Sometimes, a UI element, such as a game-over screen, needs to know when the player dies, but the UI and Player are in completely different parts of the Scene Tree. Instead of wiring them together manually, you can create an Autoload named `Events`. Then the Player can tell the hub to emit the `player_died` signal (`Events.player_died.emit()`) and the UI can connect to it (`Events.player_died.connect(show_game_over)`).

This way, the Events Autoload acts as a global message board, allowing objects to talk without knowing the other exists.

Application-level configuration

Understanding where Autoloads excel is only half the battle; knowing when to avoid them is what separates scalable games from fragile ones. To keep your architecture clean, you should actively avoid using Autoloads in the following scenarios:

- **Player or level state**: Never put your **Player** node, or variables tracking the player's immediate health and inventory, inside an Autoload. If the Player dies and returns to the **Main Menu**, that Autoload retains the data. You now must manually write code to reset the global state. Worse, if you ever decide to add local multiplayer, your global `PlayerManager` architecture will completely collapse. Use Resources or local Scene Tree passing for player data instead.
- **Heavy visual scenes**: Because an Autoload sits at the root of the Scene Tree forever, any graphics, textures, or physics nodes attached to it are permanently loaded into memory. Do not put your massive 3D **Pause Menu** or heavy particle systems in an Autoload. Instantiate these UI elements locally within the Levels that need them to keep your active memory footprint low.
- **The God Object game manager**: Avoid creating a single `GameManager` Autoload that handles enemy spawning, score tracking, weapon upgrades, and dialogue all at once. This tightly couples every system in your game to a single script. If you need to test the dialogue system, you will suddenly find it crashing because the `GameManager` is missing a reference to an enemy spawner. Keep your global managers small, focused, and single-purpose.

Now that we understand the use cases for Autoloads, it's time to see them in action.

Implementing a basic GameManager

Let's look at a common use case: a `GameManager` that handles the high-level flow of the application, for example, pausing the game or tracking high scores.

> Note
>
> **A deliberately naïve example**
>
> The initial code we are about to write is a transitional example. It is designed purely to demonstrate the mechanical setup of an Autoload in Godot. Do not copy this exact pattern directly into your production game! Once we understand how the Autoload functions mechanically, we will immediately refactor it to meet professional architectural standards.

To create an Autoload script, first make the script and call it `GameManager.gd`, then go to **Project** | **Project Settings** | **Autoload**. Now, click on the **folder** icon and select the script, and then click **Add**, as shown in *Figure 5.1*:

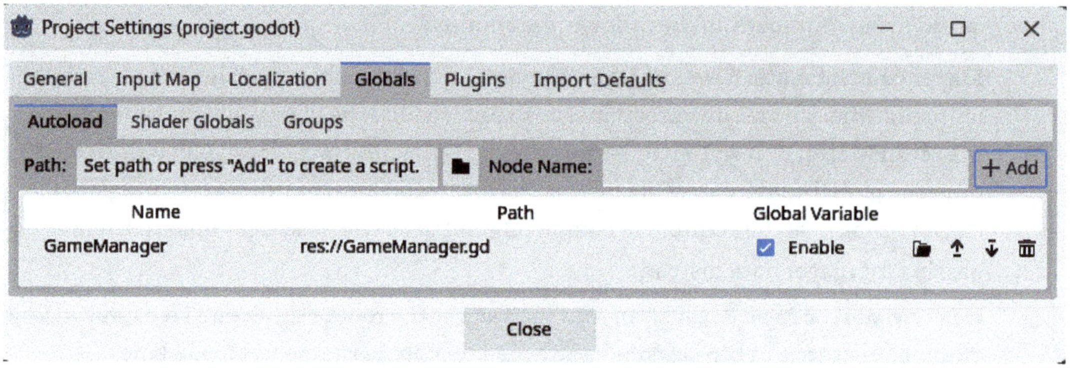

Figure 5.1 - Adding a script as an Autoload

As shown in *Figure 5.1*, the `GameManager` script is now available globally.

Now we can add some code to the `GameManager` script to give it some functionality for the purposes of our example:

```
extends Node

var score: int = 0
var is_paused: bool = false

func add_score(points: int) -> void:
    score += points
    print("Score is now: ", score)

func toggle_pause() -> void:
    is_paused = !is_paused
    get_tree().paused = is_paused
```

Even in this simple form, this `GameManager` provides two distinct pieces of global functionality:

- **Global state tracking**: By defining score and `is_paused` here, any script in the game can check or modify these values simply by calling `GameManager.score`. You no longer need to pass a score variable back and forth between the UI and the player.
- **Engine-level pausing**: The `toggle_pause()` function flips our custom Boolean and then assigns it directly to `get_tree().paused`. Because this is an **Autoload**, you can connect a physical **Pause** button on your UI, or the *Escape* key on your player controller, directly to this single function to freeze the entire game instantly.

Because Godot registers `GameManager` as a global variable, any script in your project can now directly invoke its methods without requiring a localized scene path, as seen in this `Coin` script:

```
class_name Coin extends Area2D

func _on_body_entered(body: Node2D) -> void:
    GameManager.add_score(10) # Direct global access
    queue_free()
```

Being able to trigger game logic from anywhere feels like a developer superpower. You don't have to navigate the Scene Tree, pass variables through parent nodes, or wire up complex signals to make the coin work. However, this exact frictionless ease is also the biggest architectural trap for beginner Godot developers.

Understanding the convenience and dangers of global access

In the preceding code, the `Coin` simply detects a collision and directly tells the `GameManager` to increase the score. The immediate convenience here is undeniable: we completely bypassed the need to use `get_node()`, set up export variables, or route data through parent nodes. It is fast to write.

However, from an architectural perspective, this pattern introduces a severe flaw. By hardcoding `GameManager.add_score(10)` directly inside the `Coin` script, the `Coin` class is now permanently coupled to that specific global Autoload. If you attempt to instantiate this `Coin` in an isolated test scene or migrate it to a completely different project where `GameManager` does not exist, the game will instantly crash with a missing dependency error.

While direct global access solves the immediate problem of reachability, relying on it inside low-level game objects violates the principles of loose coupling we established in *Part 1*. This approach is functionally valid for a quick prototype, but as we will see in the next section, writing code like this in a production environment is a dangerous habit that leads to rigid, untestable systems.

Avoiding Global State pitfalls

Before we fix our `Coin` script, we need to understand the traps we are trying to avoid. A global state pitfall occurs when data or logic that should be isolated is made globally accessible and modifiable from anywhere in your codebase. When any script can reach into a central manager and change a value at any time, tracking down bugs becomes difficult because the flow of information is no longer linear or predictable. Hidden dependencies begin to weave through your project, linking entirely unrelated systems together.

Let's break down exactly how the `GameManager.add_score(10)` example falls into these traps:

- **The creation of tight coupling**: In our naïve example, we forced the `Coin` script to require an exact, named external system (`GameManager`) to function. By hardcoding this specific relationship, the `Coin` can no longer operate independently. In software architecture, this unbreakable, required dependency between two distinct pieces of code is known as **tight coupling**.
- **Destroying portability**: Because of this tight coupling, the `Coin` script now explicitly depends on the existence of a Singleton named `GameManager`. If you decide to reuse this `Coin` in a different game, or even just drop it into an isolated test scene that doesn't have the `GameManager` Autoload active, the script will crash immediately upon being collected. You have made your `Coin` object completely non-portable.

  This is a severe problem because it destroys one of the greatest advantages of Godot: the ability to build a library of reusable, plug-and-play scenes. If every small prop in your game requires a massive, project-specific global manager just to exist without crashing, your development speed and flexibility will grind to a halt.

One of the most common ways this problem manifests in practice is through the God Object anti-pattern.

The God Object anti-pattern

The most common mistake that intermediate developers make is creating a `Global.gd` file and dumping everything into it. You can imagine it looking like this:

```
# Global.gd (The Anti-Pattern)

extends Node
```

```
var player_hp
var inventory_list
var current_level_name
var music_volume
var enemy_count
var is_game_over

func save_game()-> void:
    pass
func load_game()-> void:
    pass
func play_sound()-> void:
    pass
```

Looking closely at this script, the architectural failure is immediately apparent: it completely violates the **Single Responsibility Principle** and the separation of concerns we established in earlier chapters. This single file is trying to act as a database (`inventory_list`), an audio engine (`play_sound`), a state machine (`is_game_over`), and an I/O system (`save_game`). By cramming unrelated domains into one file, any minor update to the audio logic risks introducing bugs into the save system.

This is known as a **God Object**. It knows too much and does too much. This has many negative consequences, but the biggest of these is:

- **Race conditions**: If two different scripts try to modify `Global_player_hp` at the same time, you will get unpredictable bugs.
- **Memory bloat**: Everything in an Autoload stays in RAM for the entire duration of the session. If you store heavy arrays or references here, you are permanently consuming memory that is never freed.
- **Refactoring nightmares**: If you rename `player_hp` to `current_health`, you might have to update 50 different scripts scattered across the entire project!

The fundamental mistake behind the God Object is confusing global accessibility with global storage. Just because an Autoload can hold any variable doesn't mean it should act as a universal dumping ground for your game's data. When you mix static data (like player health) with active background systems (like audio players), you destroy the modularity of your codebase.

Therefore, avoiding the God Object requires more than caution; it requires a guiding principle.

To avoid pitfalls, follow this strict rule: *Autoloads should manage systems, not data*:

- **DON'T**: Add `PlayerStats` as an Autoload. Player data belongs to the Player node or a Resource.
- **DO**: Add `AudioService` as an Autoload. The ability to play sound is a system service that applies to the entire game.

To avoid these pitfalls, we need a more flexible way to manage dependencies without tightly coupling our scripts to global managers.

Using dependency injection with Singletons

To solve the tight coupling problem where our `Coin` crashes without a `GameManager`, we can employ a concept from software engineering known as **dependency injection**. In a pure dependency injection setup, an object never fetches its own dependencies (like a manager or a service). Instead, those dependencies are injected or handed to it by an external system when the object is created.

However, in Godot, implementing pure dependency injection across the entire Scene Tree can be cumbersome. Instead, we often use a closely related, lighter pattern called the **Service Locator Pattern**. While dependency injection pushes dependencies from the outside in, a Service Locator acts as a central registry that objects can query to find the services they need. In Godot, an Autoload effectively serves as a native Service Locator. The trick is to use the Autoload as a service provider while keeping our local code clean and modular.

For simple events, **signals** are the perfect solution to achieve this decoupling in Godot. The problem we are solving here is that the `Coin` needs to tell the rest of the game it was collected, but it shouldn't care who is keeping score. By using a signal, the `Coin` simply broadcasts its status, effectively saying, "I have been collected; here is my value."

Let's refactor our `Coin` script to remove the hardcoded global access and replace it with a custom signal:

```
class_name Coin extends Area2D

signal coin_collected(amount: int)

func _on_body_entered(body: Node2D) -> void:
    # Replace the hardcoded GameManager reference with a signal
    coin_collected.emit(10)
    queue_free()
```

Now that the `Coin` is broadcasting, we need a listener. The environment that groups these objects together, such as the active `Level` or the specific `CoinSpawner`, is the perfect place to wire them up:

```
class_name level extends Node2D

func _ready() -> void:
    # Level connects the specific coin to the global Manager
    $Coin.coin_collected.connect(GameManager.add_score)
```

In this script, the `Level` acts as a middleman. During its `_ready()` function, it takes the localized signal from its child `Coin` and connects it directly to the global `GameManager.add_score` function.

By adding this layer of indirection, the `Coin` is now entirely reusable. It does not care if `GameManager` exists; it simply emits a signal. The specific context (the `Level`) is responsible for wiring that local signal to the global singleton.

Injection via a Setter

While signals are excellent for simple fire-and-forget events like collecting a coin, they aren't always sufficient. If a **Player** node needs to continuously query an active system, like asking an `AudioService` to play specific footstep sounds or asking a `SaveManager` for current data, using signals becomes convoluted.

This is where **Setter Injection** becomes appropriate. Instead of hardcoding the global Autoload name directly into the player's logic functions, we define a variable to hold the service. This allows the dependency to be safely swapped out on the fly.

To do this professionally, we want to avoid Duck Typing (loosely assuming the script has the right functions). Instead, we can use Godot 4.5's `@abstract` annotation to create an **Interface**, a strict blueprint that guarantees any audio service assigned to our player will have the exact functions we expect.

First, we define the abstract interface:

```
# AudioServiceInterface.gd
@abstract
class_name AudioServiceInterface extends Node

# The contract that all audio services must follow
@abstract
```

```
func play_sfx(sound_name: String) -> void:
    pass
```

Now, we ensure our global `AudioManager` script extends this interface, and we can explicitly type our variable inside the `Player` script:

```
class_name Player extends CharacterBody2D

# Strongly typed to our interface! We get full auto-complete.
var audio_service: AudioServiceInterface

func _ready() -> void:
    # Default to the global singleton, BUT allow overrides
    audio_service = AudioManager

func jump() -> void:
    # We call the variable, not the global Autoload directly
    audio_service.play_sfx("jump")
```

In this refactored code, the `jump()` function calls `play_sfx()` on our newly created `audio_service` variable. By default, the `_ready()` function assigns our global `AudioManager` to this variable, so the game plays exactly as expected.

Testing in isolation

The main reason for following this approach is to make testing and modularity easier. If you want to write an isolated test for the player's jumping logic without initializing the entire game's heavy audio engine, you can simply inject a fake audio manager.

Because we built an interface, creating a fake audio manager (a mock or dummy) is as simple as creating a new script that extends the interface but does absolutely nothing:

```
# AudioDummy.gd
class_name AudioDummy extends AudioServiceInterface

# We satisfy the interface contract, but ignore the execution
func play_sfx(sound_name: String) -> void:
    pass
```

Now, inside your test script, you can inject this lightweight dummy object before running the test:

```
class_name TestScript extends Node

func test_player_jump() -> void:
    var player = Player.new()

    # We inject the dummy object into the variable before running the test
    player.audio_service = AudioDummy.new()

    # Won't crash - the code runs, but no actual sound files are loaded!
    player.jump()
```

By injecting `AudioDummy` into the `player.audio_service` variable before calling `jump()`, the test runs flawlessly without crashing or trying to load actual `.wav` or `.ogg` files. You have successfully decoupled your player from the global state.

Alternatives to Singletons

Before creating an Autoload, you should ask yourself, "Does this really need to be global?" Frequently, the answer will be *no*. Remember that Autoloads are simply Godot's native implementation of the Singleton Pattern. So, if we determine that a persistent, globally instanced Singleton is not the right tool for the job, what are our alternatives?

The stateless alternative (Static Functions)

If you only need a utility function (for math calculations or parsing a file), you don't need an Autoload node to process every frame. You can use a `static func` in a `class_name` script, as we discussed in *Chapter 4*.

```
class_name Utils

static func calculate_damage(a: int, b: int) -> int:
    return a - b
```

You can call `Utils.calculate_damage()` from anywhere, and it costs zero memory overhead because a node is never instantiated. This is the primary benefit of **static functions** – they are stateless and memory-efficient.

A normal Autoload is a node. Even if it does nothing, it takes up space in the Scene Tree, it has a position in memory, and it checks engine callbacks (like `_process`) every frame. A static function, however, is just a piece of code sitting in the ClassDB. It consumes zero memory until it is called, and once it finishes, it leaves no trace.

Static functions are also thread safe because they do not rely on member variables (like `var score`); they are pure functions that receive input and produce output. This makes them much safer to use in multi-threaded code (using `Thread` or `WorkerThreadPool`) because you don't have to worry about two threads trying to change the same variable at the same time.

Static functions are also portable. A script with static functions can be dragged into any project, and it just works. It doesn't require you to go into **Project Settings** and register it as an Autoload. They are perfect for building your own "Utility Library" that you can carry from game to game.

The data alternative (Resources)

As we learned in *Chapter 4*, passing a `PlayerStats` Resource to the HUD and the Player is cleaner than having a global `Global.player_hp`.

Shared Resources allow two objects (Player and UI) to communicate by observing the same data file without needing a global manager to act as a middleman. This shared reference architecture is the primary benefit of Resources.

Resources can act as a single source of truth without relying on globals. When you give a `PlayerStats.tres` resource to the Player, the HUD, and the `SaveManager`, they all point to the exact same object in memory. If the Player takes damage, the HUD sees it instantly because it is looking at the same file. You achieve the goal of global access without creating a dangerous Global namespace.

Resources also integrate with the **Inspector**, whereas Autoloads are hidden and work in the background. Resources live in your **FileSystem**. You can double-click `PlayerStats.tres` and edit the starting health, run speed, and jump height right in the **Inspector**. This separates design (data) from code (logic).

An Autoload lives forever from game start to game end. A Resource is reference-counted. If you unload the current Level and nothing else is using that specific Resource, Godot will automatically free it from memory. This prevents **memory creep**, which can be common in projects that overuse Singletons.

The decoupled alternative (Groups)

The primary benefit of the **Group System** (and signals) is decoupling (inversion of control).

If you need to send a message to all enemies or the GUI instead of routing it through a singleton, rather make use of Godot's Groups.

To demonstrate this, we could add a `die` function to the `Player` script:

```
func die() -> void:
    # Notify everyone in the game_listeners group
    get_tree().call_group("game_listeners", "on_player_died")
```

This is a fire-and-forget message. Any node can join the `game_listeners` group and define an `on_player_died()` function. The Player doesn't need to know who is listening, and the listeners don't need to know who sent the message.

Using Groups can also prevent crashes, for example, if you delete the `SoundManager` from your project, Singleton-based code (`SoundManager.play()`) would crash the game immediately. With Groups, the Player emits the message into the void. If no one is listening (because the manager was deleted), nothing happens. The game keeps running. This makes your systems robust against changes.

Groups also allow many-to-many communication. Singletons are often one-to-one (The Player tells the Manager to do something). Groups are one-to-many. One event (Player Death) can trigger 50 distinct reactions (enemies celebrate, UI fades, music changes, camera shakes, etc.) without the `Player` script needing to know about any of them.

Understanding the trade-offs

While Static Functions and Groups are powerful alternatives to Singletons, they are not silver bullets. To make the best architectural decisions, you must understand the limitations of each approach:

- **Static functions (context and lifecycle limitations)**: While Godot 4 allows you to use `static var` to maintain persistent, class-level state, static functions do not belong to a specific instantiated object in your game. Because they lack a localized `self` reference, they cannot use standard lifecycle methods like `_ready()` or `_process()`. Furthermore, while they *can* interact with the Scene Tree, they cannot do it automatically. You must explicitly pass an active Node into the function as a parameter (or query `Engine.get_main_loop()`) to give the static function a safe reference point to work from.
- **Groups (The Magic String danger)**: The biggest drawback of using Groups is their reliance on string names. Because you are broadcasting a string representation of a function (such as `"take_damage"`), your IDE cannot auto-complete the code or warn you if the target function is missing. If you misspell the function name, or if a specific

node within that group lacks that exact method, the engine will fail silently or throw a runtime error that can be frustrating to trace.

Choosing the right approach

Throughout this chapter, we have explored several ways to manage global access, data, and communication. However, Autoloads are just one piece of the puzzle. To help you make the best architectural decisions in your own projects, use this quick-reference guide when deciding how to structure your systems:

Approach	**Best for**	**Advantages**	**Drawbacks**
Autoloads (Singletons)	Persistent background systems (Audio managers, event buses, network sockets)	Survives scene changes; globally accessible without complex node paths.	Easily abused to create "God Objects"; introduces tight coupling if used for local logic.
Custom Resources	Static data, item statistics, inventory states, and configuration files	Completely decoupled from the Scene Tree; lightweight; inherently reusable.	Not designed to execute continuous logic (like `_process`); requires manual saving/loading for dynamic state persistence.
Groups	Batch operations and semantic tagging (for example, updating all `"Enemies"`, defining `"Destructibles"`)	Promotes loose coupling; bypasses complex hierarchies to command multiple nodes instantly.	Relies on "magic strings" (no IDE auto-complete); can lead to silent failures if functions are misnamed or missing.

Approach	Best for	Advantages	Drawbacks
Static Functions	Stateless utility tasks and math calculations (for example, custom RNG, specialized physics math)	Globally accessible without needing to instantiate a node; keeps utility code cleanly organized.	Cannot hold active state; cannot interact with the Scene Tree or use lifecycle functions like `_ready`.

Table 5.1 – Comparing architectural approaches for managing data and communication

With these architectural tools at our disposal, let's return to Void Defenders and see how they can be applied in a real gameplay scenario.

Void Defenders – implementing data-driven enemy spawning

Armed with these new concepts, let's jump back into *Void Defenders* and start with a way to dynamically instance enemies into the main Level scene.

Start by deleting the **BaseEnemy** and **KamikazeEnemy** nodes which we had instanced previously. The most efficient way to instance is to add a **Timer** node to the scene, which we will rename to **EnemySpawner**.

To keep our architecture strictly decoupled (avoiding fragile `$NodePaths`), we will use an exported variable to link this Timer to our script. Add a new script to the `MainLevel` node and code it as shown here:

```
class_name MainLevel extends Node2D

# Drag the EnemySpawner Timer into this slot in the Inspector!

@export var enemy_spawner: Timer
@export var enemy_scenes: Array[PackedScene] # Access to enemy types

func_ready()-> void:
    enemy_spawner.timeout.connect(_on_spawn_timer)
    enemy_spawner.start()

func _on_spawn_timer()-> void:
    # 1. Pick a random enemy from the list
```

```
    var random_enemy_scene: PackedScene = enemy_scenes.pick_random()
    var enemy: Node2D = random_enemy_scene.instantiate()
    add_child(enemy)

    # 2. Assign a random X position just off the top of the screen
    var screen_width: float = get_viewport_rect().size.x
    enemy.global_position = Vector2(randf_range(50.0, screen_width -
    50.0), -50.0)
```

Once the script is saved, click on the `MainLevel` node. In the **Inspector**, you will now see slots for your exported variables. Simply drag the **EnemySpawner** node from your Scene Tree directly into the `enemy_spawner` slot. This guarantees that even if you rename or move the Timer Node later, your code will not break!

The code above is a classic Godot 4 script for a simple spawner. It randomly selects an enemy type from a list, creates it, and drops it just above the top edge of the player's screen at a random horizontal position. There is one line of code in that block which represents a best practice, and it is this:

```
@export var enemy_scenes: Array[PackedScene] # Access to enemy types
```

Many would be tempted to use `preload` to prepare the enemy types, but when you use `preload` or `load` with a hardcoded string path, you are locking your code to your specific file structure. It would look something like this:

```
var enemy_scene = preload("res://enemies/base_enemy.tscn")
```

While this works for a quick prototype, it introduces several severe architectural bottlenecks:

- **The Magic String trap**: If you decide to reorganize your project and move `base_enemy.tscn` into a new folder, that text string might break. While Godot does try to update paths if you move things inside its own **FileSystem** dock, text-based file paths are notoriously brittle and prone to breaking during Git merges or large refactors.
- **The programmer bottleneck**: If a game designer (or even just you, three months from now) wants to test a new enemy type in the spawner, they have to open the script, locate the specific line of code, change the string path, and save the script. This forces configuration data and system logic to live in the exact same place.
- **Rigid scaling**: If you want the spawner to handle three different types of enemies, you must hardcode an array of three specific `preload` statements. Adding a fourth means going back in and rewriting code.

By using `@export var enemy_scenes: Array[PackedScene]`, you pull the data (the specific enemies) completely out of the logic (the spawning math). This approach provides three advantages:

- **Designer-friendly (Separation of Concerns)**: The script now only defines how to spawn things, not what to spawn. You can click on the **MainLevel** node, look at the **Inspector**, and visually drag-and-drop 10 different enemy scenes into the array without ever looking at a line of code.
- **Bulletproof refactoring**: When you drag a scene into an exported variable in the **Inspector**, Godot doesn't just save a fragile text path; it saves an internal Unique ID (UID). If you rename the enemy file or move it to a completely different folder, the **Inspector** keeps the reference intact perfectly. Your game won't crash.
- **Extreme reusability**: Because the script doesn't know what it is spawning, you can attach this exact same script to an entirely different node called **AsteroidSpawner**, and simply drag asteroid scenes into the **Inspector** instead of aliens. You have successfully created a universal spawner.

Another issue is that our lasers don't actually destroy enemies. We can fix this by using **Collision Layers** and **Collision Masks**. In **Project | Project Settings | Layer Names | 2D Physics**, we can give names to the different numbered collision layers. I named layer 1: `Player`, layer 2: `Projectiles`, and layer 3: `Enemies`.

Now select the **Laser** node and put it on **Collision Layer 2** and **Collision Mask 3**, set the **Player** to **Collision Layer 1**, and set the **Enemies** to **Collision Layer 3** and **Mask 1** and **2**.

Making use of **Collision Layers** and **Collision Masks** is a best practice because physics calculations are mathematically expensive. If you leave everything on the default **Layer 1** and **Mask 1**, Godot's physics engine must calculate the overlapping geometry of every single object that touches every other object in your game.

If two player lasers cross paths, the physics engine calculates a collision, generates the collision data, and sends a signal to GDScript, only for your script to ignore them.

When you use Layers and Masks, Godot filters out invalid collisions at the core C++ engine level before any complex math is done and before GDScript is ever alerted. If a laser's Mask isn't looking for other lasers, the engine treats them as thin air. This saves a massive amount of CPU overhead, especially in bullet-hell games like *Void Defenders*. Using layers and masks also unlocks complex future gameplay mechanics.

By separating what an object is from what it interacts with, you can easily create complex mechanics without writing any new code, for example:

- **Friendly fire**: Want to add a Hardcore Mode where enemies can accidentally shoot each other? Just check the **Enemies** box on the Enemy Projectile's **Collision Mask**. No code changes are required.
- **Secret walls**: A wall might be on the **World** layer, stopping the player. But if you have a Ghost power-up that temporarily removes the **World** layer from the Player's Mask, the player will walk right through walls as if they don't exist.
- **Water/lava**: An `Area2D` representing water can be on a **Liquid** layer. Only objects that have **Liquid** checked on their Mask will trigger splash effects or physics drag.

These examples highlight one of the most powerful philosophies in Godot: whenever possible, let the engine's built-in systems do the heavy lifting. Mastering collision layers and masks might require a slight shift in how you think about game physics, but it ultimately saves you from writing dozens of complex, bug-prone `if` statements just to filter out unwanted interactions. With our game objects now properly organized and interacting exactly as we intend, let's review everything we have built in this chapter.

Summary

In this chapter, we explored the powerful but often misused feature of Autoloads (Singletons). We learned that while they are technically just Nodes, they offer three distinct architectural advantages: persistence across scene changes, global accessibility from any script, and a guaranteed Singleton identity.

We identified that these traits make Autoloads the absolute best tool for specific service roles, such as:

- **Audio Managers**: To keep music playing uninterrupted between Levels
- **Scene Switchers**: To manage transitions and loading screens without being deleted
- **Event Buses**: To decouple unrelated systems like UI and Player via Global Signals
- **Configuration Managers**: To handle application-wide settings like resolution or volume

However, we also emphasized that Autoloads should manage systems, not state. We warned against the God Object anti-pattern – dumping player health, inventory, and game logic into a single `Global.gd` file – which leads to tight coupling and memory bloat.

Finally, we examined cleaner alternatives for managing game data to keep your architecture modular. These included static functions for stateless utility logic that requires no memory overhead, and Resources for sharing state, like Player stats, between objects without a global manager. We also looked at the Event Bus (Global Signals) for broadcasting fire-and-forget messages to many listeners at once.

While Godot's built-in Groups can theoretically achieve this, relying on groups often leads to fragile magic string bugs. Instead, creating a dedicated Autoload that only holds signals (an Event Bus) is a much cleaner architecture. It completely decouples your sender from your receiver while still providing full IDE autocomplete and type safety for your game-wide events.

By restricting Autoloads to their intended role as persistent services and using dependency injection or signals for communication, you ensure that your codebase remains testable, scalable, and free of spaghetti code.

In the next chapter, we will investigate the final piece of the architectural puzzle: Event-Driven Architecture, where we will master the art of using signals to make your game systems reactive and independent.

Get this book's PDF copy, code bundle, and more

Scan the QR code (or go to `packtpub.com/unlock`). Search for this book by name, confirm the edition, and then follow the steps on the page.

UNLOCK NOW

Note: Have your invoice handy. Purchases made directly from the Packt website don't require an invoice.

6

Applying Event-Driven Patterns

During rapid prototyping or small game jams, where development speed is the immediate priority, it is tempting to create hardcoded dependencies by directly targeting the specific nodes you need. For example, if the Player takes damage, you might tell it to reach across the Scene Tree by writing `get_node("../UI/HealthBar").update_value()`. If an enemy dies, it might directly modify its parent node by calling `get_parent().add_score()`.

This approach, known as **polling** or **direct reference**, works for prototypes, but it is the primary cause of death for large projects. The reason is that it creates a web of hard dependencies (everything tightly coupled) where every object needs to know the exact path and class type of every other object. If you move the `HealthBar`, the `Player` script crashes. If you delete an `Enemy` before the `ScoreManager` checks it, the game throws a `null reference error`.

The solution to this tangled web is **Event-Driven Architecture**.

In Godot, this event-driven approach is largely achieved through signals and Notifications. Instead of objects pushing data to specific targets, they broadcast events to the world, shouting, "I took damage!", "I died!", or "The level loaded!" The object broadcasting the event does not know or care who is listening. This means that if you temporarily disable your UI while testing, or if a secondary object fails to load, your game will not crash. The broadcaster simply goes about its business, resulting in a significantly more resilient and decoupled system.

In *Chapters 4* and *5*, our primary focus was bringing your ideas to life. We built out foundational mechanics and rapidly prototyped our systems to get the game running. However, as your project grows, the tightly coupled scripts that allowed for that rapid prototyping will inevitably become a bottleneck. Now that you know how to build the individual pieces of a game, it is time to learn how to wire them together for a commercial-scale project.

In this chapter, we will master the art of decoupling your systems. We will move beyond basic signal connections and explore advanced patterns like the Event Bus, Observable Resources, and lifecycle Notifications. This will transform your codebase from a fragile web into a flexible, reactive system.

We're going to cover the following main topics:

- Expanding the golden rule – Call Down, Signal Up, Event Out
- Using signals to decouple systems
- Exploring the Event Bus Pattern (publisher/subscriber)
- Void Defenders – implementing the Event Bus
- Advanced event architectures (namespacing and Event Objects)
- Applying Notifications effectively
- Observable Resources
- Void Defenders – implementing power-ups

By the end of this chapter, you will have evolved from a developer who writes rigid, fragile scripts into a systems architect who designs robust, scalable game engines. You will no longer view your game as a tangled web of nodes that must constantly micromanage one another, but rather as a highly organized network of independent systems that react intelligently to the world around them. This shift in mindset is exactly what separates amateur prototypes from professional, commercial-ready codebases.

Technical requirements

Readers should be familiar with basic Godot workflows, such as navigating the Godot editor, creating scenes, and scripting with GDScript.

You can download the example project and code for this book by following the instructions in the *Download the example code files* section in the *Preface* of this book.

This chapter's code files are included in the downloadable code bundle.

Expanding the golden rule – Call Down, Signal Up, Event Out

Before we write any code, we need a mental framework for how objects should communicate. We have already seen the common heuristic in the Godot community: **Call Down, Signal Up**.

As a quick refresher, here is how that baseline rule works to keep our node trees decoupled:

- **Call Down (Parent => Child)**: A parent node has full authority over its children. It can safely get a reference to a child node and call its functions directly. For example, the **Player** node calling `hitbox.enable()`.
- **Signal Up (Child => Parent)**: A child node should never know who its parent is. This strict rule is rooted in two core programming concepts: **decoupling** and the **Single Responsibility Principle**. A child node's only responsibility is to report what just happened to it, not to dictate how the rest of the game should react to that event. If a **HealthComponent** hardcodes a call like `get_parent().die()`, it becomes rigidly coupled to that specific parent. You could never attach that same health component to a destructible wooden crate or a boss vehicle without risking a game crash if they don't share the exact same `die()` function.

  Instead of calling a parent's function directly, the child simply emits a signal. It broadcasts that its health is depleted. And that is all. If the parent cares, it listens for that signal. For example, the **HealthComponent** emits `health_depleted`, and the **Player** node (its parent) hears it and independently reacts by playing a death animation.

However, as our game grows, we run into a third scenario: what happens when two completely unrelated branches of the Scene Tree need to communicate? Based on the advanced patterns we will learn in this chapter, we are going to expand this heuristic to: **Call Down, Signal Up, Event Out.**

Let's see how this expanded flow operates in a commercial-scale architecture:

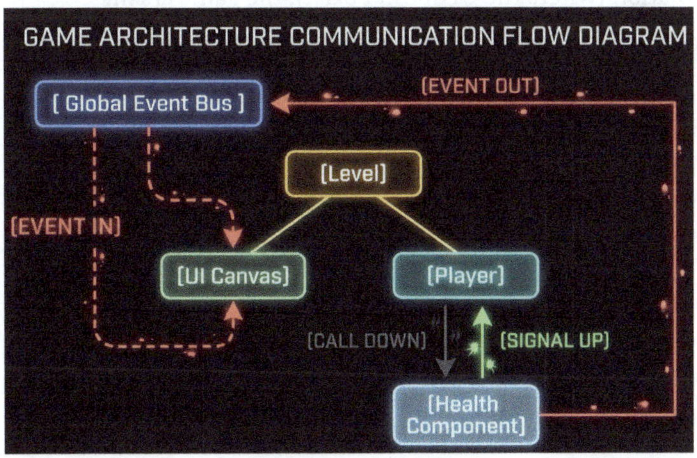

Figure 6.1 – Diagram of expanded data flow

Figure 6.1 illustrates the **Event Out (cross-system)** communication pathway. When a node needs to communicate with completely unrelated systems globally (like a UI scoreboard, an achievement tracker, or an audio manager), it does not try to find them in the Tree. Instead, it broadcasts an **EVENT OUT** to a **Global Event Bus**. For example, the **Health Component** broadcasts `player_died` to the entire game.

Keep this mental framework in mind as we progress through the chapter. Every advanced pattern and architecture we build in the upcoming sections is designed to cleanly execute one of these specific communication pathways. Let's start by looking at how to properly handle the "Signal Up" approach to decouple our child and parent nodes.

Using signals to decouple systems

To understand why signals are necessary, have a look at the problem that they solve: **Coupling**.

In a tightly coupled system, the *sender* (the object where an event happens) is responsible for pushing updates to the *receiver* (the object that needs to react). For example, a `Player` script using direct references might look like this:

```
func take_damage(amount: int):
    health -= amount
    # TIGHT COUPLING: Player must know exact path to UI
    var health_bar = get_node("../CanvasLayer/HealthBar")
    health_bar.update_health(health)
```

The preceding code is brittle. If you move the **HealthBar** node, rename it, or simply test the **Player** scene in isolation (where the UI doesn't exist), the game crashes.

The best practice approach is to use signals.

By using signals, we invert this responsibility. The Player simply broadcasts that it has changed. It is then the UI's responsibility to listen.

```
# Player.gd
signal health_changed(new_value)

func take_damage(amount: int) -> void:
    health -= amount
    # DECOUPLED: Player broadcasts, doesn't care who hears
    health_changed.emit(health)
```

Now, the **Player** scene is independent. You can drop it into any Level, even one without a UI, and it will still function. In the long term, this inversion of responsibility is what allows a commercial game to scale without collapsing under its own weight. It means your UI designer can completely overhaul the health bar's node structure without ever asking a programmer to rewrite the `Player` script. It allows you to seamlessly drop this exact **Player** scene into a completely different mini-game or sequel. By eliminating rigid dependencies early on, you prevent the tangled spaghetti code that causes cascading bugs during late-stage development.

However, in more complex scenarios, signals need to be connected dynamically through code, as we'll see in the next section.

Connecting signals via code

While connecting signals via the Godot editor interface is great for simple or static scenes, professional projects often require connecting signals dynamically via script, especially when spawning objects at runtime.

In Godot 4, the syntax for connecting signals via code is type-safe and cleaner than in previous versions:

```
# LevelManager.gd
func spawn_enemy() -> void:
    var enemy = enemy_scene.instantiate()
    add_child(enemy)

    # Connect the signal via code
    # Syntax: source_node.signal_name.connect(target_function)
    enemy.died.connect(_on_enemy_died)

func _on_enemy_died() -> void:
    score += 100
```

When you build a static Level in the editor, you can easily use the **Node** panel to connect a pre-placed button to a door. However, objects like enemies, projectiles, and loot drops don't exist until the game is actually running. You cannot connect them in the editor because there is nothing to click on!

By writing `enemy.died.connect(_on_enemy_died)`, we establish that connection the exact moment the enemy is created. Let's break down the syntax:

- `enemy`: This is our source node (the object broadcasting the event).

- `.died`: This is the specific signal we want to listen for.
- `.connect(_on_enemy_died)`: This tells Godot exactly which local function to trigger when that signal is emitted. Notice that we do not use parentheses after `_on_enemy_died`. We are passing the function itself as a reference (called a **callable** in Godot 4), rather than executing it immediately.

Connecting via code allows you to manage relationships between objects that didn't exist when you pressed **Play**. For example, in our *Void Defenders* project, we are constantly spawning new enemy ships, wave after wave. Because these enemies are created dynamically at runtime, we cannot use the Godot editor interface to pre-connect to them. By connecting to their `died` signal via code the exact moment an enemy is instantiated, we can accurately track kills, award points, and know exactly when to trigger the next wave, all without tightly coupling to objects that are constantly being created and destroyed.

Godot also allows you to use signals as **coroutines** (functions that can pause and resume execution) using the `await` keyword. This is useful for sequencing events without creating messy callback functions, as demonstrated in the code below:

```
func play_cutscene() -> void:
    animation_player.play("intro")
    # Pause execution here until the animation finishes
    await animation_player.animation_finished
    start_game()
```

Without the `await` keyword, you would have to connect the signal to a completely separate `_on_animation_finished()` function just to tell the game to start. This forces you to split a single logical sequence across multiple parts of your script. By using coroutines, you can write complex, time-based sequences in a single, top-to-bottom, easy-to-read block of code.

Signals alone are not always enough as your project grows. This becomes challenging when communication needs to cross different parts of the scene hierarchy.

Exploring the Event Bus Pattern (publisher/subscriber)

As your project scales, **Signal Up** stops being enough. This is when you encounter a deep hierarchy problem. Consider this scenario:

- Your **PlayerShip** is inside **Level** => **Entities** => **PlayerShip**
- Your **HUD** is inside **Level** => **UI** => **HUD** => **HealthBar**

If the Player takes damage, how does the **HealthBar** know? You could use the Signal Up, Call Down rule: the Player signals the Level, the Level calls a function on the UI, and the UI calls a function on the **HealthBar**. Alternatively, the Level could grab rigid node paths to both the Player and the **HealthBar** and wire their signals together directly.

But as your game grows, writing this kind of plumbing code for every single interaction becomes tedious. It bloats your Level script with hundreds of node references it shouldn't need to care about. This is where global broadcasting comes into play using the Event Bus (or Message Bus) pattern.

Think of an Event Bus as a global radio station for your game. Instead of the Player wiring a direct, physical connection through the Node Tree to reach the **HealthBar**, it simply broadcasts a message to this central radio station (I took 10 damage). The **HealthBar**, which is tuned into that specific frequency, hears the message and updates itself.

The Event Bus acts as a global middleman. The sender broadcasts, and the receiver just listens. Because neither object needs to know the other exists, you eliminate those long, fragile signal chains and rigid node paths, leaving your systems decoupled.

The Event Bus uses the publisher/subscriber paradigm. It separates who is publishing from who is subscribing. In Godot, an Event Bus is simply a global Singleton (Autoload) that acts as a central communication switchboard. Nodes don't talk to each other; they talk to the Bus.

Void Defenders – implementing the Event Bus

We created a standard script extending `Node` and named it `event_bus.gd`, and we registered it as an Autoload. Notice that the Event Bus contains no logic. It simply defines the signals:

```
# EventBus.gd (Autoload)
extends Node

signal score_changed(new_amount: int)
signal player_lives_changed(current_lives: int)
signal weapon_changed(weapon_name: String, ammo: int)
```

> **Note**
>
> Because we are only defining these signals here and emitting them from other scripts, Godot's editor might show a *yellow* warning saying the signals are "defined but never used." You can safely ignore this warning for your Event Bus or suppress it by adding `@warning_ignore("unused_signal")` at the top of your script.

Though this script is brief, every single detail serves a specific architectural purpose. Let's look at why it is built this way and how the pieces interact:

- `extends Node`: While Godot's base Object class is technically what handles signals, a script must extend `Node` to be added to the Scene Tree. By extending the base `Node` class rather than something heavier like **Node2D**, we give the Event Bus the absolute minimum functionality required to act as a global Autoload, keeping its memory footprint virtually invisible.
- **The Autoload registration**: By making this script an Autoload in our **Project Settings**, we grant it global scope. This means the Event Bus is loaded before the first Level even starts and persists until the game is closed. More importantly, it means any script in the game can access it simply by typing `EventBus`, completely eliminating the need for complex `get_node()` paths.
- **Defining the signals**: These lines establish our radio frequencies. Notice that we explicitly type our parameters (for example, `new_amount: int`). This guarantees that if a script accidentally tries to broadcast a string to the `score_changed` channel, Godot will instantly throw an error, preventing silent bugs from slipping into our game.

When an enemy is destroyed, it doesn't try to find the `LevelManager`. It just broadcasts:

```
# BaseEnemy.gd
func die() -> void:
    EventBus.score_changed.emit(score_value)
    queue_free()
```

Notice what is missing from this script. The `Enemy` broadcasts its death and immediately deletes itself. It does not wait for confirmation; it does not check if the Score UI actually exists. Broadcasting and immediately leaving the stage, the `Enemy` script remains completely independent and free of fragile dependencies.

The UI listens to that same bus:

```
# HUD.gd
func _ready() -> void:
    # Connect to the bus
    EventBus.score_changed.connect(update_score)
    EventBus.player_lives_changed.connect(update_lives)
    EventBus.weapon_changed.connect(update_weapon_display)
```

Now let's look at the other side of the equation. While the `enemy` was broadcasting, the UI was quietly listening. Here is how that connection is made:

- **Tuning in early**: By placing these connections inside the `_ready()` function, the HUD tunes into our global radio station the exact moment it is loaded into the game.
- **Making the connection**: The line `EventBus.score_changed.connect(update_score)` tells Godot: whenever anyone, anywhere in the game, broadcasts a `score_changed` event, immediately run the local `update_score` function and pass along the number.
- **Total independence**: Notice what is missing here, too. The `HUD` script never searches for the Player or the Enemies. It only knows about the Event Bus.

By utilizing this pattern, we have completely severed the physical ties between the objects creating the data (the dying enemy) and the objects displaying the data (the UI). You can now delete the UI, swap it out for a completely different design, or spawn 1,000 enemies at once, and your codebase will remain perfectly stable because the sender and receiver never actually touch.

We have successfully crossed a massive system boundary, from gameplay entities to UI, without a single direct dependency. While this approach is powerful, it's important to understand its trade-offs before applying it more broadly.

Trade-offs of Event-Driven Architecture

It would be irresponsible to say Event-Driven Architecture is completely flawless. Be aware of these three major risks and how to actively prevent them in your projects:

- **Cascading events (Spaghetti Logic)**: If Event A triggers a function that emits Event B, which triggers Event C, debugging becomes nearly impossible. You cannot read the code linearly, and you risk creating an infinite loop that crashes your game.
  How to avoid it: Enforce a **One-Hop Rule**. An event should trigger a final reaction (like updating UI, playing a sound, or changing a single state), not more events. If multiple things must happen in a strict chain, a dedicated Manager node should listen to the initial event and then explicitly execute the subsequent steps via direct function calls.

- **System ordering**: Because the Event Bus broadcasts to everyone at once, you cannot easily guarantee which listener will process the event first. If system execution order strictly matters (for example, the `ScoreManager` must update the internal score before the `LevelManager` checks if the victory threshold is met), you run into race conditions.

  How to avoid it: Never use the Event Bus for sequential, dependent logic. If Object A relies on Object B finishing its math first, use standard Call Down or explicit function delegation. Reserve the Event Bus for parallel, independent reactions where order doesn't matter (like the UI updating at the exact same time an explosion sound plays).

- **Traceability (The Bad Actor Problem)**: Because the Event Bus is global, any script can trigger any event. A stray bullet script could accidentally emit `EventBus.level_completed.emit()`, causing the game to end prematurely. However, the true danger here isn't just that the game ended; it is that finding the culprit is difficult. Because the Event Bus completely decouples your code, you don't have a clear, direct path to trace backward. The debugger will just tell you the Event Bus fired the signal, leaving you to hunt down exactly who was broadcasting. To mitigate this, a common best practice is to require a `source` or `reason` parameter for major global events:

  ```
  # EventBus.gd
  signal level_completed(source: Node, reason: String)
  ```

  Now, any script that wants to end the Level must identify itself:

  ```
  # BossEnemy.gd
  func die() -> void:
      EventBus.level_completed.emit(self, "Boss defeated")
  ```

  If the game ends randomly, your `LevelManager` can simply print that `source` and `reason` to the console, allowing you to instantly track down the rogue script.

  How to avoid it: Discipline your architecture by establishing strict ownership over events. For critical game-state changes, require the sender to pass itself as an argument (for example, `signal level_completed(sender: Node)`). This allows the listening script to verify that the sender is the authentic `LevelManager` before it executes the win screen.

Advanced Event architectures (namespacing and Event Objects)

As your project grows, organizing a large number of events within a single Event Bus can quickly become difficult to manage. If you have 50 different signals all mixed, finding the right one becomes a chore, and you risk naming collisions (like accidentally mixing up an `enemy_died` signal with a `player_died` signal).

To keep your system maintainable at scale, we need better ways to structure and organize events. This is where namespacing and Event Objects come into play.

In programming, **namespacing** simply means grouping related items under a specific category or label to keep them separated. Think of it like organizing your computer: instead of dumping 1,000 files directly onto your desktop, you group them into specific folders (like Invoices, Family Photos, or Game Assets). Namespacing does the exact same thing for your code, allowing you to categorize your global signals into logical folders like Audio, UI, or Combat.

This approach has not been used in *Void Defenders*, but it could look similar to this:

```
# EventBus.gd (Autoload)
extends Node

class PlayerEvents:
    signal health_changed(new_health: int)
    signal died

class WorldEvents:
    signal asteroid_destroyed(size: int)
    signal sector_cleared

# Instantiate the inner classes so they can be accessed globally
var Player = PlayerEvents.new()
var World = WorldEvents.new()
```

Let's break down exactly how this Godot-specific namespacing works:

- `class PlayerEvents:` **(Inner Classes)**: GDScript allows you to define a class *inside* another script. Think of these inner classes as mini-blueprints for specific categories. By grouping our signals inside these classes, we keep the main script clean.

- `var Player = PlayerEvents.new()` **(Instantiation)**: This is the most critical step. An inner class is just a theoretical blueprint; it doesn't exist in the game's memory yet, meaning it cannot emit signals. We must use the `.new()` keyword to build a real object from that blueprint and store it in a variable (`Player`).
- `EventBus.Player...` **(The Dot Notation)**: Because our `EventBus` is a global Autoload, any script can call it. By typing `EventBus.Player`, we are accessing the specific `PlayerEvents` object we instantiated, giving us exclusive access to the `health_changed` signal inside it.

Now, when a player takes damage, the code is beautifully organized: `EventBus.Player.health_changed.emit(health)`.

Advanced pattern: the changing signature problem

One of the biggest headaches with Event-Driven Architecture is refactoring. Let's say the `enemy_destroyed` signal currently passes an `int` for the score. Later, you decide you also want it to pass the `Vector2` position of the enemy so the UI can spawn a floating **+50** text effect.

If you change the signal signature to `enemy_destroyed(points: int, pos: Vector2)`, every single script that is currently listening to that signal will throw an error because their callback functions are only expecting one argument.

To solve this, professional teams often pass *Event Objects* rather than discrete arguments.

An **Event Object** is simply a custom data container, often a lightweight class or a Dictionary, that bundles all the event information together. Instead of passing multiple separate variables through the signal, you pass this single object. If you need to add more data later, like the enemy's position, the type of weapon that killed it, or the item it dropped, you just add new properties to the Event Object. Because the signal signature never actually changes (it is always just passing one object), your existing listener's scripts will never break.

Now, let's look at the implementation here:

```
# enemy_death_event.gd (A custom class)
class_name EnemyDeathEvent extends RefCounted

var points: int
var position: Vector2
var enemy_type: String
```

Let's look at how this custom class functions in practice:

- **The concept (the envelope)**: Think of this class as a custom envelope. `extends RefCounted` simply tells Godot to manage its memory automatically (deleting it when it is no longer needed). Instead of handing the Event Bus three loose pieces of paper (`points`, `position`, and `enemy_type`), you place them all safely inside this `EnemyDeathEvent` envelope.
- **During emission**: When an enemy dies, it creates a new instance of this envelope, fills out the details, and passes the single envelope to the Event Bus:

```
var death_event = EnemyDeathEvent.new()
death_event.points = 100
death_event.position = global_position

EventBus.enemy_destroyed.emit(death_event)
```

- **For the listeners**: The UI script listening to this signal only needs to expect one argument: the event object. It can then open the envelope and grab only the specific data it cares about using dot notation:

```
func _on_enemy_destroyed(event: EnemyDeathEvent) -> void:
    score += event.points
    # The UI ignores event.position
```

  Now, your signal looks like this: `signal enemy_destroyed(event: EnemyDeathEvent)`.

If you ever need to add more data to the event (like the `enemy_type`), you just add it to the `EnemyDeathEvent` class. The signal signature never changes, and your subscriber functions never break.

Namespacing versus Event Objects

Because we introduced these two patterns back-to-back, it is easy to mix them up. Remember that they solve entirely different problems:

- Use *Namespacing* when you have too many signals and need to organize the communication channels (for example, grouping all audio signals together).
- Use *Event Objects* when a single signal carries complex *data* (or data that changes frequently), and you need to organize the payload.s

Professional projects almost always use both together. You will frequently broadcast an Event Object (the payload) over a namespaced signal (the channel).

While these patterns help us manage our own events more effectively, Godot also provides a built-in system for handling engine-level events. Let's explore this next.

Applying Notifications effectively

While signals are excellent for gameplay events, things that we define, Godot has a separate system for engine events called **Notifications**. Think of Notifications as mandatory memos sent directly from the Godot engine to your scripts. Instead of you wiring up custom signals for fundamental lifecycle changes, Godot automatically notifies a node when important, under-the-hood things happen to it.

For example, the engine sends a specific Notification when a node is first added to the Scene Tree, when it is about to be deleted from memory, when the game is paused, or when the player clicks the **X** to close the application window. By tapping into this system, your code can cleanly react to the engine's core state without requiring any complex plumbing or custom Event Buses.

Every Object in Godot receives notifications from the engine when its status changes. You are likely already using them without realizing it: `_ready()`, `_process()`, and `_enter_tree()` are actually helper functions that wrap the underlying Notification system. Sometimes, you may need to hook into lifecycle events that don't have dedicated helper functions. You can do this by overriding the `_notification()` function.

One common use case for Notifications is detecting when the game window loses focus (for example, the player *Alt-Tabs* away) or when the OS tries to close the game. Let's look at the code for this as follows:

```
func _notification(what: int) -> void:
    match what:
        NOTIFICATION_WM_FOCUS_OUT:
            # Auto-pause game when game window minimized
            get_tree().paused = true
            print("PAUSED")

        NOTIFICATION_WM_CLOSE_REQUEST:
            # Save data before game quits
            save_game()
```

To understand how this powerful engine function works, let's look at its three main components:

- **The `what` parameter**: Every time Godot sends a Notification, it passes an integer (a whole number) representing the exact event that just occurred. For example, the engine might send the number `1004` when the window loses focus. The `what` variable simply catches that number.
- **The `match` statement**: This is GDScript's version of a switch statement. Instead of writing a massive, messy chain of `if/elif` statements to check what number the engine just sent, `match` cleanly compares the incoming `what` integer against a list of specific outcomes.
- **The constants (`NOTIFICATION_WM_...`)**: Memorizing random ID numbers like `1004` is impossible. To fix this, Godot provides built-in, human-readable constants to represent these integers. `WM` stands for `Window Manager`:
    - `NOTIFICATION_WM_FOCUS_OUT` triggers when the player clicks on another monitor or *Alt-Tabs* out of the game, making it the perfect place to trigger an auto-pause.
    - `NOTIFICATION_WM_CLOSE_REQUEST` triggers when the player clicks the system **X** to close the application window, giving you a final fraction of a second to save their progress before the engine forcefully shuts down.

Since it is not always easy to know when to define your own signal and when to rely on built-in Notifications, you can use *Table 6.1* to help you decide:

Feature	**Signals**	**Notifications**
Direction	One object speaks, and many listen.	The engine tells a specific object that something happened.
Customization	You define the name and arguments (for example, `health_changed(50)`).	You must use the integer constants provided by Godot.
Performance	Slightly slower (parsing overhead)	Extremely fast (C++ level calls).

Feature	Signals	Notifications
Best used for	Gameplay logic, UI updates, quest triggers.	Memory management, OS interactions, Object cleanup (`_exit_tree`).

Table 6.1 – Signals versus Notifications decision checklist

So far, we've focused on reacting to events. But what about managing persistent state? Let's move on to the next section.

Observable Resources

While the Event Bus is fantastic for ephemeral, moment-to-moment events (like an enemy exploding), Godot 4 offers another powerful pattern for persistent state: *Observable Resources*.

What is an Observable Resource? At its core, this pattern is a Godot-specific implementation of the classic Observer Design Pattern. In software engineering, the **Observer Pattern** is a system where one central object (the *subject*) maintains a list of dependents (the *observers*) and automatically notifies them the moment its internal state changes. Think of it like subscribing to a newsletter; instead of constantly checking a website for new articles, the website simply pushes the news to your inbox the second it is published.

An **Observable Resource** takes this exact concept and applies it to a custom Godot Resource. It holds specific data (such as a player's health, current XP, or an inventory list) and is explicitly programmed to emit a signal the exact moment that data changes.

Instead of UI nodes or managers constantly checking the player's health every single frame (a costly practice known as *polling*, mentioned earlier in the chapter), those systems subscribe to the health resource. When the resource's internal data updates, it automatically pushes a notification to every subscribed node.

It is easy to confuse the Event Bus and Observable Resources architectures, but the distinction comes down to *actions* versus *state*:

- **Use the Event Bus for Actions (Verbs)**: The player jumped, the boss died, or a bullet was fired. These are fleeting events that happen once and vanish.
- **Use Observable Resources for State (Nouns)**: Player Health, Current Ammo, or Master Volume – these are values that must be stored, saved, and constantly referenced by multiple UI elements, gameplay systems, and save-game managers.

By pulling this persistent data out of your individual node scripts (like `player.gd`) and placing it into an independent, Observable Resource, your core game state becomes completely decoupled from your Scene Tree. You can delete the player, swap levels, or rebuild the UI, and the underlying data remains intact and ready to notify any new systems that subscribe to it.

In *Void Defenders*, you might decide to have a `Resource` that tracks player upgrades. By defining custom signals inside a `Resource`, you can make your data reactive using Godot's setter functions. Let's see how in the code below:

```
# player_stats.gd (Custom Resource)
extends Resource
class_name PlayerStats

signal shield_capacity_changed(new_capacity: int)

@export var max_shield: int = 50:
    set(value):
        max_shield = value
        shield_capacity_changed.emit(max_shield)
```

This script might look short, but it completely automates the synchronization between your game data and your UI. Let's walk through the mechanics of how it achieves this:

- **The Custom Blueprint (**`class_name PlayerStats`**)**: By defining this as a custom class, you can create and save an actual data file (like `player_stats.tres`) in your Godot project. You can then plug this same file into your **Player** node, your **Upgrade Menu**, and your HUD. They are all looking at the same piece of data.
- **The Interceptor (**`set(value):`**)**: This is Godot 4's inline setter syntax. Think of it as a bouncer guarding the `max_shield` variable. Whenever *any* script in your entire game tries to change this number (for example, a power-up script running `stats.max_shield += 25`), Godot intercepts that change and routes it through this `set()` block first. The new requested number is passed in as the `value` parameter.
- **The State Update (**`max_shield = value`**)**: Inside the setter, we first take the incoming value and apply it to the `max_shield` variable, permanently updating the resource's underlying data.
- **The Automatic Broadcast (**`emit`**)**: Immediately after updating the number, the resource automatically emits the `shield_capacity_changed` signal, pushing the new number out to anyone listening.

Because of this mechanism, your gameplay code never has to worry about manually updating the UI. An upgrade station simply writes `stats.max_shield = 100`, and the `Resource` itself handles the responsibility. This ensures your frontend display and backend data are always perfectly synchronized without requiring a tangled web of central managers.

Whenever any script upgrades the `max_shield` variable, the `Resource` automatically emits a signal. Any UI element can listen directly to this `Resource`, ensuring your UI and backend data are always perfectly synchronized without requiring a central manager.

Void Defenders – implementing power-ups

Now that we have explored the theory behind decoupled systems, it is time to put these event-driven patterns into practice.

In this section, we will implement a modular power-up system for *Void Defenders*. By combining basic node inheritance with our newly created Event Bus and Observable Resources, we will build collectible items that can alter the player's shield, speed, and weapons without ever directly coupling to the player's internal scripts. This will perfectly demonstrate how to broadcast ephemeral gameplay events and maintain a strictly decoupled architecture in a real-world scenario.

Building the base power-up system with inheritance

For the vertical slice of *Void Defenders*, it would be good to have some power-up collectibles. I've chosen a shield, which temporarily protects the player's ship; a fuel canister, which temporarily boosts the ship's speed; and a plasma cell, which gives the player limited shots with a high-powered plasma weapon. Create the **BasePowerUp** scene from which the others will inherit as follows:

1. Create a new scene with **Area2D** as the root. Rename it to `BasePowerup`.
2. Add **Sprite2D**, **CollisionShape2D**, and **VisibleOnScreenNotifier2D** nodes as children.
3. For the **Sprite2D** texture, assign a basic texture like `star_gold.png`.
4. For the **CollisionShape2D** node, choose a basic rectangle and enclose the texture.
5. Select the **BasePowerup** root node and set the **Collision Layer** to `5` (**Powerups**) and the **Mask** to `1` (**Player**).
6. For the **VisibleOnScreenNotifier2D** node, enclose the texture.
7. Add a new script to the **BasePowerup** node.

The script for **BasePowerup** node is as follows:

```
class_name BasePowerup extends Area2D

@export var speed: float = 100.0
```

```
# Grab a reference to the notifier node so we can connect its signal
@onready var screen_notifier: VisibleOnScreenNotifier2D =
$VisibleOnScreenNotifier2D

func _ready() -> void:
    # Connect both signals consistently via code
    body_entered.connect(_on_body_entered)
    screen_notifier.screen_exited.connect(_on_screen_exited)

func _physics_process(delta: float) -> void:
    position.y += speed * delta

func _on_screen_exited() -> void:
    queue_free()

func _on_body_entered(body: Node2D) -> void:
    if body.is_in_group("Player"):
        apply_powerup(body)
        queue_free()

# This is a "Virtual Function" meant to be overwritten by children
func apply_powerup(_player: Node2D) -> void:
    pass
```

In the preceding code, note the virtual function at the end of the script. This function doesn't do anything; instead, it acts as a contract. Because **BasePowerup** is a template, it doesn't know what it is supposed to do to the player. So, it just uses the `pass` keyword, which tells Godot to do nothing and move on.

The magic will happen when we create the inherited child script. When we make the script for the Shield power-up, for example, we don't need to rewrite any of the movement or collision code. We can simply extend the base class and override that one virtual function. We will see this in action next.

To create the shield power-up:

1. Click on the **Scene** menu and select **New Inherited Scene**, then select the `base_powerup.tscn` file.
2. In the new scene, rename the root node from **BasePowerup** to **ShieldPowerup**.

3. Substitute the `star_gold.png` texture for the `powerupGreen_shield.png` texture.
4. Next, look at the **Inspector** panel. Instead of disconnecting the script from the root node, click on the existing **Script** property and select **Extend Script...** from the dropdown menu.

This will safely generate a new script that automatically inherits all the logic from our base class! Thanks to inheritance, this one is much smaller:

```
extends BasePowerup


func apply_powerup(player):
    player.activate_shield()
```

This script works. However, it is unsafe – it uses a **direct call**. It blindly trusts that whatever object is passed in as the `player` variable absolutely has a function named `activate_shield()`. If an object touches this power-up and doesn't have that exact function, the entire game will instantly crash with a **Method not found** error.

Improving safety with Static Typing

One way to fix this is to use **defensive programming** or **Duck Typing** (if it walks like a duck and quacks like a duck, it's a duck). Before trying to run the code, we ask the engine if the object knows how to run it. We could refactor the code as follows:

```
extends BasePowerup

func apply_powerup(player):
    # Safely check before executing
    if player.has_method("activate_shield"):
        player.activate_shield()
```

By wrapping our function call in an if statement using `has_method()`, we are performing a safety check. We are essentially asking Godot if the object has the `activate_shield` function built into it. If the answer is yes, the code runs. If the answer is no, it simply ignores the collision, saving our game from a fatal crash.

While Duck Typing is a valid form of defensive programming, it has a major flaw: it relies on magic strings (like `activate_shield`). If you accidentally make a typo and write `activte_shield`, Godot will not warn you; the power-up will just silently fail to work when you play the game, leading to frustrating debugging sessions.

In modern Godot 4, a much stronger, safer, and more professional approach is to use **Static Typing**. Instead of checking if an unknown object happens to have a specific method at runtime, we can use Static Typing to strictly define exactly what *type* of object is allowed to interact with our power-up in the first place.

Here is how we refactor the power-up system to use Godot 4's Static Typing.

Open the `player_ship.gd` script and define a `PlayerShip` class:

```
class_name PlayerShip extends CharacterBody2D
```

Now we can refactor the `base_powerup.gd` script and replace the Group Check (`is_in_group`) with a Type Check using the `is` keyword:

```
func _on_body_entered(body):
    # Instead of checking a string group, we check the actual Class
    # Type
    if body is PlayerShip:
        apply_powerup(body as PlayerShip)
        queue_free()

# We enforce that this function will ONLY accept a PlayerShip object
func apply_powerup(player: PlayerShip) -> void:
    pass
```

Let's break down exactly what this new syntax is doing and why it is better than our previous approach:

- **The `is` keyword**: Instead of relying on a magic string to check if the `body` is in the `"Player"` group (which can easily be misspelled), `body is PlayerShip` checks the actual, structural blueprint of the object. Godot mathematically verifies that the colliding object was built using the `PlayerShip` class.
- **Safe casting (`as PlayerShip`)**: The body parameter is generic, Godot just knows it's a physics body. By writing body as `PlayerShip`, we are explicitly telling the engine that we have verified this is a `PlayerShip`, so treat it exactly like one.
- **Strict parameters (`player: PlayerShip`)**: By defining the expected type in the function signature, we establish an unbreakable rule. If you ever accidentally try to pass an enemy or a stray asteroid into `apply_powerup()`, the Godot editor will instantly flag it as a red error before you even run the game.

Now we can fix the `shield_powerup.gd` script, and it is very satisfying:

```
extends BasePowerup

func apply_powerup(player: PlayerShip):
    player.activate_shield()
```

Because we have strictly typed the `player` parameter, Godot now knows exactly what this object is capable of. When you type `player.` in the editor, a dropdown menu will immediately appear, auto-suggesting `activate_shield()` alongside every other custom variable and function inside your `Player` script. You no longer must guess function names, cross-reference scripts, or worry about silent typos. The code is clean, completely crash-proof, and self-documenting.

We can apply the same process for any other power-ups we choose to add to the game. Below are the scripts that I used for a speed boost and a temporary weapon upgrade:

```
# speed_powerup.gd

extends BasePowerup
func apply_powerup(player: PlayerShip):
    player.activate_speed_boost()

# weapon_powerup.gd

extends BasePowerup
func apply_powerup(player: PlayerShip):
    player.upgrade_weapon()
```

Static Typing is a great architectural upgrade for a few reasons:

- **IntelliSense/Autocomplete**: Because you defined `player: PlayerShip`, the moment you type `player.` In the Godot editor, Godot will immediately pop up a list of every variable and function inside the `PlayerShip` script. This speeds up development massively and prevents typos.
- **Compile-time safety**: If you accidentally type `player.upgrad_weapon()`, the editor will immediately highlight it in *red* and refuse to run the game. With Duck Typing, the

engine wouldn't catch the typo until the player touched the power-up during gameplay (which might take 10 minutes of testing to reach).

- **Performance**: GDScript 2.0 is highly optimized for Static Typing. When the engine knows exactly what type of object it is dealing with beforehand, it can execute the code significantly faster than when it must guess at runtime.

Of course, like most things in game development, there is a trade-off for why you might not use it. Static Typing introduces tighter coupling.

By demanding a **PlayerShip**, this power-up can only ever be picked up by that specific class. If you add a **SupportDrone** or a **PlayerTwoRover** that has different base classes, they will bounce right off this power-up, even if they do have an `upgrade_weapon` function.

When deciding between the two approaches, the choice depends on your priorities:

- Use *Duck Typing* (`has_method`) when you want extreme flexibility and have lots of totally unrelated objects interacting with the same systems.
- Use *Static Typing* (`: PlayerShip`) when you want safety, performance, and a highly structured, autocomplete-friendly codebase.

Spawning power-ups and building the HUD system

Now that we have some power-ups, let's reuse our spawning logic to populate space with some random power-ups dynamically rather than placing them in the Level by hand. Follow these steps:

1. In the **MainLevel** scene, add another **Timer** node as a child and rename it to **PowerupSpawner**.
2. Adjust the `main_level.gd` script to include an exported reference to the new spawner and an exported array for the power-up scenes.
3. Connect the timeout signal of the power-up spawner in the `_ready` function and code the timeout function to randomly spawn power-ups.
   Here is how your updated `main_level.gd` script should look to bring all these pieces together. (Remember to drag your new **PowerupSpawner** node into the **Inspector** slot after saving.)

```
class_name MainLevel extends Node2D

# Drag the Timers into these slots in the Inspector!

@export var enemy_spawner: Timer
@export var powerup_spawner: Timer
```

```
@export var enemy_scenes: Array[PackedScene]
@export var powerup_scenes: Array[PackedScene]

func _ready() -> void:
    enemy_spawner.timeout.connect(_on_spawn_timer)
    enemy_spawner.start()

    powerup_spawner.timeout.connect(_on_powerup_timer_timeout)
    powerup_spawner.start()

func _on_spawn_timer() -> void:
    # Pick a random enemy from the list
    var random_enemy_scene: PackedScene = enemy_scenes.pick_random()
    var enemy: Node2D = random_enemy_scene.instantiate()
    add_child(enemy)

    # Assign a random X position just off the top of the screen
    var screen_width: float = get_viewport_rect().size.x
    enemy.global_position = Vector2(randf_range(50.0,
                        screen_width - 50.0), -50.0)

func _on_powerup_timer_timeout() -> void:
    # Pick a random powerup from the list
    var random_powerup_scene: PackedScene =
    powerup_scenes.pick_random()
    var powerup: Node2D = random_powerup_scene.instantiate()
    add_child(powerup)

    # Assign a random X position just off the top of the screen
    var screen_width: float = get_viewport_rect().size.x
    powerup.global_position = Vector2(randf_range(50.0,
                            screen_width - 50.0), -50.0)
```

This script is a perfect example of how decoupled architecture makes your life easier as a developer. Let's break down exactly what is happening here:

- **How the system works**: We are utilizing Godot's built-in `Timer` nodes to handle our spawn delays. When a timer finishes its countdown, it emits a `timeout` signal that triggers our custom spawn functions. The script then uses `.pick_random()` to grab one scene from our exported array, instantiates it into the game world, and places it just above the top edge of the screen (`-50` on the *Y*-axis) at a random horizontal position so it can drift downward.

- **Why this pattern is used**: By mirroring the exact same logic we used for the enemies, we keep our codebase consistent and easy to read. Furthermore, by relying on signals and standard `Timer` nodes, we avoid writing complex, manual countdown logic inside a `_process()` function.
- **The main takeaway**: Notice the ultimate benefit of this setup: the `Main Level` script has absolutely no idea what a power-up is! It doesn't know about shields, fuel canisters, or plasma cells. It just blindly takes a `PackedScene` from a list and drops it into the game. Because of this decoupled design, you can create 50 brand-new power-up types and add them to the game entirely through the Godot **Inspector**, without ever needing to open or rewrite this code again.

Finally, we should work on a heads-up display (HUD) to serve as the UI for the game. This can be achieved by following the steps below:

1. Create a new scene with **CanvasLayer** as root; rename it to `UI`.
2. Add a **Control** node as a child and rename it to `HUD`. Set its **Anchors Preset** to **Full Rect**.
3. Add a **MarginContainer** as a child of the **HUD**, set its **Anchors Preset** to **Top Left**, and set its size to `60 x 25`.
4. Add an **HBoxContainer** as a child of **MarginContainer**. Rename it to `ScoreContainer`, set its **Alignment** property to `End`.
5. Add an **HBoxContainer** as a child of **HUD** and rename it to `LivesContainer`. Set its **Layout Mode** to **Anchors** and set its **Anchors Preset** to **Top Right**.
6. Add an **HBoxContainer** as a child of **HUD** and rename it to `WeaponContainer`. Set **Layout Mode** to **Anchors** and its **Anchors Preset** to **Center Top**, set its size to `145 x 70`.
7. Add a **Label** as a child of **WeaponContainer** and rename it to `WeaponLabel`. Set the default **Text** to `LASER`. In the **Inspector**, create a new **LabelSettings** resource and click to expand. Set **Font Size** to `48px`.

Add a new Script to the **HUD** node. We will use the ship's texture to represent the player's lives, and we can also make use of the digit textures to represent the score. We can export an array for the digit textures. First, let's set up the foundational variables for our HUD. We need references to where our UI elements will be drawn, as well as the actual textures we will use to draw them:

```
extends Control

# Container references for dynamic UI instantiation
@onready var score_container: HBoxContainer = $MarginContainer/ScoreContainer
@onready var lives_container: HBoxContainer = $LivesContainer
@onready var weapon_label: Label = $WeaponContainer/WeaponLabel

# Data-driven UI: Textures are injected via the Inspector rather than hardcoded.
# 'digit_textures' should map strictly from indices 0-9 to match
@export var life_texture: Texture2D
@export var digit_textures: Array[Texture2D]

var score: int = 0
```

Let's understand what this code does:

- `@onready` **variables**: These grab references to our UI containers so we can easily add or remove elements from them later.
- `@export` **variables**: Instead of hardcoding image file paths into our script, we export a `life_texture` and an array of `digit_textures`. This is a data-driven design. It allows your artists to swap out the UI fonts or life icons directly in the Godot **Inspector** without ever touching your code.

Next, we need to initialize the **HUD** when the game starts. Because the **HUD** might load after the Event Bus or the Player, we must both fetch the current state and listen for future updates:

```
func _ready() -> void:
    # 1. Subscribe to future updates (PUSH)
    EventBus.score_changed.connect(update_score)
    EventBus.player_lives_changed.connect(update_lives)
    EventBus.weapon_changed.connect(update_weapon_display)

    # 2. Fetch the initial state from a global authority (PULL)
    var initial_lives = EventBus.current_lives
    var initial_score = EventBus.current_score

    # 3. Initialize the UI with that true data
    update_weapon_display("LASER CANNON", -1)
```

```
    update_score(initial_score)
    update_lives(initial_lives)
```

This `_ready()` function demonstrates a robust Push/Pull architecture:

- **Push**: By connecting to the Event Bus, we guarantee the HUD will automatically update whenever the game state changes in the future. The HUD passively waits for these signals to be pushed to it.
- **Pull**: However, what if the player already scored 500 points before this specific **HUD** node was loaded into the tree? The Event Bus doesn't hold data; it only broadcasts it. By manually pulling the current values from our global `GameState` Autoload and passing them into our update functions, we guarantee the UI instantly displays the correct information on frame one.

Now let's build the individual update functions, starting with the simplest one: the weapon Label:

```
func update_weapon_display(weapon_name: String, ammo: int) -> void:
    # We use -1 as a sentinel value for infinite ammo weapons.
    if ammo < 0:
        weapon_label.text = weapon_name
    else:
        weapon_label.text = weapon_name + " (" + str(ammo) + ")"
```

This function updates a standard text Label, but it introduces a smart programming pattern: the **sentinel value**. Since ammo can never naturally be negative, we establish -1 as a secret code for "infinite ammo." If the UI sees a negative number, it simply hides the ammo counter entirely.

To make our score look like a retro arcade game, we aren't using a standard text font. Instead, we are procedurally spawning individual images for every digit:

```
func update_score(amount: int):
    score += amount

    for child in score_container.get_children():
        child.queue_free()

    var score_str = str(score)

    # Rebuild the score dynamically by mapping each character
```

```
    # to its corresponding texture in the exported array.
    for character in score_str:
        var digit_index = int(character)

        var texture_rect = TextureRect.new()
        texture_rect.texture = digit_textures[digit_index]

        score_container.add_child(texture_rect)
```

First, we clear out any old score digits using `queue_free()`. Then, we convert our total score integer into a String. This allows us to loop through it character by character. If the score is "150", the loop reads "1", then "5", then "0". It converts those characters back into integers and uses them as an index to grab the exact matching image from our `digit_textures` array, dynamically spawning a new **TextureRect** for each number.

Finally, we apply a very similar procedural approach to display the player's remaining ships:

```
func update_lives(count: int) -> void:
    # Clear existing life icons
    for child in lives_container.get_children():
        child.queue_free()

    # Procedurally generate TextureRects for the current life count
    for i in range(count):
        var icon = TextureRect.new()
        icon.texture = life_texture

        # Programmatically configure sizing constraints
        icon.expand_mode = TextureRect.EXPAND_KEEP_SIZE
        icon.stretch_mode =
            TextureRect.STRETCH_KEEP_ASPECT_CENTERED
        icon.custom_minimum_size = Vector2(32, 32)

        lives_container.add_child(icon)
```

Just like the score, we wipe the container clean. We then use a `for` loop to spawn a new `TextureRect` for every life the player has remaining. The key takeaway here is the *programmatic configuration*. Because these icons are spawned via code (instead of in the editor), we have to manually tell Godot how to size them. Setting the `custom_minimum_size` and `stretch_mode` ensures our ship icons don't warp or stretch awkwardly inside the UI container.

Note

Architectural alternative: Lightweight UI scenes

While configuring nodes programmatically is an essential skill to understand, many professional developers strongly prefer a visual approach for UI. Instead of building the **TextureRect** via code, you could create a new, lightweight scene (for example, `life_icon.tscn`) containing just a single, pre-configured **TextureRect**. By doing this, you can simply `instantiate()` that scene inside your loop. This editor-driven approach prevents your scripts from bloating with UI configuration data and allows you to visually tweak the icon's size and stretch settings without having to run the game to test your changes.

To ensure that the player life icons display correctly whenever the player takes damage, we need a way to automatically notify the UI.

It might be tempting to add `current_lives` directly into our `Event Bus` script, but if you recall our earlier lessons, an Event Bus should be completely stateless; it is merely a radio station that broadcasts messages. To keep our architecture clean and adhere to the Single Responsibility Principle, we are going to let our `PlayerStats` Resource handle the actual data (the state), but we will wire its setter functions to broadcast through our global `EventBus`.

First, ensure your `EventBus` Autoload remains stripped down to its purest form. It should contain absolutely no variables, only the signal definitions:

```
============================================
EVENT BUS (Stateless Autoload)
============================================
extends Node

# --- SIGNALS ---
@warning_ignore("unused_signal") signal score_changed(new_amount: int)
@warning_ignore("unused_signal") signal player_lives_changed(current_lives: int)
@warning_ignore("unused_signal") signal weapon_changed(weapon_name: String, ammo:
int)
```

Next, open your `PlayerStats` resource script. We will use Godot 4's powerful setter functions to guarantee that whenever a variable is changed, it automatically pushes that update out to the global Event Bus.

```
==========================================
PLAYER STATS (Stateful Resource)
==========================================
class_name PlayerStats extends Resource

# --- STATE VARIABLES & AUTOMATIC SIGNALS ---
# By using Godot 4 setter functions, any time a script changes these variables,
# the Resource updates its internal state AND tells the global EventBus to
broadcast it.

@export var current_score: int = 0:
    set(value):
        current_score = value
        EventBus.score_changed.emit(current_score)

@export var current_lives: int = 3:
    set(value):
        current_lives = value
        EventBus.player_lives_changed.emit(current_lives)
```

By structuring our code this way, we get the absolute best of both worlds. Our data is cleanly encapsulated inside a reusable Godot Resource, but our programmatic UI icons can still instantly react to changes just by listening to the global Event Bus.

Let's break down exactly what changed in this refactor and why this new architecture is crucial for a stable game:

- **What changed (Stateless to Stateful)**: Previously, our Event Bus was purely a router. It held no actual data; it just provided the communication channels. Now, we have transformed it into a stateful Autoload. It physically stores the authoritative `current_score` and `current_lives` variables for the entire game.
- **How the Setter solves the problem**: By using Godot's `set(value):` syntax, we turn standard variables into reactive data. Now, a script no longer needs to manually emit a signal. If the player takes damage, the script simply runs `EventBus.current_lives -= 1`. The setter instantly intercepts this math, permanently updates the value, and

automatically broadcasts the `player_lives_changed` signal to the UI. It combines data manipulation and event broadcasting into one unbreakable step.

- **Why this prevents Race Conditions**: A *race condition* (further explained in the next section) happens when your game's logic depends on unpredictable timing. For example, if your **Player** node loads first and broadcasts "I have 3 lives," but the HUD hasn't finished loading yet, the **HUD** misses the broadcast completely and displays 0 lives. Because our Event Bus is an Autoload (meaning it loads before anything else in the game), it always holds the correct `current_lives` value. When the HUD finally loads, it doesn't have to wait for a signal—it can simply "pull" the starting value directly from the Event Bus on frame one, guaranteeing the icons display perfectly every time.

The fatal flaw of pure event-driven systems is that statelessness means there is no history. Because the Event Bus previously only held signals and no variables, it acted like a radio tower. When the **PlayerShip** broadcast that it had 3 lives a fraction of a second before the **HUD** turned on its radio, the message would be lost forever.

Architectural note: race conditions

The scenario we just described, where a signal fires into the void before the listening node has had time to connect to it, is what programmers call a **race condition**. It occurs whenever your game's logic depends on the unpredictable timing of events to function correctly. It is a literal race during the game's startup sequence: will the Player finish loading and broadcast its signal first, or will the **HUD** finish loading and start listening first? Because of the order in which Godot initializes the Scene Tree (children run `_ready` from bottom to top), you can never guarantee which node will win this race, leading to a UI that randomly displays 0 lives.

The solution, as seen above, is the Push/Pull architecture utilizing our `PlayerStats` Resource. By using Godot 4's setter functions inside the Resource, it acts as our single source of truth. The HUD can confidently subscribe to the Event Bus for future updates (Push), while safely pulling the current, guaranteed state directly from the `PlayerStats` variables during `_ready()` (Pull).

Summary

In this chapter, we learned how to untangle our projects by abandoning brittle direct node references.

By following the Call Down, Signal Up, Event Out rule, we shifted the responsibility of communication from the object performing the action to the objects that need to react to it. We implemented the Event Bus pattern to cross system boundaries, learned how to future-proof our signals using Namespaces and Event Objects, and utilized Observable Resources to create reactive data.

By adopting these event-driven patterns, a project can be transformed from a fragile house of cards into a robust, scalable system ready for commercial development.

In the next chapter, we will take this decoupled foundation and apply it to implementing State and Strategy Patterns, replacing massive, tangled `if/else` statements with clean, modular logic to manage complex behaviors like Enemy AI and dynamic Player states.

7

Implementing State and Strategy Patterns

As your game grows, so does the complexity of your logic. This is a natural evolution. As you implement more ideas, they interact with other parts of your game. This can lead to knock-on effects, which make things complicated.

In the early stages of *Void Defenders*, when it was simple and easier to prototype, we might have programmed the enemy ship behavior like this:

```
func _physics_process(delta: float) -> void:
    if hp > 50 and distance_to_player > 300:
        # fly around
    elif hp > 50 and distance_to_player < 300:
        # shoot at player
    elif hp < 50:
        # run away
    elif is_stunned:
        # do nothing
```

This can quickly grow into a giant switch-case or spaghetti conditional trap. As you add more features (like shields, EMP blasts, or dodging), this single function will bloat into hundreds of lines of fragile code. If you want to change how the enemy shoots, you must carefully navigate a minefield of `if/else` statements, hoping that you don't break the movement logic.

This is what is known as the **prototype wall**. Development starts very fast: you create a **Player** node, attach a script, and start adding variables. For the first few weeks, everything works perfectly. But as the project grows into a commercial-scale game, that single `player.gd` script bloats to 1,500 lines of code. Suddenly, fixing a bug takes days instead of minutes. You have hit the wall, and your code is no longer an asset; it is a liability.

This is where design patterns come in to save your project. Specifically, to solve the nightmare of overgrown conditionals, we need to look at a specific category known as *behavioral patterns*.

While creational patterns deal with how objects are made, and **structural patterns** deal with how they are organized, **behavioral patterns** focus purely on communication and the assignment of responsibilities between objects. They define exactly how objects act, react, and change their logic on the fly.

In gameplay systems, mastering behavioral patterns is absolutely critical. Games are highly dynamic by nature: an enemy might need to seamlessly switch from a passive patrol to an aggressive chase, or a player might need to instantly swap a rapid-fire Laser for a heavy Plasma Cannon. If you try to manage all these shifting behaviors by checking dozens of Boolean flags (`is_patrolling, has_plasma_cannon`) inside a single monolithic script, you hit the prototype wall we just discussed.

By applying behavioral patterns, specifically the **State Pattern** and the **Strategy Pattern**, we can extract those messy conditionals entirely. We take behaviors that used to be tangled inside a giant `match` statement and turn them into modular, interchangeable objects. The main script is stripped of its complex logic and simply acts as a manager, delegating the actual work to these specialized behavior objects.

In *Chapter 6*, we already explored conditional and structural patterns when we implemented Singletons (Autoloads) and the Observer Pattern via the Event Bus. In this chapter, we are going to focus on behavioral patterns with the goal of structuring behaviors as interchangeable, highly organized objects.

In this chapter, we will cover:

- Understanding design patterns
- Building a state machine in Godot using the State Pattern
- Organizing state transitions
- Using the Strategy Pattern for gameplay variations
- Implementing weapon strategies
- Refactoring conditionals into patterns

By the end of this chapter, you will have crossed a critical threshold in your development journey: transitioning from a beginner who writes rigid, tangled scripts into an intermediate software architect capable of building professional, highly scalable game systems.

Technical requirements

Readers should be familiar with basic Godot workflows, such as navigating the Godot editor, creating scenes, and scripting with GDScript.

You can download the example project and code for this book by following the instructions in the *Download the example code files* section in the *Preface* of this book.

This chapter's code files are included in the downloadable code bundle.

Understanding design patterns

Now that we've introduced the role of design patterns in managing complexity, let's take a closer look at what they are and why they are so effective.

Rather than being a specific piece of code, design patterns are a proven, standardized solution to a common architectural problem. They are generalizations since developers realized that whether you are building banking software, an operating system, or a space shooter, you are ultimately solving the same underlying logic puzzles – answering questions like:

- How do I make objects talk to each other without hardcoding paths?
- How do I change objects' behavior at runtime?
- How do I ensure only one instance of a manager exists?

Instead of reinventing the wheel every time you face one of these puzzles, you apply a design pattern.

Design patterns are essential for large projects because they help to transform your codebase from a tangled web into a modular, professional system. Design patterns have many benefits, but the fundamental ones are:

- **Extreme scalability**: Patterns force you to write modular code. If you use the Strategy Pattern (which we will build later in this chapter) for your weapons, adding a fiftieth weapon to the game is exactly as easy as adding a second. You don't have to touch the `Player` script at all; you just drop in a new module.
- **Enhanced maintainability (decoupling)**: Patterns isolate failures. If your AI's Flee state has a bug, the State Pattern (explained in the next section) guarantees that the bug is physically isolated inside the `flee_state.gd` file. You can fix it without any fear of breaking the `Attack` or `Patrol` logic.
- **Improved communication**: Design patterns give developers a universal language. If you bring a second programmer onto your team and tell them that the `AudioManager` is

a Singleton and the weapons use a Strategy Pattern, they can easily understand the entire architecture of those systems before even reading a single line of code.

- **Removing spaghetti conditionals**: As humans, we can only hold so many logic threads in our heads at once. Patterns eliminate the cognitive load of tracking massive, nested `if/elif/else` blocks, allowing you to focus purely on creating fun gameplay.

To handle changing behaviors cleanly, we turn to the State Pattern. Let's see how to implement this in Godot using a reusable state machine.

Building a state machine in Godot using the State Pattern

The **State Pattern** is an object-oriented way to implement a concept known as a **Finite State Machine** (**FSM**).

In computer science, an FSM is a system that has a limited, strictly defined number of states (like Idle, Walking, or Jumping), and it dictates that an object can only ever be in exactly one state at a time. It cannot be both idle and jumping simultaneously. It moves between these states using defined rules called transitions.

The State Pattern connects to this concept by turning those abstract states into physical, interchangeable objects. Instead of a single, massive script trying to juggle all a ship's behaviors with fragile `if/else` checks, we separate each behavior into its own dedicated script.

Conceptually, the architecture looks like this:

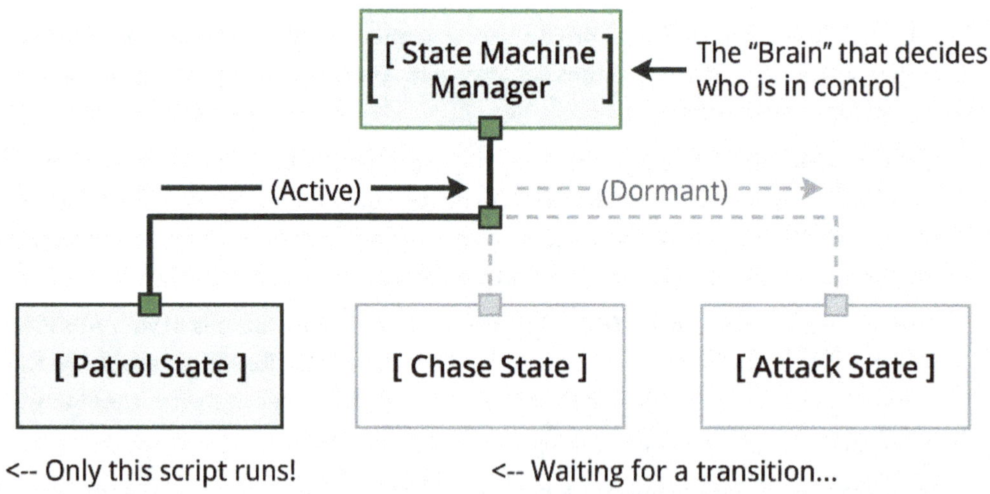

Figure 7.1 – An example of a state machine

In Godot, the most intuitive way to build an FSM is by using Nodes. While you could technically write a state machine using pure code (basic data objects or custom classes), using Godot's Node hierarchy leverages the engine's greatest strengths.

> Note
>
> **Architectural note**
>
> In *Chapter 5*, we established a golden rule: *Use code for logic and Nodes for structure.* At first glance, using Nodes to build a state machine might feel like breaking that rule. However, it is actually the ultimate expression of it! An FSM is the structural architecture of your entity's brain. We aren't using these Nodes to calculate math or handle raw data; we are using them to structurally organize and encapsulate isolated behaviors. The moment-to-moment logic still lives in the code, but the structure of those behaviors is handled by the tree.

Here is why utilizing Nodes for your state machine is the preferred Godot methodology:

- **Visual organization**: You can look directly at your Scene Tree and see the exact list of behaviors an entity possesses. The architecture documents itself.
- **Native game loops**: Because states are Nodes, they naturally hook into Godot's built-in processing loops (`_process` and `_physics_process`). They can handle their own movements and timers without complex workarounds.
- **Easier debugging**: When your game is running, you can open Godot's **Remote Scene Tree**, look at the state machine, and immediately see which State node is currently active and processing, making bug hunting really fast.

The big idea is to create a **StateMachine** parent node and then attach **State** child nodes to it. To demonstrate this in action, add a new enemy to *Void Defenders* that has three distinct behaviors: `Patrol`, `Chase`, and `Attack`. We will call this enemy the `Elite Cruiser`.

First, we need a template that all states will follow, and we do this by creating a new script called `state.gd`. This will form our virtual base class using the code shown as follows:

```
# State.gd
class_name State extends Node

# Custom ID to prevent brittle node-name dependencies
@export var state_id: String = ""

# Emitted when this state wants the manager to change the active state signal
```

```
transition_requested(state: State, new_state_name: String)

# Virtual functions to be overridden by specific child states
func enter() -> void:
    pass

func exit() -> void:
    pass

func update(_delta: float) -> void:
    pass

func physics_update(_delta: float) -> void:
    pass
```

In the preceding code, the `enter` function is called when the state becomes active, the `exit` function is called when the state is about to change, `update` is called by the state machine's `_process` function, and `physics_update` is called by the state machine's `_physics_process`.

But why create a script full of empty functions? This structure establishes a strict contract for our architecture. Because every specialized state we build later (like `Patrol` or `Attack`) will inherit from this base `State` class, our state machine manager never has to guess what functions are available. It can blindly call `current_state.physics_update(delta)` with absolute certainty that the game won't crash, even if that specific state doesn't need to use physics that frame. This guarantees that our manager remains completely decoupled from the specific behaviors of the states it is managing.

The reason I refer to a state machine is that it is the brain that will manage different states. In effect, it uses the `state` class, which we have just defined. It will keep track of the active state and will call the correct functions when needed. The `state machine` class, which we will create below, will be the parent of all the states:

```
# StateMachine.gd
class_name StateMachine extends Node

@export var initial_state: State
var current_state: State

# Strictly typing our dictionary for better auto-complete and safety
var states: Dictionary[String, State] = {}
```

```
func _ready() -> void:
    # Loop through all children to map out our available states
    for child in get_children():
        # Guard clause: Skip if it isn't a State
        if not child is State:
            continue

        # Determine the key for our dictionary
        var key: String = child.name
        if child.state_id != "":
            key = child.state_id

        states[key.to_lower()] = child

        # Connect to our state's request signal
        child.transition_requested.connect(on_state_transition_requested)

    if initial_state:
        initial_state.enter()
        current_state = initial_state

# Delegate the engine's built-in processing to the active state
func _process(delta: float) -> void:
    if not current_state:
        return
    current_state.update(delta)

func _physics_process(delta: float) -> void:
    if not current_state:
        return current_state.physics_update(delta)

# Handle the transition logic
func on_state_transition_requested(state: State, new_state_id: String) -> void:
    # Guard clause: ignore delayed signals from old states
    if state != current_state:
        return
    var new_state: State = states.get(new_state_id.to_lower())

    # Guard clause: exit if the requested state doesn't exist
    if not new_state:
        push_warning("State does not exist: ", new_state_id)
```

```
        return

    # Execute the transition
    current_state.exit()
    new_state.enter()
    current_state = new_state
```

In the above code, the `state_machine` script acts purely as a manager whose only job is to route traffic and ensure that exactly one behavior is active at a time. Here is how that logic maps directly to the structure of the script:

- **Initialization (`_ready`):** When the Elite Cruiser spawns into the game, the state machine runs its setup. Rather than forcing us to manually type out a list of every state, the script uses `get_children()` to look at the Scene Tree, finds every child node that extends the `State` class, and dynamically adds it to a `states` dictionary.
- **Delegation (`_process` and `_physics_process`):** Every frame, the Godot engine tells the state machine to update. The manager doesn't run any movement or attack logic itself; it simply passes the engine delta time down to whatever the `current_state` is. This ensures only active behavior is executed, saving CPU cycles.
- **Switching gears (`on_state_transition_requested`):** When an active state finishes its job (like spotting the player), it emits a signal that triggers this function. The manager safely calls `exit()` on the old state, calls `enter()` on the new state, and updates the `current_state` variable to officially hand over control.

Then we connect the `transition_requested` signal for each state to our transition function. This allows states to signal when they are finished, and the manager can take over. The core of the State Pattern is *delegation*. Godot is telling the `state_machine` to process every frame. Instead of running a massive `if/else` block, the state machine just passes `delta` time down to whatever state is currently active. If the `current_state` is the **Patrol** node, only the `Patrol` code runs. The **Chase** and **Attack** nodes sit idle; this saves CPU resources and prevents logical conflicts.

When an active state decides that it is time to change, such as when the `Patrol` state spots the **Player**, it emits the `transition_requested` signal. Using a signal here rather than directly calling a function on the parent node (like `get_parent().change_state()`) is the ultimate form of decoupling. The `Patrol` script does not need to know that the `StateMachine` manager exists, nor does it need to know how the manager handles the physical swapping of states.

While the `Patrol` script *does* need to know what state it wants to transition to next (for example, requesting to go to `idle`), it relies entirely on the conceptual `state_id` we set up earlier. Because it is completely decoupled from the actual Node names in the Scene Tree, a designer can rename or reorganize the state nodes at any time without breaking the `Patrol` script's transition request. It simply broadcasts that it is finished and recommends changing to the `Chase` state. It trusts that the manager is listening and will handle all the complex logistics safely.

This function handles the swap safely. Sometimes an old state may be in the middle of a delayed animation or a timer function when it is deactivated. The check `if state != current_state: return` prevents ghost transitions where an old state suddenly emits a transition signal. Once the transition is validated, the manager calls `exit()` on the old state, which allows it to clean up timers or reset variables. Then it immediately calls `enter()` on the new state, which allows it to acquire targets or play animations. Finally, the `current_state` variable is updated, which completes the entire transition cycle.

Now that we have our state script as a base for all states and our `state_machine` script to control state changes, we can use them in a new enemy type: the Elite Cruiser.

1. Create a new scene with **CharacterBody2D** as the root and rename it to `EliteCruiser`.
2. Add a **Sprite2D** and **CollisionShape2D** nodes as children.
3. Set the `texture` of the **Sprite2D** node (I used `enemyBlue4.png`).
4. Set the shape of the **CollisionShape2D** node to rectangle and enclose the sprite.
5. Add a new **Node** node as a child and rename it to `StateMachine`.
6. Add three new nodes as children of **StateMachine** and name them `Patrol`, `Chase`, and `Attack`.
7. Attach `state_machine.gd` to the **StateMachine** node.
8. Create new scripts for the **Patrol**, **Chase**, and **Attack** nodes. Let them all inherit from `state.gd`.

The result is shown in *Figure 7.2* as follows:

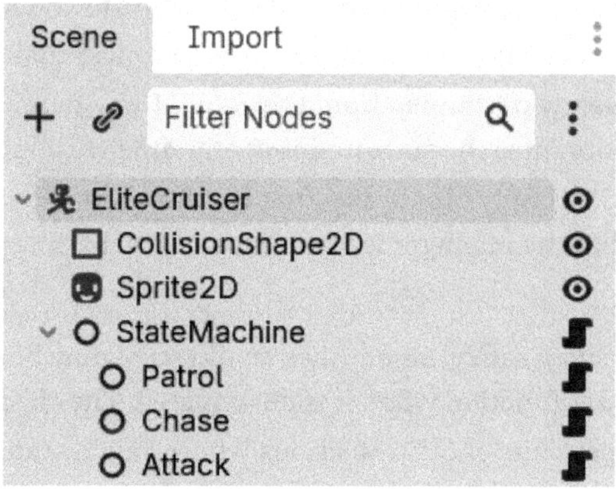

Figure 7.2 – Framework for the EliteCruiser with state machine

Because we created an export variable for the initial state, we should assign that to the **Patrol** node so that the Elite Cruiser starts off in **Patrol** mode. This can be seen in *Figure 7.3* as follows:

Figure 7.3 – Assigning the initial state of the machine

Now that we have the state machine framework in place, let's focus on how individual states define their behavior and handle transitions.

Organizing state transitions

Now that our state machine architecture is securely in place, we need to define the rules for how the Elite Cruiser uses it. A state machine is only as powerful as the logic that governs how it moves from one state to the next.

In this section, we will explore how to cleanly organize these state transitions by writing the `Chase` logic. As you read through the upcoming script, pay close attention to what is absent. Notice that there is not a single line of code dedicated to patrolling or firing weapons. This perfectly illustrates the concept of *state-level responsibility*: an individual state script should only care about executing its unique behavior and determining the exact moment it needs to pass the baton to a different state.

Because each state must only be concerned with its own behavior, the script for each state is clean and simple. This is the advantage of isolating states; the Chase state does not have to worry about patrolling or firing weapons; it only cares about hunting the player and deciding when to transition. This is demonstrated in the code for the `Chase` state:

```
class_name Chase extends State

@export var actor: CharacterBody2D
@export var speed: float = 150.0
@export var attack_range: float = 200.0

# Variable to control how fast the elite cruiser can turn

@export var rotation_speed: float = 3.0

var target: Node2D

func enter()-> void:
    target = get_tree().get_first_node_in_group("Player")

func physics_update(delta:float)-> void:
    if not target:
        transition_requested.emit(self, "Patrol")
        return

    var distance =
    actor.global_position.distance_to(target.global_position)

    if distance <= attack_range:
        transition_requested.emit(self, "Attack")
        return

    # 1. Calculate the ideal direction to the target
    var direction = (target.global_position -
    actor.global_position).normalized()

    # 2. Smoothly rotate the actor to face that direction
    # We add PI/2 (90 degrees) because sprites face UP by default
    var target_rotation = direction.angle() + PI/2
    actor.rotation = lerp_angle(actor.rotation, target_rotation,
    rotation_speed * delta)

    # 3. Move the actor "Forward"
```

```
    # The ship moves wherever its nose is pointing
    var forward_direction = Vector2.UP.rotated(actor.rotation)
    actor.velocity = forward_direction * speed
    actor.move_and_slide()
```

Most of the heavy lifting for this behavior happens inside the `physics_update` function. It runs every physics frame and is split into two distinct phases: **decision-making** and **movement execution**. We'll explore these in detail in the subsequent sections.

Phase 1: The guard clauses (decision-making)

Before the ship even thinks about firing its thrusters, it asks itself if it should still be chasing the player. It does this using guard clauses at the very top of the function:

- **Target verification:** `if not target:` checks if the player still exists (perhaps they were destroyed or cloaked). If the target is gone, the state emits a signal to transition back to patrol and immediately calls return to stop the rest of the code from running.
- **Range checking:** Next, it calculates the distance between itself and the player. If the ship gets close enough (`distance <= attack_range`), it emits a signal to swap to the attack state and returns.

By placing these decisions at the top, we save valuable CPU cycles and prevent the movement math from running if the ship is about to change states.

Phase 2: Steering and thrust (movement execution)

If the guard clauses pass, the cruiser is cleared to move. Because we want our Elite Cruiser to feel weighty and realistic, we don't just snap it directly to the player's location. Instead, we break the flight math into three steps:

1. **Calculate direction**: We find the absolute straight line to the player by subtracting our position from the target's position and using `.normalized()` to turn it into a pure directional arrow.
2. **Smooth rotation**: We find the angle of that direction. Note that we add `PI/2`, or `90` degrees, to this angle. Because Godot's 2D *Y*-axis points *down*, positive angles rotate *clockwise*. Our sprite is natively drawn facing up, but Godot considers `0` degrees to be pointing right. Adding `PI/2` rotates the sprite `90` degrees clockwise so its nose perfectly aligns with the mathematical angle. We then use `lerp_angle()` (Linear Interpolation)

to smoothly swing the cruiser's nose toward the target over time, governed by our `rotation_speed`.

3. **Forward movement**: Finally, instead of just sliding along the *X* or *Y* axis, we tell the ship to move forward relative to wherever its nose is currently pointing. We calculate this `forward_direction`, apply our speed to the body's velocity, and execute `move_and_slide()`.

   If you are relatively new to Godot, `move_and_slide()` is a powerful built-in physics function. Instead of just teleporting the node, it calculates the movement, checks for obstacles in the way, and automatically handles collisions, allowing our ship to smoothly slide against walls instead of glitching through them or coming to a jarring halt.

This script has single responsibility and therein lies its power: its sole job is to hunt the target. When the state machine switches to the `Chase` state, the manager calls `enter()` exactly once. It is within this `enter()` function that the state locates and locks onto the player.

But hunting the target also means knowing exactly when to stop. Inside the `physics_update()` function, the script constantly evaluates its transition logic. If the player is destroyed or lost, it emits a signal to return to the `Patrol` state. If the cruiser gets close enough to strike, it emits a signal to seamlessly switch to the `Attack` state. By isolating both the movement and the transition rules inside this single file, we have completely self-contained and modular behavior.

Isolating the transitions in this way ensures single responsibility, which helps with locating bugs. If something is off with the shooting, we know exactly which script to open: `attack.gd`. You don't have to scroll through 400 lines of patrol and movement code to find the weapon logic. Furthermore, if you want to create a new Flee state, you simply add a new node to the state machine. You don't have to touch or risk breaking any of the existing states.

Note that in the `chase.gd` script, we have two distinct entities:

1. `@export var actor: CharacterBody2D` **(The body being controlled)**: Since the `Chase` state is just a general node, it doesn't have its own physical `position` or `velocity`. It needs to know what physical body it is supposed to be moving around the screen. In this case, we called the variable actor, and we dragged the **Elite Cruiser** root node into the **Inspector** as shown in *Figure 7.4*, as follows:

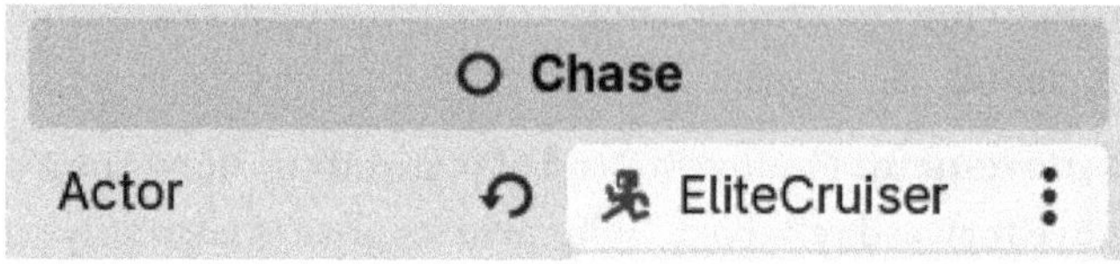

Figure 7.4 – Actor represents the enemy ship running this script

2. `var target: Node2D` **(The player)**: This is the object the Elite Cruiser is trying to hunt down. We find it by looking for the first node in the `Player` group.
   So, when the code says `actor.velocity = forward_direction * speed`, it means that we are setting the Elite Cruiser `velocity` to move toward the player.

Before we move on, let's reflect on the core architectural philosophy we just applied: **Separation of Concerns**. By stripping the state machine manager of any actual game logic and stripping the individual states of any management logic, we have created a system that is robust. If a bug occurs while the cruiser is attacking, you know with absolute certainty that the bug lives inside the `Attack` state script, nowhere else. This isolation is the true power of the State Pattern.

With the state machine gracefully handling the complex transitions of our enemy AI, we can now apply a similar modular thinking to the player's abilities by utilizing the Strategy Pattern.

Using the Strategy Pattern for gameplay variation

While the State Pattern is great for managing what an object is currently doing, the Strategy Pattern is designed to manage how an object does something.

Before we write the code, let's look at a brief comparison to help you decide which pattern is right for your specific gameplay feature.

State versus Strategy patterns: Which should I use?

Here are some practical guidelines to help you decide which pattern to use:

- **Use the State Pattern** when an object goes through distinct phases or moods. States are usually mutually exclusive, and the object frequently transitions between them based on internal rules. For example: An enemy swapping from *Patrol* to *Chase* to *Attack*.
- **Use the Strategy Pattern** when an object performs a specific, consistent task, but you want to easily swap out the algorithm it uses to complete that task. Strategies rarely manage their own transitions; they wait to be called by a parent. For example, a player

pressing **Fire**, and the game seamlessly swaps between a Single Shot strategy and a Spread Shot strategy based on their equipped weapon.

With these guidelines in mind, let's dive into implementing our first Strategy Pattern to give our player multiple weapon types without cluttering their main movement script.

Understanding the Strategy Pattern in Godot

The Strategy Pattern allows you to define a family of algorithms, encapsulate each one, and make them interchangeable at runtime. In Godot 4, the optimal way to implement the Strategy Pattern is by using *Custom Resources*.

At its core, a Resource is an independent object designed solely to hold information. Rather than living inside the active Scene Tree like a standard Node, it resides quietly in the engine's memory. It doesn't have a physical position, and it doesn't natively process every frame. A **Custom Resource** is simply a script you write that extends the `Resource` class. It allows you to package your own custom variables and functions together, save them as `.tres` files in your project folder, and instantly snap them into your nodes as lightweight, interchangeable modules.

We could make use of the Strategy Pattern as an alternative way to handle the player ship's weapons in *Void Defenders*. Instead of writing complex logic inside `player_ship.gd` to handle Lasers, Spread Shots, and Plasma Cannons, or using rigid arrays of packed scenes, we can extract the firing logic into a Strategy Resource.

But what exactly is a *Strategy Resource*, and how does it fit into the pattern?

In traditional software engineering, the Strategy Pattern relies on creating separate, interchangeable classes for each behavior (for example, a `LaserStrategy` class and a `SpreadShotStrategy` class) that all follow the same strict rules. In Godot, we bring this concept to life by writing scripts that extend the `Resource` class.

A **Strategy Resource** is simply a custom data container that holds both the variables for a specific weapon (like `fire_rate` or `energy_cost`) and the unique algorithm required to fire it (the `fire()` function).

How this fits into the pattern is beautiful: by assigning this Resource to an exported variable on the **PlayerShip** (or its **Blaster** component), the ship itself never needs to know how the weapon fires. When the player clicks the mouse, the ship simply tells its currently equipped Strategy Resource to execute its `fire()` function. If the player picks up a power-up, you just swap the underlying Resource file, seamlessly changing the ship's firing behavior at runtime without touching a single line of the player's movement logic.

Defining the weapon strategy base

The first thing we should do is to create a script to represent the general strategy for weapons. Because weapons will become Custom Resources, this script will extend `Resource` instead of Node:

```
class_name WeaponStrategy extends Resource

@export var fire_rate: float = 0.5
@export var energy_cost: int = 10

# Virtual function meant to be overridden by specific weapon strategies
# spawn_location: Where the projectile originates
# direction: The directional vector the weapon is aiming
# parent_container: Where the projectile should be added in the Scene Tree
func fire(
    spawn_location: Vector2,
    direction: Vector2,
    parent_container: Node
) -> void:
    push_error("Abstract method fire() must be overridden!")
```

You might be thinking that the `weapon_strategy.gd` script is incomplete, since it has variables, yet its only function simply throws an error. This is entirely intentional. The `weapon_strategy` script is not meant to be used directly in the game; instead, it acts as an abstract base class or an interface. Its entire purpose is to define a strict contract that all future weapons must follow.

By extending `Resource`, we create a Pure Data Object, so it does not need a `_process` function, it doesn't sit in the Scene Tree, and it takes up almost no memory at all. We can now save our strategies as `.tres` files and hot swap them into the **Blaster** component instantly!

The variables in the base `weapon_strategy` script ensure that every weapon we create will have a `fire_rate` and an `energy_cost`. This guarantees that the **Blaster** component can confidently ask for the `fire_rate` from any weapon without worrying about whether the variable actually exists.

The most important part of the script is the virtual function. This defines the contract of the strategy. It dictates that any script inheriting from `WeaponStrategy` must contain a fire function that accepts a location, direction, and parent container. You will notice that there is no bullet spawning logic here; instead, it uses Godot's `push_error()` function. This is a defensive programming mechanism, because if a game designer accidentally drags this empty `weapon_strategy.gd` blueprint into the Player's weapon slot instead of a real `Laser`, the game won't know what to do. By using `push_error()`, we create an immediate warning in the Godot console, which will alert us to create a child class that overrides this function with actual shooting logic.

Implementing weapon strategies

The next step is to implement specific strategies to differentiate our weapons. Because our strategies are Resources, they exist entirely outside the Scene Tree. They don't inherently know where the game world is.

Rather than forcing the Resource to blindly hunt down the root of the scene to dump its projectiles, we will add a `parent_container` parameter to our `fire()` function. This allows whoever is shooting the weapon (like the Player) to pass in a specific organizational Node (like an empty Projectiles **Node2D**) to keep our Scene Tree clean.

Here is the script for our first variant, a basic `Laser`:

```
class_name LaserStrategy extends WeaponStrategy

@export var laser_scene: PackedScene

# Notice the parent_container parameter

func fire(spawn_location: Vector2, direction: Vector2, parent_container:Node)->
void:
    var laser: Node2D = laser_scene.instantiate()
    laser.global_position = spawn_location
    laser.rotation = direction.angle() + (PI / 2.0)

    # Add the laser to the specific container passed by the caller
    if parent_container:
        parent_container.add_child(laser)
    else:
        push_warning("LaserStrategy fired without a valid
        parent_container!")
```

Notice how we safely spawn the Laser using `parent_container.add_child(laser)`. If you are familiar with writing scripts inside standard Godot nodes, you might be wondering why we didn't just use standard `add_child(laser)` or `get_tree().root.add_child(laser)`. To understand why we must explicitly pass a container into this function, we must look at two major architectural hurdles: the **Relative Movement Problem** and the **Resource Isolation Problem**.

First, if we simply called `add_child(laser)` directly inside the **Player** or **Blaster** node, Godot would attach the Laser as a direct child of the player. Because children inherit the transforms (position and rotation) of their parents, the fired Laser would physically travel with the ship. If the player dodged to the left, all Lasers currently on screen would instantly slide left. To fix this relative movement problem, projectiles must be spawned in a neutral container at the top of the Scene Tree, completely detached from the ship that fired them.

Second, because our `WeaponStrategy` is a Resource, it suffers from the resource isolation problem. Resources exist purely in memory; they are not Nodes, they do not sit in the Scene Tree, and they completely lack access to built-in functions like `add_child()` or `get_tree()`. By forcing the active Node (the **Blaster**) to pass a valid `parent_container` directly into the Resource's `fire()` function, we elegantly bridge the gap between our isolated data and the active game world.

With our understanding of how to safely bridge the gap between Resources and the physical game world, we can add a strategy for a Spread Shot Laser. Notice how it strictly follows the same interface contract as the basic Laser:

```
class_name SpreadShotStrategy extends WeaponStrategy

@export var laser_scene: PackedScene
@export var spread_angle: float = 15.0

func fire(spawn_location: Vector2, direction: Vector2, parent_container:Node)->
void:
    # Fire 3 lasers at different angles
    var angles = [-spread_angle, 0, spread_angle]

    for angle in angles:
        var laser = laser_scene.instantiate()
        laser.global_position = spawn_location

        var rotated_dir = direction.rotated(deg_to_rad(angle))
        laser.rotation = rotated_dir.angle() + PI/2

        if parent_container:
            parent_container.add_child(laser)
        else:
```

```
        push_warning("SpreadShotStrategy fired without a
        valid container!")
```

In the Spread Shot Strategy code above, instead of firing a single bullet, this strategy runs a for loop to instantiate three separate projectiles simultaneously. All the complexities of vector math, looping, and instantiation are locked away inside this one file to simplify the job of the `Blaster` script.

Let's break down exactly how this code works under the hood:

- **The pattern array**: First, we define an array of three angles: one angled to the left (`-spread_angle`), one firing straight ahead (0), and one angled to the right (`spread_angle`).
- **The trajectory math**: Inside the loop, we instantiate a Laser for each angle and calculate its unique flight path. We use `direction.rotated(deg_to_rad(angle))` to take the ship's base forward direction and tilt it by our target angle. Notice that we use `deg_to_rad()` to convert our human-readable degrees into radians, which Godot's internal math engine requires.
- **The visual alignment**: We then set `laser.rotation` to match that new trajectory so the bullet doesn't fly sideways. We add `PI/2` (`90` degrees) to ensure the sprite's nose points in the direction of travel, compensating for Godot's default 2D right-facing orientation.

Injecting strategies into the Player

It is now time to inject the strategy into the **Player**. Our `Blaster` script is made simpler since instead of using arrays of scenes and strings, we can just export slots for our strategy resources. Refactor the `Blaster` script as shown so that we can fire basic Lasers and Spread Shot Lasers:

```
class_name Blaster extends Node2D

# --- STRATEGY INJECTION ---
# Instead of arrays of scenes and strings,
# we just export slots for our strategy resources!
@export var basic_weapon: WeaponStrategy
@export var upgraded_weapon: WeaponStrategy

@onready var muzzle: Marker2D = $Muzzle
@onready var cooldown_timer: Timer = $CooldownTimer
@onready var fire_sound: AudioStreamPlayer2D = $FireSound
```

```
# The Blaster's brain. Holds whatever strategy is currently active.
var current_strategy: WeaponStrategy
var special_ammo: int = 0

func _ready() -> void:
    # Default to the basic weapon on startup
    current_strategy = basic_weapon
    EventBus.weapon_changed.emit("LASER CANNON", -1)

func fire() -> void:
    if not cooldown_timer.is_stopped():
        return

    if not current_strategy:
        push_error("Blaster has no strategy assigned!")
        return

    # DELEGATION: The Blaster doesn't calculate bullet math anymore.
    # We pass the muzzle position, facing direction, and the active scene
    # as the safe parent_container to hold the projectiles.
    current_strategy.fire(
        muzzle.global_position,
        Vector2.UP.rotated(global_rotation),
        get_tree().current_scene
    )

    fire_sound.play()

    # Pull the specific fire_rate from the strategy resource
    cooldown_timer.start(current_strategy.fire_rate)

    # --- AMMO TRACKING ---
    if current_strategy == upgraded_weapon:
        special_ammo -= 1

        if special_ammo <= 0:
            downgrade_weapon()
        else:
            EventBus.weapon_changed.emit(
                "SPREAD SHOT",
```

```
            special_ammo
        )

func upgrade_weapon() -> void:
    # Swap the strategy resource seamlessly
    current_strategy = upgraded_weapon
    special_ammo = 5

    EventBus.weapon_changed.emit(
        "SPREAD SHOT",
        special_ammo
    )

    print("Blaster strategy swapped to: Spread Shot")

func downgrade_weapon() -> void:
    current_strategy = basic_weapon

    EventBus.weapon_changed.emit(
        "LASER CANNON",
        -1
    )

    print("Blaster strategy swapped to: Basic Laser")
```

Here is a walkthrough of the key mechanics driving this script:

- **Strategy Injection (`@export`)**: Instead of hardcoding which weapons the player can use, we expose `basic_weapon` and `upgraded_weapon` to the Godot **Inspector**. This allows you to simply drag and drop your `.tres` Resource files right into the player's weapon slots without touching the code.
- **Pure delegation (`current_strategy.fire`)**: This is the heart of the pattern. When the player pulls the trigger, the **Blaster** doesn't calculate bullet math. It just delegates the task by passing its current location and rotation to the active strategy. The Resource handles the actual spawning of the projectiles.
- **Dynamic properties**: Notice that we start the cooldown timer using `current_strategy.fire_rate`. Because every Strategy Resource holds its own fire rate,

a heavy Plasma Cannon will naturally fire slower than a basic Laser, and the `Blaster` script doesn't have to manage any of those timings.

- **Seamless swapping**: When the player grabs a power-up, the `upgrade_weapon()` function doesn't need to toggle any complex Boolean flags (like `is_using_spread_shot = true`). It simply overwrites the `current_strategy` variable with the new Resource. The next time the player clicks, the new algorithm runs automatically.

Because we added export variables for the different weapon strategies in the `blaster.gd` script, the **Blaster** node is now ready to receive Resources directly in the Godot **Inspector**. We need only to create these Custom Resources and plug them in for the system to work.

Let's walk through the exact steps to build these Strategy Resources and assign them to the player:

1. In the **FileSystem** dock, right-click and select **Create New** and then **Resource**.
2. Search for the `LaserStrategy` class and create it. Name the file `basic_laser.tres`.
3. Create another Resource, search for `SpreadShotStrategy`, name it `spread_shot.tres`.
4. Double-click both `.tres` files to open them in the **Inspector**. Assign the **Laser** scene to both and tweak their fire rates as you desire.
5. Finally, select your **Blaster** node in the Scene Tree.
6. In the **Inspector**, click on the dropdown next to **Basic Weapon**, and choose **LaserStrategy** and assign **SpreadShotStrategy** to **Upgraded Weapon**. This is shown in *Figure 7.5* as follows:

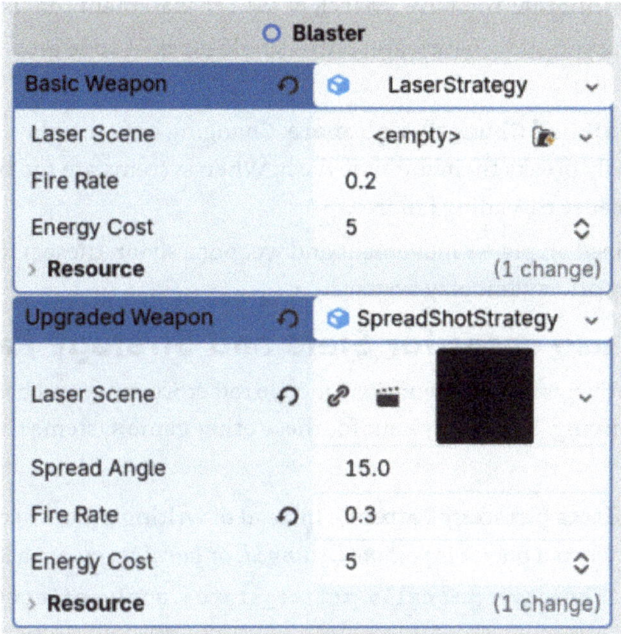

Figure 7.5 – Assigning weapon strategies in the Inspector

The `fire()` function in the `Blaster` script has no idea what a Spread Shot Strategy is. It is unaware of the loops, angles, or instantiation required to create the shot. By applying the Strategy Pattern, all the complexity is locked inside `spread_shot_strategy.gd`. If you ever want to add more weapons, perhaps a homing missile, you just create a new `homing_strategy.gd`, make a `.tres` file Resource, and plug it in. The `player_ship` and `Blaster` scripts will never need to be modified for this purpose again.

Both the State and Strategy patterns help us move away from large, complex conditional logic by organizing behavior into modular components. But how do we identify when our existing code actually needs this kind of refactoring?

You don't want to over-engineer a simple game, so you should wait until your codebase starts exhibiting certain warning signs, often called **code smells**. Here are the three biggest indicators that it is time to refactor:

- **The Boolean trap**: You have half a dozen Boolean flags (`is_jumping`, `is_attacking`, `is_crouching`), and you must constantly check and uncheck them to prevent bugs (for example, making sure a player can't attack while crouching).

- **The mega-match**: You have a `match` or `switch` statement that is over 50 lines long. Every time you add a new feature, this single block of code grows larger and harder to read.
- **The "One Small Change" nightmare**: Changing how the player's double-jump works accidentally breaks their ability to dash. When systems are too tightly tangled, isolated changes cause cascading failures.

While we've focused on player movement and weapons so far, these patterns are just as powerful in many other gameplay systems.

Additional use cases for State and Strategy Pattern

There are some other common scenarios for code refactoring beyond basic player movement and weapon swapping. Keep an eye out for these other game systems that heavily benefit from these patterns:

- **Status Effects (Strategy Pattern)**: Instead of writing a giant script to handle what happens when a player is *poisoned*, *stunned*, or *burning*, create a `StatusEffect` strategy Resource. The player just `calls active_status.apply_effect()`.
- **Multi-Phase Boss Fights (State Pattern)**: Bosses often change entirely when their health drops below 50%. Separating *Phase 1*, *Phase 2*, and *Phase 3* into distinct states prevents their massive AI script from collapsing under its own weight.
- **Interactable Objects (Strategy Pattern)**: Instead of checking if an object is a `Door`, a `Chest`, or a `Switch` when the player presses *E*, give each object an `InteractStrategy` Resource. The player just says `target.interact()`, and the object handles the rest.

Trade-offs and limitations (when NOT to use them)

Design patterns are powerful tools, but they are not silver bullets. It is equally important to know when a pattern is too much. You should carefully weigh these trade-offs before implementing them in your game:

- **Beware of over-engineering:** If you have a simple mechanical door that only ever opens and closes, building a full state machine with `open_state.gd` and `closed_state.gd` scripts is a massive waste of time. A simple `is_open` Boolean is perfectly fine. Only reach for patterns when the complexity of the feature demands it.
- **File fragmentation:** While patterns remove 1,000-line "spaghetti" scripts, they replace them with dozens of smaller files. If you aren't careful with your folder

organization, finding the exact script you need among 50 tiny strategy files can actually *increase* your development time.

- **Performance overhead:** In Godot, nodes and objects have a tiny memory footprint, but it is not zero. If you have 5,000 asteroid debris particles flying through space, attaching a dedicated **StateMachine** node to every single one of them will unnecessarily drain your game's performance. Keep these patterns reserved for complex entities like players, bosses, and advanced AI.

Now that you understand where these patterns apply, and where they don't, the next step is learning how to recognize when your existing code needs to be refactored using them.

Refactoring conditionals into patterns

Knowing *how* to write the State and Strategy patterns is only half the battle. Knowing *when* to use them is what defines an architect. When reviewing your codebase, look for **code smells**; as discussed previously, these are signs that a script is doing too much.

The most common smell is the presence of an `enum` coupled with a `match` (`switch`) statement. An example of this spaghetti architecture could be the use of an `enum` to define different movement types:

```
enum MovementType { NORMAL, BOOSTING, DISABLED }
var current_movement = MovementType.NORMAL

func _physics_process(delta):
    match current_movement:
        MovementType.NORMAL:
            speed = 300
            process_normal_input()
        MovementType.BOOSTING:
            speed = 600
            process_boost_input()
            drain_energy()
        MovementType.DISABLED:
            speed = 0
            play_sparks_effect()
```

At first glance, this may seem fine; however, the problem arises when you want to add new movement types. Adding an `EMP_STUNNED` movement type requires opening the file, modifying the `enum`, adding a new `match` case, and adding new variables (like `stun_duration`) to the `Player` script, bloating the file further. By refactoring this enum-and-match structure into a state machine, the `player_ship.gd` file is stripped of all movement logic. It delegates processing to its child State nodes (**NormalState**, **BoostState**, **DisabledState**). If you wanted to add an EMP effect, you would create `emp_state.gd`, attach it to the state machine, and that is all. The `player_ship` file remains untouched.

The advantages of replacing large conditional blocks with structural patterns are threefold:

- **Enforces the Open-Closed Principle:** Without patterns, you must modify the `player_ship.gd` script, risking breaking other behaviors or components. With patterns, you extend the game by creating new scripts and Resources. The original `player_ship.gd` file is completely closed to modification. This is the holy grail of safe game development.
- **Reduces cognitive load:** The human brain can only hold about seven different pieces of information at one time. When you read a 300-line `match` statement nested inside an `if`-block, your brain must attempt to remember the entire context of the game's state to understand what is happening. Patterns chunk this logic. When you open `patrol_state.gd`, your brain only needs to think about patrolling.
- **Isolates debugging:** If the player gets stuck in a wall while boosting, and your movement logic is a giant conditional soup, the bug could be anywhere. If you use a state machine, you know the bug is mathematically guaranteed to be inside `boost_state.gd`. You can fix it without touching the normal movement code.

So, how do we spot the refactor or sniff out the code smells?

There are some warning signs that your code is about to collapse under its own weight:

- **Problem: enum and match trap**: The first of these is the **enum and match trap**. As I mentioned before, if you find yourself creating an `enum` and then writing a massive `match` statement inside `_physics_process`, then you are manually writing a bad state machine.
  Solution: Refactor this conditional movement system into a true Node-based State Pattern.
- **Problem: Boolean soup (flag blindness)**: The second problem is **Boolean soup** or **flag blindness**. If you have a cluster of Boolean flags at the top of your script to check `is_moving`, `is_shooting`, and `is_stunned`, and your `_process` function is filled with conditional checks, then your logic is extremely fragile. Each flag you add will double the complexity of every if-statement.

Solution: Refactor this flag-based conditional logic into a State Pattern so that the entity can only physically be in one defined state at a time, eliminating the need for complex flag combinations.

- **Shotgun surgery**: The third and final problem is **shotgun surgery**. This is when you want to make a single change to your game, but doing so forces you to make changes and add many variables in multiple different places. You must fire a shotgun blast of edits across your whole project just to add one feature.
  Solution: Refactor the code into the Strategy Pattern. By encapsulating the specific algorithm into its own standalone `Resource`, you condense all those widespread changes into a single, modular file.

To make this process easier, let's look at a quick reference you can use when deciding whether to refactor and which pattern to apply in the next section.

The refactoring quick check

If you are ever staring at your screen, unsure whether you need to build a design pattern or just stick to simple code, use this quick rule of thumb:

Scenario	**Common examples**	**Recommended solution**
Tracking moods or phases	Idle, Chase, Attack	State Pattern
Tracking variations of a tool	Lasers, Missiles, Shields	Strategy Pattern
Massive conditional blocks	`If/else` or `match` blocks > 50 lines	Refactor
Simple, binary toggles	Open/Closed door	Booleans

Table 7.1 – Refactor quick check table

By learning to recognize these code smells and proactively applying the right design pattern, you are doing more than just cleaning up your scripts; you are future-proofing your entire game. Refactoring often feels like taking a step backward because you aren't immediately adding new features to the screen, but it is one of the most crucial steps forward you can take as a developer. It transforms a fragile, rigid prototype into a robust, professional codebase, ensuring that when it is finally time to add that next massive boss fight or a wild new weapon type, your architecture is ready to handle it effortlessly.

Summary

In this chapter, we confronted the prototype wall and conquered the complex conditional logic that often causes growing projects to collapse. We learned how to identify critical code smells, such as Boolean traps and massive `match` statements, and explored how to untangle them using behavioral design patterns.

First, we implemented the *State Pattern* by building a Finite State Machine using Godot's node hierarchy. By breaking down the Elite Cruiser AI into isolated states like Patrol, Chase, and Attack, we enforced the Single Responsibility Principle. Each state now governs its own logic and safely manages its own transitions. This guarantees that a bug in one behavior will never cascade and break another.

Next, we tackled gameplay variations by utilizing the *Strategy Pattern*. We leveraged Godot's Custom Resources to build a highly modular, plug-and-play weapon system for the `PlayerShip`. Instead of writing complex firing math inside the main `Player` script, we delegated that responsibility to interchangeable Strategy objects. This allowed us to swap from basic Lasers to complex Spread Shots seamlessly at runtime without altering the player's movement code.

Ultimately, by prioritizing composition and delegation over monolithic scripts, we have ensured that our game remains easy to debug, infinitely logical to expand, and fundamentally crash-resistant.

Now that we have mastered separating and swapping behaviors, it is time to take our modular architecture even further. In the next chapter, we will explore how to decouple fundamental properties. You will learn how to build reusable, bite-sized nodes, such as a **HealthComponent** or a **HitboxComponent** that can be instantly snapped onto any entity in your game. Instead of rewriting the taking-damage logic for the player, the enemies, and the destructible asteroids, you will learn how to write it exactly once, keeping your codebase DRY (Don't Repeat Yourself) while supercharging your development speed.

Get this book's PDF copy, code bundle, and more

Scan the QR code (or go to `packtpub.com/unlock`). Search for this book by name, confirm the edition, and then follow the steps on the page.

UNLOCK NOW

Note: Have your invoice handy. Purchases made directly from the Packt website don't require an invoice.

8

Creating Component-Based Systems

As games, like *Void Defenders*, grow from simple prototypes and more features are added, major architectural decisions must be made. You need to decide how to organize the sprawling web of nodes and scripts, determine which node should handle collision, and consider questions like, "Should a defensive turret know about the alien ship that it is shooting at?" If you aren't careful, it is very easy to turn your game into a big bowl of spaghetti, a tangled mess where every script directly references every other script.

In *Chapter 7*, we tamed complex entity behaviors using Finite State Machines (FSM) and encapsulated our game rules using the Strategy Pattern. While those patterns perfectly organize *how* our entities act and think, we are now faced with a structural problem: how do we organize what our entities *are*?

As your game grows, relying on traditional object-oriented inheritance (for example, writing `class Boss extends Enemy extends Character`) quickly leads to a brittle codebase. You end up with deep, rigid family trees in which changing a feature in a base class accidentally breaks a dozen unrelated child objects. In this chapter, we will break free from rigid class hierarchies and tangled dependencies by adopting the **Entity-Component (EC) Pattern**.

The Entity-Component Pattern is an architectural philosophy that favors *composition* over *inheritance*. In this system, an entity (such as a Player, an Enemy, or a destructible crate) is essentially just a container. We bring that entity to life by attaching small, independent, single-purpose nodes called components (such as a **HealthComponent**, a **HitboxComponent**, or a **MovementComponent**).

Understanding this pattern at this stage of your journey is critical. Now that you know how to decouple your game's communication with an Event Bus (see *Chapter 6*) and isolate your logic with state machines (see *Chapter 7*), the EC Pattern is the final architectural pillar you need to confidently scale your project.

The overall goal of this chapter is to teach you how to shift your mindset from "what is this object?" to "what can this object do?" We will build a library of modular, plug-and-play components that you can mix and match to rapidly prototype and create complex entities, often without writing a single line of new code.

In this chapter, we will cover the following topics:

- Understanding the limits of inheritance
- Designing modular components
- Composing complex behaviors
- Refactoring to the Entity-Component Pattern

By the end of this chapter, you will learn how to break down complex game objects into tiny, reusable, attachable behaviors. We will build modular systems where health, movement, and damage are separate components, allowing you to mix and match features to create infinite variations of enemies without writing duplicate code.

Technical requirements

Readers should be familiar with basic Godot workflows, such as navigating the Godot editor, creating scenes, and scripting with GDScript.

You can download the example project and code for this book by following the instructions in the *Download the example code files* section in the *Preface* of this book.

This chapter's code files are included in the downloadable code bundle.

Understanding the limits of inheritance

In Object-Oriented Programming, the first tool that developers use to share behavior is *inheritance*. In *Chapter 5*, for *Void Defenders*, we created a `BaseEnemy` class that handled health and movement, and then had `KamikazeEnemy` inherit from it. This works brilliantly for simple hierarchies, but as your game design becomes more ambitious, inheritance quickly hits a brick wall known as the *deep inheritance trap*.

The **deep inheritance trap** occurs when a family tree of classes becomes so tall and rigid that sharing behaviors becomes impossible without causing unintended side effects. You might need a new enemy to inherit a specific attack from one class and a movement style from another. However, because a script can only extend a single parent, you are forced to either duplicate code or inherit a massive chain of unwanted features just to get the one function you need.

Let's walk through a practical scenario for *Void Defenders.* Consider that we want to expand our game with several new enemy types using standard inheritance. We might start by building a family tree that looks like this:

- `BaseEntity`: Handles basic health and taking damage.
- `MovingEnemy` **(extends** `BaseEntity`**)**: Adds flight logic and engine thrusters.
- `ShootingEnemy` **(extends** `MovingEnemy`**)**: Adds weapon cooldowns and projectile spawning.

So far, this structure seems logical. But what happens when the game's design requirements inevitably expand?

- **The Turret problem**: We decide to add a stationary defense turret that shoots at the player. We cannot inherit from `ShootingEnemy` because the turret would accidentally inherit the flight logic from `MovingEnemy.` To fix this, we are forced to create a separate `StationaryEnemy` branch and copy-paste all our shooting code into it.
- **The Drone problem**: Next, we want a support drone that flies around and heals allies, but has no weapons. We have to inherit from `MovingEnemy` and write brand-new healing logic.
- **The Asteroid problem**: Finally, we want an asteroid that moves, cannot shoot, but splits into smaller pieces when destroyed.

Inheritance forces us to define strictly *what an object is*. However, this system breaks down the moment objects need to share isolated features across different branches of the family tree. We are forced to choose between two bad options: write highly duplicated code, or create a massive god class that contains every possible feature (movement, shooting, healing, exploding) controlled by a messy web of Boolean flags, such as `is_moving = false` and `can_shoot = true`. Fortunately, Godot is built from the ground up to support a much better approach: favoring composition over inheritance.

Instead of relying on deep class inheritance, we can use composition. **Composition** defines an object not by *what it is*, but by *what it has*. In an entity-component architecture, the entity is just an empty container. In Godot, this is usually an empty **Node2D** or **CharacterBody2D** node. The components are specialized child nodes containing pure data and isolated behavior. If you want a turret that shoots and takes damage, you simply attach a **ShootingComponent** and a **HealthComponent** to it. If you want a flying drone that shoots, takes damage, and moves, you attach a **ShootingComponent**, a **HealthComponent**, and a **MovementComponent**.

This is the exact design philosophy Godot itself uses (for example, attaching a **CollisionShape2D** component to give a node a physical form). Let's learn how to write our own components.

Designing modular components

Ideally, a **component** should work independently of all other components around it. It should know as little as possible about its parent entity or the game world. We should start by designing the most universal component for *Void Defenders* – the health component.

Rather than writing health logic inside every ship, asteroid, and turret script, we will extract it into a *pure component*. In this context, a **pure component** is a completely self-contained node that has exactly one responsibility (managing health) and relies on zero external dependencies to do its job. It does not care if it is attached to the player or a rock; it simply tracks numbers and broadcasts a signal when those numbers reach zero.

First, create a new script called `health_component.gd` and extend `Node`. You can save this empty script since you don't necessarily need a dedicated scene for simple logic components; the script alone can be attached to any node. Now, fill out the script with the logic as follows:

```
# health_component.gd
class_name HealthComponent extends Node

# Emitted when health drops to 0
signal died

# Emitted when health changes, useful for updating UI health bars
signal health_changed(new_health: float, max_health: float)

@export var max_health: float = 100.0
var current_health: float

func _ready() -> void:
    current_health = max_health

func take_damage(amount: float) -> void:
    current_health -= amount
    health_changed.emit(current_health,max_health)

    if current_health <= 0:
        died.emit()
```

At first glance, the script seems simple. However, its architectural brilliance lies not in what it does, but in what it doesn't do. By extending `Node` rather than a 2D- or 3D-specific class, we guarantee this component has no physical presence in the game world. It is purely a logic and data container. By defining a `class_name`, this script is registered globally within your project.

This is a powerful Godot feature: it means you can now open the **Add Node** menu in any scene, search for your new class by name, and add it just like a built-in node (such as a **Timer** or **Sprite2D**). When you do this, Godot automatically creates a new node matching the base type you defined in your `extends` statement and automatically attaches your custom script to it.

Combined with exporting the `max_health` variable, which allows us to tweak the health value directly in the **Inspector** without touching the code, we have transformed a basic script into a highly reusable, custom node.

Signals are used to broadcast changes to the UI listening for them. When the `take_damage()` function is called, the component handles the calculations and then broadcasts the results again via signals. Since we discussed the `EventBus` (or global signal hub) in previous chapters, you might be wondering: Why don't we just broadcast `health_changed` directly to the `EventBus` so the UI can easily reach it? The answer comes down to *reusability* and *encapsulation*.

A `HealthComponent` is designed to be completely modular; you should be able to drop it onto the player, an enemy, or a destructible barrel without changing the code. If you hardcode a global `EventBus.emit()` inside this component, you tightly couple it to this specific project's Autoload. Worse, you will suddenly flood your global event channels with the health data of every single barrel and minor enemy in the game. To solve the UI reachability problem without breaking modular architecture, we could use the parent node as a relay:

1. The `HealthComponent` emits its local `health_changed` signal.
2. The parent node (for example, `player_ship.gd`) connects to this local signal.
3. Because the player's health is globally important to the HUD, `player_ship.gd` catches the local signal and relays it to the global `EventBus`.

The code for this would look like this:

```
# Inside player_ship.gd
@onready var health_component: HealthComponent = $HealthComponent

func _ready() -> void:
    # 1. Listen to the local component
    health_component.health_changed.connect(_on_health_changed)
```

```
func _on_health_changed(current: float, max: float) -> void:
    # 2. Relay the important data to the global EventBus for the UI
    EventBus.player_health_updated.emit(current, max)
```

This strategy ensures your components remain completely isolated and reusable, while still getting critical data exactly where it needs to go.

Most importantly, notice what is completely absent from this function. There is no call to `queue_free()` to delete the object. There is no logic to spawn explosion particles. There is no code to drop a scrap metal collectible for the player. The `HealthComponent` does not and should not know what it is attached to. Its only job is to manage a value and `emit` when that number reaches zero.

Our next modular component is the `Hitbox` component. To make our game robust, we should separate the concept of *health* (*data*) from *taking damage* (*physics*). We will create a `HitboxComponent` that extends the `Area2D`. Its job is to detect incoming lasers and forward that damage to the `HealthComponent`.

So, let's create a new scene with an `Area2D` node as the root and name it `HitboxComponent`. Then, attach a script to it named `hitbox_component.gd`:

```
# hitbox_component.gd
class_name HitboxComponent extends Area2D

# Export reference to HealthComponent so Hitbox knows where to send
# damage
@export var health_component: HealthComponent

func damage(attack_damage: float) -> void:
    if health_component:
        health_component.take_damage(attack_damage)
    else:
        push_warning("Took damage, but has no HealthComponent")
```

If the `HealthComponent` is the invisible brain that tracks vitality, the `HitboxComponent` is the physical skin that interacts with the world around it. By separating these two concepts, we gain the ability to give a single ship multiple hitboxes that all feed into the same central health pool.

Unlike the `HealthComponent`, the `HitboxComponent` needs a physical presence in the game world. By extending the `Area2D` node, this component gains the ability to hold a `CollisionShape2D` and detect when a laser overlaps with it. By exporting the `HealthComponent`, we make it available for assignment in the **Inspector**.

But how does the `damage()` function actually get triggered? To keep our architecture clean and as modular as possible, the `HitboxComponent` must remain completely ignorant of the outside world. It does not know what a laser, a missile, or an asteroid is; it only knows how to receive a number and pass it along to the health pool.

If we reversed this design and forced the `Hitbox` to detect incoming collisions, the `Hitbox` would have to constantly ask, *"What just hit me and how much damage did it do?"* This would force the component to know the specific details of every weapon in your game, instantly creating a tangled, tightly coupled mess.

By making the projectile the active agent, our components stay perfectly modular.

When the projectile's script detects the overlap, it calls the `damage()` function on our `HitboxComponent`. In our initial script above, the hitbox received that damage and directly called `health_component.take_damage()`. While this direct reference works for simple prototypes, it creates a rigid dependency. If a developer forgets to assign the **HealthComponent** in the Inspector, the script will trigger the warning and fail to apply the damage.

To achieve true modularity, we must remove this dependency entirely. Our `HitboxComponent` should not calculate anything, nor should it interact directly with the health pool. Instead, we can refactor the component so that the `damage()` function acts purely as an alarm. We remove the exported reference and replace it with a signal:

```
class_name HitboxComponent extends Area2D
# HitboxComponent.gd

signal hit_received(damage_amount: float)

func damage(amount: float) -> void:
    # We do not calculate anything, and we do not know what Health is.
    # We just ring the alarm.
    hit_received.emit(amount)
```

By refactoring to rely on a signal, the `HitboxComponent` remains completely blind to the rest of the entity. It does not need a direct reference, nor does it need to know if a `HealthComponent` even exists on the object. It simply broadcasts that it was hit for a specific amount of damage, allowing the parent entity to route that signal to the health pool.

This is a good example of delegation. The `HitboxComponent` is responsible for physics, asking "Where did the laser hit?", while the `HealthComponent` is responsible for the data, asking "Did that hit kill us?" By keeping these responsibilities strictly separated, the code becomes easier to read, debug, and expand.

You could create an enemy with a heavily armored hull, perhaps a hitbox that halves incoming damage before sending it to the `HealthComponent`, and a glowing weak spot, a separate hitbox that doubles incoming damage. Both of these would feed the exact same `HealthComponent`.

Now that we have built individual components, let's see how to combine them to create complete game entities.

Composing complex behaviors

Before we build our next enemy, we should review composition in greater detail.

As mentioned before, composing complex behaviors is a professional alternative to deep inheritance. Instead of asking, *"What is this object?"* (*Inheritance*), we ask, *"What can this object do?"* (*Composition*).

Think of composition like building with LEGO® bricks. Instead of writing one massive script that controls movement, health, shooting, and animations, we break those behaviors down into tiny, independent, single-purpose nodes (components).

But how do these isolated bricks actually work together to create a cohesive enemy? The secret lies in multi-component interactions driven by signals.

The motherboard approach

In an Entity-Component architecture, the parent entity (for example, the `Asteroid` or `KamikazeEnemy` node) contains almost no logic of its own. Instead, it acts like a computer motherboard. Its only job is to hold the components and use its `_ready()` function (or **Inspector** assignments) to wire their signals together.

Let's look at a complex interaction scenario. Imagine we want to create a **Shielded Stun Cruiser**, an enemy that absorbs a few hits, gets temporarily stunned when its shield breaks, flashes white, and then finally takes real damage. If we were using standard inheritance, this would require a massive, tangled script. With composition, we simply snap together these independent components.

- **MovementComponent**: Handles the underlying velocity, steering, and pathing toward the player
- **HitboxComponent**: Detects the physical laser collision
- **ShieldComponent**: Intercepts damage, tracks its own separate health pool
- **HealthComponent:** Tracks the ship's actual core health
- **StunComponent**: Listens for the shield to break, and temporarily disables the **MovementComponent** for a set duration when triggered
- **FlashComponent**: Turns the sprite white for a fraction of a second

Simply attaching these six independent components to an enemy doesn't automatically create a Stun Cruiser; to make them function as a cohesive unit, we need a way to trigger them in the correct sequence.

The chain reaction

Because we designed these as pure components, they don't explicitly know each other. Instead, they rely on a chain reaction of signals wired up by the parent entity. To see this in action, we need to step outside of the isolated components and look at the brain of the operation.

Let's explore how the parent Controller script (`stun_cruiser.gd`) acts as a master switchboard, routing these signals to assemble our complex enemy behavior step-by-step:

1. The laser strikes the `HitboxComponent`, which broadcasts its `hit_received` alarm.
2. The Controller catches this alarm. Because this specific enemy has a shield, the Controller's script intercepts the damage and uses an `if` statement to decide where to route it.
3. If the shield is up, the damage goes to the `ShieldComponent`. If the shield's health drops to zero, it emits a `shield_broken` signal.
4. The Controller has wired that `shield_broken` signal directly to the `StunComponent` and `FlashComponent`, triggering them instantly.
5. Any future damage detected by the Hitbox is automatically routed by the Controller directly to the `HealthComponent`, completely bypassing the broken shield.

Here is what that switchboard logic could look like inside the Stun Cruiser's main script:

```
class_name StunCruiser extends CharacterBody2D
# StunCruiser.gd - The Controller Script

@onready var hitbox: HitboxComponent = $HitboxComponent
@onready var shield: ShieldComponent = $ShieldComponent
@onready var health: HealthComponent = $HealthComponent
@onready var stun: StunComponent = $StunComponent
@onready var flash: FlashComponent = $FlashComponent

func _ready() -> void:
    # 1. Route the hitbox alarm to the Controller's own routing function
    hitbox.hit_received.connect(_route_incoming_damage)

    # 2. Wire the destruction directly to the reaction components
    shield.shield_broken.connect(stun.trigger_stun)
    shield.shield_broken.connect(flash.trigger_flash)

func _route_incoming_damage(amount: float) -> void:
    # 3. Controller decides where damage goes based on the current state
    if shield.current_health > 0:
        shield.take_damage(amount)
    else:
        # 4. The shield is down, so the hull takes direct damage
        health.take_damage(amount)
```

By keeping the routing logic inside the `Controller`, the components remain dumb. The Hitbox component doesn't need to know that a shield exists, and the Shield component doesn't need to know how to stun the ship. The parent script glues them together to create a unique, highly specific enemy.

By designing your game this way, you can create limitless combinations. For example, if you want an asteroid that flashes when hit but has no shields, you can just attach the Hitbox, Health, and Flash components. If you want a boss that gets stunned every time it takes 100 damage, you can wire the `HealthComponent`'s damage signal to the `StunComponent`.

You are no longer writing custom logic for every new enemy; you are simply plugging different wires into your existing components. Let's understand the significance of this by building our next enemy in the following section.

Understanding the benefits of composition

The shift to composition offers several practical benefits:

- **Ultimate reusability**: If you build a completely independent `HealthComponent`, you don't just use it on your enemies. You can drop that exact same node onto the Player, a boss, a breakable asteroid, or an explosive barrel, and it will work perfectly without changing a single line of code.
- **Isolated debugging**: If your enemy stops moving, you don't have to scroll through a 500-line enemy script. You know exactly where the problem is: the `MovementComponent`.
- **Fearless iteration**: If you want to make a variant of the Alien Drone that doesn't shoot but moves twice as fast, you don't need to write a new class. You just delete the `ShooterComponent` from the scene and tweak the variables on the `MovementComponent`. You can invent completely new enemies in seconds just by snapping different components together in the Godot editor.

Now that we have reviewed the practical benefits of the Entity-Component Pattern, let's put it to the test.

Applying composition in practice

We will build an Alien Drone. Let's construct a fully component-driven enemy from scratch to see exactly how these isolated pieces wire together to create a living entity. Follow these steps:

1. Create a new scene with a **CharacterBody2D** root and name it `AlienDrone`.
2. Add a **Sprite2D** node and a **CollisionShape2D** node as children to handle the basic visuals and physics.
3. Because we registered our scripts using `class_name`, you do not need to create empty nodes. Simply open the **Add Node** menu, search for `HealthComponent`, and add it directly to your scene as a child of the root.
4. Open the **Add Node** menu again, search for `HitboxComponent`, and add it. Add a **CollisionShape2D** as a child of this Hitbox so that incoming lasers can physically detect it.
5. Finally, we need a Controller to link our new components. Attach a new script (`alien_drone.gd`) to the root **CharacterBody2D** node. Inside its `_ready()` function, wire the Hitbox's `hit_received` signal directly to the Health pool's `take_damage` function.

The **AlienDrone** scene structure is shown in *Figure 8.1*:

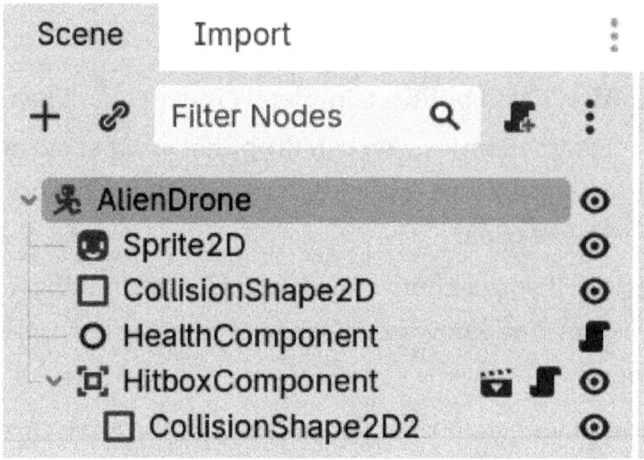

Figure 8.1 – Scene Tree for the Alien Drone

Because the components handle the mechanics, the actual `alien_drone.gd` script is lightweight. It simply acts as the glue that listens to its components, as shown in the following script:

```
# alien_drone.gd
class_name AlienDrone extends CharacterBody2D

@onready var health_component: HealthComponent = $HealthComponent

func _ready() -> void:
    # Connect the component's signal to the drone's death sequence
    health_component.died.connect(on_death)

func on_death() -> void:
    # We can spawn explosions, drop scrap metal, and free the node.
    print("Alien Drone destroyed!")
    queue_free()
```

When a laser is fired at the drone, how does the laser know that it hit the drone's hitbox without causing spaghetti dependencies? There are two techniques to counter this: **Groups** (telling friend from foe) and **Duck Typing** (executing behavior safely).

Select the **AlienDrone**'s **HitboxComponent**. Now add it to a group called `"enemy"`.

In the `laser.gd` script, under the `_on_area_entered` function, you can verify the target's group and check for the correct method before delivering damage:

```
# laser.gd
var damage_payload: float = 10.0

func _on_area_entered(area: Area2D) -> void:
    if area.is_in_group("enemy"):
        if area.has_method("damage"):
            area.damage(damage_payload)
            queue_free() # laser deletes itself after a successful hit
```

In this example, `is_in_group("enemy")` uses Groups to identify valid targets, while `has_method("damage")` uses Duck Typing to safely execute the damage behavior without needing to know the object's exact class or type. Notice the elegance of this loose coupling: The laser doesn't know it hit an **AlienDrone**. It doesn't know what a `HealthComponent` is. It simply asks the physics engine if it hit an enemy, delivers its damage payload, and deletes itself. Decoupling your systems like this is a core best practice in Godot. Because the `laser`'s logic is entirely independent, you can add fifty new enemy types, destructible asteroids, or giant bosses to your game later, and you will never have to open or modify the `laser` script again.

Best practice: Avoiding magic strings

While typing `"enemy"` and `"damage"` directly into your code is quick for prototypes, relying on these hardcoded **magic strings** can introduce frustrating bugs. If you accidentally type `"enemy"` in another script, the editor won't warn you, but the collision will silently fail. As your project grows, consider creating a global Constants Autoload (for example, `GameGlobals.gd`) that holds variables like const `GROUP_ENEMY = "enemy"`. By checking `area.is_in_group(GameGlobals.GROUP_ENEMY)` instead, you allow Godot's auto-complete to catch typos for you.

Now that we've seen how components interact in practice, let's look at how to refactor existing systems into a Component-Based Design. In this chapter, we'll achieve Component-Based Design by applying the Entity-Component Pattern, one of the most common ways to build component-driven architectures.

Refactoring to the Entity-Component Pattern

Before we dive into the code and begin tearing apart our existing scripts, we need to understand exactly why we are doing this. Refactoring your project from deep inheritance trees to the **Entity-Component Pattern** is a major structural shift.

Up until now, we have largely written monolithic scripts. If an enemy can move, shoot, and take damage, all that logic lives inside a single `enemy.gd` file. While this is easy to read from top to bottom, it scales poorly. If you want a destructible asteroid that takes damage but doesn't move or shoot, you have to rewrite the health logic all over again in a new `asteroid.gd script`.

Component-Based Design (CBD) solves this by chopping that monolith into tiny, single-purpose pieces. Create a standalone `HealthComponent`, a `MovementComponent`, and a `ShooterComponent`. An enemy is no longer a massive script; it is just an empty physical body with these three components snapped onto it like LEGO® bricks. The asteroid is just a physical body with only the `HealthComponent` snapped on.

Evaluating Component-Based Design

Like all architectural approaches in game design, CBD comes with benefits and trade-offs, which I have represented in *Table 8.1* as follows:

Benefits	**Trade-offs**
Logic is written once and reused.	The Scene Tree becomes increasingly dense.
Bugs are quarantined and easier to find.	Passing data becomes more complex.
Different behaviors can be worked on simultaneously by different team members because they live in different files.	Development can be slowed down by building complex, generic components that do not get reused.

Table 8.1 – Benefits and trade-offs of Component-Based Design

Ultimately, while composition offers unmatched flexibility and safer debugging, it requires disciplined organization. You must constantly balance the desire to make everything a highly reusable component against the risk of cluttering your Scene Tree and overcomplicating your game's communication flow.

While these trade-offs help us understand the impact of CBD, the next question is when it should be used in practice. Godot's Node system is inherently built for composition, but you should use it strategically since there are times when it is not warranted. *Table 8.2* provides a simple guideline for making that decision:

When to use composition	When NOT to use composition
There are complex and multifaceted entities sharing overlapping behaviors.	You have simple, single-purpose objects.
You have universally shared mechanics.	You have a one-off object.
Your environmental objects are highly interactive.	Do not build a complex, generic component architecture just because you think you might need it in the future. If a single, lightweight script solves a simple problem today, use it.

Table 8.2 – When to use Component-Based Design

Always apply the **YAGNI** principle: **You Aren't Gonna Need It**. In game development, it is tempting to architect a massive, flexible system for features you think you might want later. However, building a generic, highly reusable `HealthComponent` is a waste of time if your game currently only features a single enemy type.

In that scenario, it is much faster and cleaner to just write a health variable directly inside that enemy's script. Start simply. Wait until your design expands, and a second or third object desperately needs that exact same health logic. Once you feel the urge to copy and paste code, you have encountered the other side of the programming coin: **DRY (Don't Repeat Yourself)**.

While YAGNI tells you not to build systems prematurely, DRY tells you that once you are repeating the exact same logic across multiple scripts, it is time to consolidate. That is the exact moment to extract the logic and refactor it into a reusable component. Balancing these two principles keeps your codebase lean. YAGNI prevents you from wasting hours building complex systems for a future that never arrives, while DRY ensures your active, expanding systems remain clean and maintainable.

Handling communication between components and systems

To gain a well-rounded understanding of the Entity-Component architecture, we must address how components interact not just with each other, but with the broader game world. In a traditional monolithic script, if an enemy dies, it might directly call `GameManager.add_score(10)`. This forces the enemy to be permanently, tightly coupled to your `GameManager` script. If you drop that enemy into a different level that doesn't have a `GameManager`, the game will crash. The solution to this is to refactor deep hierarchies into component-based signal relays. Now, instead of an enemy reaching up into the global game state, the systems that spawn the enemies should listen to their broadcasts. An `EnemySpawner` component, which acts as a signal relay, could be scripted as follows:

```
# EnemySpawner.gd
class_name EnemySpawner extends Marker2D
@export var enemy_scene: PackedScene
@export var spawn_interval: float = 2.0
# A designer can choose where enemies are spawned in the Scene Tree
@export var spawn_container: Node

# We relay the death of our spawned units up
signal enemy_defeated(score_value: int)
func _ready() -> void:
    var timer = Timer.new()
    timer.wait_time = spawn_interval
    timer.timeout.connect(spawn_enemy)
    add_child(timer)
    timer.start()

func spawn_enemy() -> void:
    var new_enemy = enemy_scene.instantiate()
    var health = new_enemy.get_node_or_null("HealthComponent")
    if health:
        health.died.connect(_on_spawned_enemy_died)

    # Determine safe parent using a standard if/else block
    var parent_node: Node
    if spawn_container:
        parent_node = spawn_container
    else:
        parent_node = get_parent()

    parent_node.add_child(new_enemy)

    new_enemy.global_position = global_position

func _on_spawned_enemy_died() -> void:
    # Relay the event upward
    enemy_defeated.emit(100)
```

This script transforms a simple `Marker2D` node into an automated, self-contained enemy factory. Rather than forcing a global manager to constantly check if new enemies need to be spawned or if existing enemies have died, this spawner handles both the creation and the communication internally. The script makes use of dynamic timers. Instead of requiring you to manually attach a **Timer** node in the Godot editor, the `_ready()` function creates one purely through code. It applies your exported `spawn_interval`, connects the timeout signal, and starts the loop automatically. This makes the spawner portable; you can drop it into any scene, and it will just work.

Smart instantiation is another element of this script. Inside `spawn_enemy()`, the script creates a new instance of your chosen enemy. However, before letting it loose in the game world, it performs a crucial architectural step: it searches the new enemy for a `HealthComponent`. If the `HealthComponent` is found, the spawner immediately connects to its died signal. This ensures that the spawner is constantly listening to the exact enemies it created, without the enemies needing to know the spawner even exists.

For positioning, notice that we added an exported `spawn_container` variable. A common beginner mistake is to add the new enemy as a direct child of the spawner (`add_child()`), but this means if the spawner moves, the enemy will be dragged along with it! Conversely, simply adding it as a sibling (`get_parent().add_child()`) can be brittle if your Scene Tree is deeply nested. By exposing an optional `spawn_container`, you give the level designer the power to cleanly organize all spawned enemies into a specific folder node (like an **Entities** node) in the Scene Tree, falling back to the parent safely if left blank.

When a spawned enemy dies, the spawner's `_on_spawned_enemy_died()` function is triggered. The spawner then emits its own custom `enemy_defeated` signal, passing along a score value (`100`). But who is listening to this signal? This script demonstrates the **Event Relay Pattern** (often called **Event Bubbling** or **Signal Bubbling**). It is an architectural technique used to manage how different parts of a system communicate by using a middleman. The spawner acts as this middleman; it listens to a low-level, specific event from its children (a specific drone exploding), and then turns around to broadcast a new, broader event to the level's overarching scripts.

To see this in action, imagine a `LevelManager.gd` script sitting at the very top of your Scene Tree. It doesn't care about individual drones, but it does care about the spawner:

```
# LevelManager.gd
extends Node

@onready var alien_spawner = $AlienSpawner
```

```
func _ready() -> void:
    # The LevelManager listens to the Spawner's broad relay signal
    alien_spawner.enemy_defeated.connect(_on_enemy_defeated)

func _on_enemy_defeated(score: int) -> void:
    # Now we can safely update the global game state!
    GameManager.add_score(score)
    print("Level score updated by: ", score)
```

Through this relay, our architecture remains completely decoupled. The enemy only knows about its own health. The spawner only knows about the enemies it created. The Level Manager only knows about the spawner. No single script is overwhelmed, and every piece can be reused independently. Instead of every part of a program being directly connected to every other part, information travels up a chain of command using signal relays. We can see this exact chain of command again in our **AlienDrone** example:

- **The Child Component (The Trigger)**: The `HitboxComponent` has one simple job. When a laser touches it, it detects the physical collision and forwards the damage value.
- **The Middleman (The State Tracker)**: The `HealthComponent` receives this damage, subtracts it from its internal pool, and emits a specific signal (`died`) when that pool reaches zero.
- **The Parent Node (The Coordinator)**: The `AlienDrone` script acts as the overarching coordinator. It listens for the `died` signal and executes the result (playing an explosion and removing the enemy from the game).

In this scenario, the `AlienDrone` does not need to know how the collision math works, what Collision Layer the hitbox is on, or how the math for subtracting health is calculated. If you completely rewrite how the `HitboxComponent` works tomorrow, the `AlienDrone` script doesn't have to change at all. The components act as relays, taking a low-level physics event (an overlapping area) and translating it into a high-level game event (`died`) that the parent node cares about.

The advantages of using the Event-Relay Pattern are shown in *Table 8.3* as follows:

Advantage	Description
Translation	Converts low-level generic technical events into meaningful and context-specific events
Encapsulation	The middleman acts as a gateway for communication, keeping the parent's code clean.
Decoupling	Components only ever communicate with their direct neighbors in the hierarchy. This allows individual parts of the system to be safely replaced, upgraded, or deleted without breaking the entire application
Scalability and maintenance	As applications grow, managing direct connections between hundreds of distinct components becomes a tangled nightmare. A relay chain organizes communication hierarchically, making the codebase vastly easier to trace and debug.

Table 8.3 – Advantages of using the Event-Relay Pattern

In our case, the low-level `HealthComponent` only knows it ran out of health. It is the spawner's job to hear that broadcast, translate it, and shout a higher-level message to the rest of the game that an enemy was destroyed, and `100` points should be awarded. This keeps your components entirely decoupled from your scoring system.

Understanding decoupled interactions in action

Let's review the chain of events that occurs when a laser hits an enemy, and look at how perfectly decoupled every step is:

1. **The** `LaserProjectile` **moves independently**: It detects a collision with a node in the `"enemy"` group. It calls `damage()` and destroys itself.
2. **The** `HitboxComponent` **receives the damage**: It knows nothing about lasers. It blindly passes the math to the `HealthComponent`.
3. **The** `HealthComponent` **subtracts the damage**: It realizes health is zero. It emits the `died` signal. It knows nothing about the ship it is attached to.

4. **The** `alien_drone` **script hears died**: It triggers its explosion animation and destroys the physical node via `queue_free()`.
5. **The** `EnemySpawner` **hears the same** `died` **signal**: It emits `enemy_defeated(100)` up to the main game loop, which updates the player's score.

At no point does any script hard-reference another script's unique logic. You can take this exact `HealthComponent` and `HitboxComponent` and drag them onto a giant space station, a destructible meteor, or even the Player's own ship.

By prioritizing composition over inheritance, you have transformed *Void Defenders* from a rigid block of code into a modular sandbox. Your game design is no longer limited by the constraints of your class hierarchy.

Summary

In this chapter, we tackled one of the most significant leaps in game architecture: moving away from rigid, monolithic scripts and embracing Component-Based Design (CBD).

By prioritizing composition over inheritance, we learned how to treat our game logic like LEGO® bricks. We broke down massive god scripts into small, single-purpose, and highly reusable nodes like `HealthComponent` and `MovementComponent`. We discussed how this modular approach enables ultimate reusability, isolates bugs, and allows for fearless iteration when designing new entities. Just as importantly, we examined the stark trade-offs of this architecture, establishing the YAGNI principle to ensure we only implement components when they genuinely benefit the project, rather than falling into the trap of over-engineering simple objects.

With our entities broken into modular pieces, we then solved the resulting communication overhead by implementing the Event Relay Pattern. We built an automated Enemy Spawner that dynamically instantiates complex entities, safely wires up their internal signals, and acts as a middleman. By doing so, we learned how to encapsulate and translate low-level, generic events (like a health component's died signal) into high-level, context-specific broadcasts (like `enemy_defeated(100)`), keeping our global game managers clean and decoupled.

Through these techniques, we have successfully transformed our entities from tangled, fragile scripts into scalable, interconnected systems.

Right now, we know how to build modular enemies using components, and we know how they should communicate. However, as our game scales, manually snapping together 10 or 15 different components in the Godot editor for every single new enemy, item, or weapon variant will quickly become a tedious and error-prone chore.

In *Chapter 9*, we will solve this exact problem. We will shift our focus from how objects behave to how objects are created. Building directly on the dynamic spawning logic we just wrote, we will introduce industry-standard creational patterns.

Get this book's PDF copy, code bundle, and more

Scan the QR code (or go to `packtpub.com/unlock`). Search for this book by name, confirm the edition, and then follow the steps on the page.

UNLOCK NOW

Note: Have your invoice handy. Purchases made directly from the Packt website don't require an invoice.

Part 3

Advanced Data Architecture

Part 3 shifts the focus toward how your game generates objects and handles complex information under the hood. You will explore advanced creational patterns like Factories and Builders to automate complex scene instancing and configure gameplay systems dynamically at runtime. From there, we transition into data management, detailing how to separate configuration data from execution logic using custom Godot Resources. Finally, you will learn how to take your project outside the engine by building a secure, zero-trust modding pipeline capable of safely validating and parsing external data files.

This part of the book includes the following chapters:

- *Chapter 9, Using Factory and Builder Patterns*
- *Chapter 10, Applying Command and Service Patterns*
- *Chapter 11, Adopting Data-Driven Design*
- *Chapter 12, Structuring Gameplay Logic*

9

Using Factory and Builder Patterns

We have seen that as projects scale, we need to come up with more efficient ways to complete repetitive tasks. In *Void Defenders*, you may have noticed by now that spawning objects has become a recurring and repetitive chore. Whether we are firing lasers, spawning enemies, or dropping power-ups into the game world, the underlying code is always mostly the same: `instantiate()` the scene, set its position, inject some starting data, and add it as a child to the Scene Tree.

When you only have a few objects, scattering logic across your player, level, and enemy scripts is fine. But on a commercial scale, this scattered instantiation becomes a liability. If you decide that all spawned enemies need to be added to a specific **EnemyContainer** node instead of the main Scene Tree, you suddenly must track down and rewrite the instancing logic in twenty different scripts.

When instantiation logic is scattered across multiple scripts, your codebase becomes highly brittle and violates the DRY (Don't Repeat Yourself) principle.

The **Factory Pattern** solves this problem by moving the responsibility of creating an object out of the scripts that *need* the object, and into a dedicated script whose sole job is to *build* the object. While the Factory Pattern is perfect for churning out standard objects on demand, we will also explore the **Builder Pattern**. The Builder Pattern takes creation a step further by handling objects that require complex, multi-step configurations, such as assembling dynamic UI menus or constructing highly customized boss enemies piece by piece.

Gaining proficiency in these creational patterns is critical for long-term project maintenance, team collaboration, and scalability. By centralizing how objects are built, you drastically reduce merge conflicts in collaborative environments, as teammates aren't constantly modifying the same level scripts. Furthermore, as your game scales to include hundreds of different entities, your codebase remains flexible; when you inevitably need to change how an object initializes, you must only update a single file instead of hunting down brittle dependencies scattered across your entire project.

In this chapter, we are going to eliminate boilerplate and focus on fundamental structural designs by covering the following main topics:

- Implementing a Factory Pattern for Nodes
- Building complex objects with the Builder Pattern
- Centralizing object creation
- Procedural generation with Factories
- Choosing between Factory and Builder patterns

By the end of this chapter, you will understand how to delegate tedious object creation to specialized components, keeping your codebase clean and strictly modular. You will be able to dynamically construct complex UI elements using the Builder Pattern and leverage decoupled Factories to drive procedural generation. Ultimately, you will transform your rigid, manual instancing into a highly automated, commercial-grade assembly line, saving you countless hours of debugging and refactoring as *Void Defenders* continues to grow.

Technical requirements

Readers should be familiar with basic Godot workflows, such as navigating the Godot editor, creating scenes, and scripting with GDScript.

You can download the example project and code for this book by following the instructions in the *Download the example code files* section in the *Preface* of this book.

This chapter's code files are included in the downloadable code bundle.

Implementing a Factory Pattern for Nodes

The **Factory Pattern** is exactly what it sounds like: a system dedicated entirely to assembling and outputting products. Instead of your `Player` script manually building a laser beam from scratch, the player simply presses a button, and a dedicated **LaserFactory** node handles the messy reality of memory allocation, positioning, and Scene Tree management.

In Godot, the Factory Pattern is typically implemented as a specialized Node2D component, which game developers commonly call a "Spawner."

To clarify the terminology: **Factory** is the formal software engineering name for the architectural design pattern, while **Spawner** is simply the practical, industry-standard term for a node that executes this exact pattern by generating entities in the game world. Moving forward in *Void Defenders*, these terms are functionally interchangeable; our Spawners *are* our Factories.

Because Godot uses `PackedScene` (which are reusable scene templates that can be instantiated at runtime and already contain their complete internal node hierarchies), our Factory doesn't need to manually assemble the underlying nodes from scratch. Its job is to handle the environment setup: where the object goes, what container it belongs to, and broadcasting that it exists. To appreciate the value of this pattern, let's look at a quick before-and-after comparison. Without a Factory, every script that needs to create a laser (the player, enemies, automated turrets) must duplicate the same setup logic:

```
# BEFORE: Scattered and duplicated logic in the Player script
func fire_laser() -> void:
    var laser = laser_scene.instantiate()
    get_tree().current_scene.add_child(laser)
    laser.global_position = global_position
    laser.global_rotation = global_rotation
```

If you ever want to change how lasers are added to the game, you have to hunt down this block of code in every single script. By introducing a Factory, all that setup logic is centralized, and the calling script is simplified to a single, decoupled command:

```
# AFTER: Clean, factory-based instantiation in the Player script
func fire_laser() -> void:
    $LaserSpawner.spawn()
```

We can see this in action by building a universal **Spawner** component for *Void Defenders*. We will construct this script piece by piece to understand exactly how a Factory operates.

Let's create a new scene with **Node2D** as the root. We'll rename it to `Spawner`. Then, we'll attach a new script to the **Spawner** node and code it as shown here:

```
# spawner.gd (A universal Factory component)
class_name Spawner extends Node2D

# The Product: What are we building?
@export var product_scene: PackedScene

# The Container: Where should it live in the Scene Tree?
@export var parent_container: Node
```

```
signal product_created(product: Node)
```

By assigning a class name, we turn our script into a custom Godot node. Now we can search for a **Spawner** node in the **Add Node** menu just as we do for a standard **Sprite2D** or **Timer**. By using export variables, we can drag and drop scenes directly into the Godot **Inspector**. This makes our **Spawner** node flexible; it does not hardcode what it builds – we tell it what to build and where to organize it in the Scene Tree. Finally, our custom signal will broadcast the exact moment a new object is finished being built.

Next, we'll implement the `spawn()` function, which validates the assigned scene and creates a new instance of the product at runtime:

```
func spawn() -> Node:
    if not product_scene:
        push_error("No product_scene assigned!")
        return null

    var product = product_scene.instantiate()
    return product
```

The `spawn` function is set up to warn us if we forget to assign a scene in the Godot editor. The `instantiate()` function is used to create the object in the game's memory.

This centralization is the core purpose of the Factory Pattern. By wrapping the raw instantiation process inside this dedicated function, we create a single point of control for object creation. If we later decide that every spawned entity needs randomized starting stats, a specific collision layer, or a custom scale applied before entering the game world, we must add that logic right here. The rest of the game remains completely decoupled from this process; a `Player` script simply calls `spawn()` and receives a fully prepared entity, unaware of the complex steps that may have occurred behind the scenes.

Once the product has been instantiated, the Factory must decide where the new object belongs in the Scene Tree and safely attach it to the game world:

```
    # 1. Determine the parent
    var container: Node
    if parent_container:
        container = parent_container
    else:
        container = get_tree().current_scene
```

```
    # 2. Add to tree
    container.add_child(product)
```

Now that the object is in memory, we can add it to the Scene Tree. If a specific `parent_container` was assigned, the object is placed there; if not, it defaults to the main Scene Tree root using `get_tree().current_scene`.

> Note
>
> **Spawning during Physics calculations**
>
> In 99% of cases, standard `add_child()` works perfectly. However, if your Factory is triggered directly by a physics callback (for example, spawning a particle explosion directly inside an `_on_area_entered` signal), Godot may throw an error because the engine is currently busy calculating physics collisions.
>
> Only in those specific cases should you defer the spawn until the physics step finishes by replacing `add_child` with: `container.call_deferred("add_child", product)`.

With the product safely added to the Scene Tree, the final step is to position it in the game world and notify other systems that the spawning process has completed:

```
# 3. Position the product at the Spawner's exact location
    if product is Node2D:
        product.global_position = global_position
        product.global_rotation = global_rotation

    # 4. Announce the creation
    product_created.emit(product)

    return product
```

Finally, we physically place the object in the game world using `global_position` and tell the rest of the game that the Factory has finished its work using our custom signal. The **Spawner** node snaps the products' position and rotation to exactly match its own. This means that wherever you place the **Spawner** node on your level, that is exactly where the spawned objects will appear.

The `Spawner` script is designed to promote reusability. The `PackedScene` represents the final product. By exporting the `product_scene`, this **Spawner** node is agnostic. You can attach this script to an asteroid generator, a player's weapon, or a loot chest. It doesn't care what it is spawning; it only knows how to spawn it.

The spawner also introduces new objects safely using `call_deferred`. If you try to spawn a physics object during a physics calculation frame, Godot will throw an error. By using `call_deferred` we can guarantee that the object is added safely at the end of the frame. We also use signals to announce when the product has been created. The Factory emits this signal the moment the product is ready. This is crucial for injecting data later without hardcoding dependencies into the **Spawner** itself.

That said, not every object needs a dedicated Factory. If you are ever unsure whether to build a Spawner component or just write the code directly inside your current script, consult *Table 9.1* to help you decide:

Decision factor	**Direct script spawning**	**Factory Pattern**
Complexity of creation	Object only needs one or two lines of code to set up	Object requires multi-step initialization, data injection, or randomized properties
Scale of use	Object is only ever spawned by one specific script in the game	Many different scripts across the game need to spawn the same type of object
Object variety	Script always spawns the same scene every time	Spawned object changes based on data, random chance, or exported arrays
Hierarchy management	Spawned object is added directly as a child of the node that created it	Object needs to be routed to a separate container
Coupling	Script needs to know how the object works to function	Script does not need to know how the object is made; it just needs the final product.

Table 9.1 – Choosing between direct script spawning and the Factory Pattern

A helpful rule is to start simply. Default to direct script spawning when you are prototyping. The exact moment you find yourself copying and pasting that same spawning logic into a second or third script, you should stop. That is the signal to refactor that code into a Factory.

> **Note**
>
> While the Factory Pattern is powerful, do not fall into the trap of using it for every single object in your game. If your game only ever spawns a single, unique Final Boss at the end of a specific level, building a dedicated `BossFactory` is over-engineering. Adding unnecessary patterns to simple, one-off problems clutters your Scene Tree, creates unnecessary files, and makes your code harder to read. Always let the pain of duplicated code dictate when a pattern is actually needed.

Factories work well for rapidly creating standardized objects, but some systems require more detailed configuration. To handle these scenarios, we can use the Builder Pattern to assemble objects step by step. Let's understand this pattern in the next section.

Building complex objects with the Builder Pattern

While the Factory is well-suited for stamping out identical clones (like asteroids), it struggles when an object requires complex, multi-step configuration. This is where the Builder Pattern shines. The Builder separates the construction of a complex object from its final representation. Instead of passing ten different arguments into a single `_init()` function, which makes it very difficult to read and understand, a Builder allows you to construct an object step-by-step using method chaining.

You might be wondering that since Godot has a fantastic visual UI editor, why would we build UI entirely in code? While static menus (like a Main Menu) should be built visually, dynamic menus, like generating 50 different item tooltips on the fly or creating custom plugins for your development team, benefit massively from code generation.

To demonstrate this, we will build a `MenuBuilder` to handle procedural UI generation, and then combine it with Godot's `@tool` annotation so we can see our Builder's output previewed live in the editor!

First, we need to define our class and establish the foundational UI node that will hold all our generated menu items:

```
# menu_builder.gd
class_name MenuBuilder extends RefCounted

var _menu_root: VBoxContainer

func _init():
```

```
    _menu_root = VBoxContainer.new()
    _menu_root.alignment = BoxContainer.ALIGNMENT_CENTER
```

In the preceding code, by extending `RefCounted` we ensure that, unlike our Factory spawner, this Builder is not a node. It does not exist in the Scene Tree. It is simply a lightweight data object residing in memory. Godot will automatically delete it from memory the moment it is no longer being used, preventing memory leaks. The `VBoxContainer` is the invisible box that will stack our UI elements vertically. Our `_init()` function is our constructor; the exact moment a script creates a `new() MenuBuilder`, it automatically generates the `VBoxContainer` and sets its alignment to center everything. Next, we need functions to add elements to our container. Let's start with a simple label:

```
# Step 1: Add a title
func add_title(text: String) -> MenuBuilder:
    var label = Label.new()
    label.text = text
    label.horizontal_alignment = HORIZONTAL_ALIGNMENT_CENTER
    _menu_root.add_child(label)
    return self # Returning 'self' is the secret to method chaining.
```

This function creates a new Label node via code, applies the text passed into the function arguments, centers the text, and safely adds it as a child to our `_menu_root` container. The most important part of this entire script is the final line: `return self`. Instead of returning nothing, the function returns the Builder object itself. This is the secret sauce of the Builder Pattern. It allows us to chain multiple commands together in a single continuous line of code later.

Of course, the menu isn't very good without buttons to make selections. We need a way to dynamically generate interactive buttons and tell them what to do when clicked:

```
# Step 2: Add a configured button
func add_button(text: String, callable: Callable) -> MenuBuilder:
    var btn = Button.new()
    btn.text = text
    btn.pressed.connect(callable)
    _menu_root.add_child(btn)
    return self
```

Just like the title, this function generates a Button node and sets its text. However, it also introduces a `Callable` parameter. A `Callable` is simply a reference to a function. By passing a `Callable` into the Builder, we can dynamically wire the button's pressed signal directly to a specific function (like `_on_upgrade_purchased`) exactly when the button is created. Finally, just like the previous step, we return self to keep the chain going.

We have added all of our pieces to the container, but right now, that container is still just trapped inside our custom `RefCounted` object. We need a way to extract the finished product so we can put it on the screen:

```
# Step 3: Finalize and return the product
func build() -> Control:
    return _menu_root
```

Here, the `build()` function marks the end of the construction process. Instead of returning self, it returns the fully assembled `_menu_root` (our `VBoxContainer` packed with labels and buttons). Because it returns a standard Godot `Control` node, any other script in your game can take this finished product and add it directly to the Scene Tree.

Previewing the Builder with @tool

Now that we have a Builder, we can move on to how to use it. Because every configuration function returns self (the Builder itself), we can chain these commands together in a beautifully readable sequence.

To solve the issue of not having visual feedback, we will use Godot's `@tool` annotation. By adding `@tool` to the very top of a script, the code will execute inside the Godot editor without you having to press **Play**. Let's create an `autoshop_terminal.gd` script and attach it to a blank **Control** node in our scene:

```
@tool
extends Control
# autoshop_terminal.gd

# Clicking this checkbox in the Inspector will trigger the menu generation!
@export var generate_preview: bool = false:
    set(value):
        _build_shop_ui()

func _build_shop_ui() -> void:
    # 1. Clear out any old previews
    for child in get_children():
        child.queue_free()

    # 2. Use the Builder Pattern to generate the new UI
```

```
    var upgrade_menu = MenuBuilder.new() \
        .add_title("Ship Upgrades") \
        .add_button("Upgrade Shields ($500)", _on_shield_upgrade) \
        .add_button("Upgrade Lasers ($800)", _on_laser_upgrade) \
        .build()

    # 3. Add the fully built menu to the scene
    add_child(upgrade_menu)

func _on_shield_upgrade() -> void:
    print("Shields upgraded!")

func _on_laser_upgrade() -> void:
    print("Lasers upgraded!")
```

Save the script, and look at your **Inspector**. You will see a new checkbox named **Generate Preview**. If you click it, the `@tool` script triggers the `set(value)` function, which calls `_build_shop_ui()`. Instantly, your code-driven Builder generates the `VBoxContainer`, the title, and the buttons, and drops them directly into your Godot editor Viewport! Take a look at the Builder syntax block. In GDScript, the backslash (\) is the line continuation character. Normally, Godot assumes a command is finished when it hits a line break. The \ symbol tells Godot to treat the next line as if it were still on this same line.

We create a brand new instance of our `MenuBuilder`. Because we are starting a chain, we end the line with the \ character. Next, we call `.add_title()`. Remember that this function does its job and then returns self. Because it returns the Builder, we can instantly call `.add_button()` on the very next line. The last line of the chain is `.build()`. This stops returning self and instead returns the fully assembled `VBoxContainer` UI node. All the labels and buttons we just chained together are neatly packed inside this container, which gets saved into our `upgrade_menu` variable and added to the scene.

By using the Builder Pattern, we keep our configuration totally dynamic and easy to read, while hiding the tedious `Node.new()` and `add_child()` boilerplate safely inside the Builder class. Now that we have reusable Factory and Builder components in place, let's explore how centralizing object creation can simplify gameplay scripts and improve maintainability across larger projects.

Centralizing object creation

Now that we have our **Spawner** component, we can dramatically simplify our existing game logic through centralization. By moving all instantiation logic out of our individual scripts and into a dedicated Factory, we instantly achieve several core architectural best practices:

- **Single source of truth (maintainability)**: If you need to change how an entity is spawned (for example, adding a brief invincibility flash upon creation), you only have to update the `Spawner` script, rather than hunting down dozens of spawning functions scattered across your project.
- **Decoupled dependencies**: The player and enemy scripts no longer need to understand the complex setup requirements of a laser or a power-up. They simply call a single function and receive the product, keeping their own code clean and focused on their specific behaviors.
- **Consistent safety**: Because the Spawner uniformly handles tree insertion via `call_deferred()`, you guarantee that every single object created by this system avoids Godot's common physics-frame errors.
- **Effortless extensibility**: Centralization gives you a perfect choke point to inject dynamic data later. If you eventually decide to apply randomized stats or scale variations to every spawned object, you have one clear, dedicated place to add that logic.

Think about environmental hazards in *Void Defenders*. When you boil it down, an asteroid field is just a timed asteroid spawner. Previously, we would have created a `LevelManager` or `AsteroidSpawner` script to handle the countdown timers, the randomization math, and the manual instantiation, positioning, and Scene Tree management of the asteroid scene.

By utilizing our new Factory component, we can strip the messy creation boilerplate out of our manager scripts entirely.

Let's look at how an **AsteroidManager** (a dedicated node acting as a high-level gameplay system) would handle spawning by using a Factory to do the heavy lifting.

First, we establish the variables our manager needs to control the game's difficulty, as well as a reference to the Factory node itself:

```
# asteroid_manager.gd
extends Node2D
```

```
@export var base_speed: float = 150.0
@onready var asteroid_factory: Spawner = $AsteroidFactory
```

We export the `base_speed` variable so game designers can easily tweak how fast asteroids fall without opening the script. Then we create a ready variable called `asteroid_factory` to grab a reference to the **Spawner** node attached to this manager. Instead of loading a `PackedScene` directly, the manager only needs to know that the Factory exists.

Next, we connect a standard **Timer** node's `timeout` signal to trigger our spawn function. But notice what we aren't doing here: we aren't instancing scenes or calling `add_child`:

```
func _on_spawn_timer_timeout() -> void:
    # 1. The manager delegates the actual creation to the Factory
    var asteroid = asteroid_factory.spawn()

    # 2. Safety check in case the factory lacks a product_scene
    if not asteroid:
        return
```

Here, we delegate—the manager simply commands the Factory, `asteroid_factory.spawn()`. The Factory handles all the messy Scene Tree math, memory allocation, and `call_deferred` safety checks we wrote earlier. However, because our Factory is designed to return `null` if it forgets its blueprint, the manager needs to check if the asteroid actually exists. If it equals null, the return statement immediately cancels the rest of the function, preventing the game from crashing.

Now that the Factory has successfully built and placed the asteroid in the game world, the manager can step back in to do what it does best: *manage gameplay*.

```
    # 3. The manager only handles gameplay-specific logic
    # Randomize the asteroid's downward trajectory and spin
    var speed_variance = randf_range(base_speed * 0.8, base_speed
    * 1.5)

    asteroid.velocity = Vector2.DOWN * speed_variance
    asteroid.angular_velocity = randf_range(-3.0, 3.0)
```

Because the Factory returned a reference to the newly minted asteroid, we can instantly modify its properties. We generate a random speed based on our `base_speed` variable and give the asteroid a random spin (`angular_velocity`), so every rock feels unique. The manager no longer cares how an asteroid is made; it only cares about how fast it falls. By isolating the creation logic inside the Factory, this script becomes clean, readable, and focused purely on fun gameplay mechanics.

Notice how clean the script is. The `AsteroidManager` script no longer cares about the messy details of instantiation, loading packed scenes, or finding the correct parent in the Scene Tree. It simply delegates the heavy lifting to the `Spawner`, and then focuses entirely on its own responsibility: modifying and managing the resulting product. This centralization is a massive win for the design team. Because the `AsteroidManager` doesn't strictly dictate what is being spawned, you can create completely different hazards entirely through the Godot **Inspector**.

Want to swap standard rocky asteroids for explosive space mines or crystal comets? You just change the `product_scene` inside the **AsteroidFactory** node. You can radically alter the feel of a level without touching a single line of the manager's code.

Beyond clean code and design flexibility, isolating creation logic provides a massive advantage when testing and debugging your game. When object instantiation is scattered across multiple scripts, tracking a missing node reference or a physics crash requires hunting through dozens of files. With a Factory, if a spawned object behaves incorrectly or fails to enter the Scene Tree, you have a single point of failure. You instantly know exactly where to look: the `Spawner` script.

Furthermore, this decoupling makes isolating bugs straightforward. If you want to test the `AsteroidManager`'s wave-timing math, but your complex, fully animated asteroid scenes are currently broken and crashing the game, you can temporarily swap the `product_scene` in the **Inspector** to a simple, lightweight placeholder scene (like a basic **Sprite2D**). You can verify that your wave logic functions perfectly without the broken assets getting in the way, proving that your gameplay systems are truly independent.

Centralizing object creation already makes our gameplay systems cleaner and easier to maintain. However, the real strength of the Factory Pattern emerges when we combine these reusable components to generate dynamic, procedural gameplay systems at runtime.

Procedural generation with Factories

The ultimate test of a Factory is **procedural generation**. Because our **Spawner** is decoupled and broadcast-driven, we can combine it with other modular components to build complex, dynamic encounters like asteroid fields or endless enemy waves.

Let's say we want to spawn a circular ring of asteroids around a space station. We can pair our **Spawner** with a new component: a **RadialPositionRandomizer**. This component will listen to the Factory and reposition whatever it creates.

First, we should define our script and the variables that will control the size of the asteroid field:

```
# radial_randomizer.gd
extends Node

@export var spawner: Spawner
@export var min_radius: float = 100.0
@export var max_radius: float = 300.0
```

Notice that this isn't a Node2D. This script doesn't need its own physical position in the game world; it is purely a mathematical brain. We use export variables to get a reference to our **Spawner** and define the `min_radius` and `max_radius` in the Godot editor. Think of this like a donut: we want asteroids to spawn somewhere inside the dough of the donut, not too close to the center and not too far away.

Because we are using an event-driven Factory Pattern, this script doesn't need to know when an asteroid is made or how it is made. It just needs to listen for the announcement:

```
func _ready() -> void:
    # We listen to the Factory's announcement
    spawner.product_created.connect(_on_product_created)
```

As soon as the game starts, this script wires itself to the **Spawner**'s `product_created` signal. Now, it can sit back and wait. Every time the Factory spits out a new object, this script will automatically trigger our custom `_on_product_created` function.

When the Factory announces it has made something, it passes the new object along with the signal. We need to catch that object and make sure it is something we can actually move.

```
func _on_product_created(product: Node) -> void:
    if product is Node2D:
```

We receive the newly minted product. We use the `is Node2D` safety check because you can only change the `global_position` of 2D objects. If the Factory accidentally spawns a standard UI Control node or a basic Node, this script will safely ignore it instead of crashing.

Now for the core logic. We need to pick a random spot inside our donut boundary:

```
# Generate a random angle and distance
        var random_angle = randf() * TAU
        # TAU is 2 * PI (a full circle)
        var random_distance = randf_range(min_radius, max_radius)

        # Calculate the offset
        var offset = Vector2(cos(random_angle), sin(random_angle)) *
        random_distance
```

In the preceding code, `TAU` is Godot's built-in constant for a full 360-degree circle (in radians). Multiplying a random fraction (`randf()`) by `TAU` gives us a completely random direction to point in. Next, we pick a random distance between our inner limit and outer limit. Finally, we use basic trigonometry (Cosine for the *X*-axis, Sine for the *Y*-axis) to turn the random angle into a normalized direction vector. We then multiply it by a random distance. This gives us the exact coordinates of our new random spot.

If this trigonometry feels intimidating, don't worry. Mastering procedural math is not required to use these design patterns. The *core takeaway* here is architectural: notice how the Factory Pattern provides a perfectly isolated environment to execute complex, specialized logic without cluttering the rest of your game's codebase.

Lastly, we apply this calculated spot to the object:

```
# Reposition the product relative to the Spawner's center
        product.global_position += offset
```

Remember that our **Spawner** automatically places all new objects exactly at its own center. By taking the asteroid's current position and adding our new mathematical `offset` to it, we instantly teleport the asteroid out of the center and into its new, randomized place in the asteroid ring.

To create our asteroid field, we don't write a massive `AsteroidFieldManager` script. Instead, we use Composition to snap our components together in the Scene Tree:

1. We create a generic **Timer** node set to loop 10 times.
2. We connect the **Timer**'s `timeout` signal to our `Spawner.spawn()` method.
3. The **Spawner** instantiates the Asteroid.

4. The **Spawner** emits `product_created`.
5. The **RadialRandomizer** hears the signal, catches the newly spawned Asteroid in mid-air, and mathematically offsets it into a ring formation.

This is the true power of the Factory Pattern. We have created a dynamic, procedural asteroid field without writing a single script specifically for asteroids. By treating the game world as an assembly line of specialized components, we have automated our instancing, eliminated boilerplate, and unlocked a highly scalable, commercial-grade architecture.

However, it is important to strike a practical balance. While decoupling your systems is powerful, taking it to the extreme can lead to excessive fragmentation. If you break your game down into too many micro-components, where firing a single laser requires tracing logic through five different scripts and three separate Factories, your project will become difficult to debug.

The goal of any architectural pattern is to make your codebase easier to read and maintain, not to hide the logic behind an endless maze of tiny files.

Choosing between Factory and Builder patterns

While both the Factory and Builder patterns help you create objects, they handle different levels of complexity. It is important to note that these patterns are not mutually exclusive; in fact, a Builder is essentially just a highly specialized Factory with step-by-step customization capabilities.

If you are ever unsure which end of the creation spectrum you need for a specific system, use *Table 9.2* as a guide:

Decision factor	Factory Pattern	Builder Pattern
Primary goal	Quickly generating fully formed and ready-to-use objects	Step-by-step assembly of a single, highly configured object
Construction process	You call one function, such as `spawn()` or `create()`, and receive the final product immediately.	You call several chained functions such as `set_size()` and `add_title()` before finally calling `build()`.

Decision factor	Factory Pattern	Builder Pattern
Object complexity	The objects are mostly identical.	The object has many optional parts or nested children.
Encapsulation focus	The messy boilerplate of memory allocation, hierarchy management, and instantiation is hidden.	Injecting properties, linking dependencies, and structural layout are hidden.
Common use cases	Spawning enemies, generating particle effects	Generating procedural levels
Common mistake	Building a dedicated Factory for a unique object (like a Final Boss) that only appears once in the entire game.	Using a Builder for a simple object that only needs one or two basic properties set, where a Factory or direct instantiation would suffice.

Table 9.2 – Choosing between Factory and Builder Patterns

There is a common scenario where a simple Factory feels too restrictive, but a full Builder Pattern feels like overkill. Imagine you are using a Factory to spawn a laser projectile, but you suddenly realize you need to customize its speed, color, scale, and damage value. Passing all of these into a single function creates a massive list of arguments (`spawn(10.0, Color.RED, 2.0, 50)`), which is a code smell known as **constructor telescoping**.

Before reaching for the Builder Pattern, consider using a **Configuration Object** (also known as the **Parameter Object Pattern**). You can create a lightweight class or Custom Resource that holds all the default values, and simply pass that object into your Factory:

```
# ProjectileConfig.gd
class_name ProjectileConfig extends RefCounted

# Holds all customization parameters with sensible defaults
var speed: float = 500.0
var color: Color = Color.WHITE
var scale: float = 1.0
var damage: int = 10
```

Now, your spawning script can simply tweak the specific variables it cares about before passing the configuration into the standard Factory:

```
# Weapon.gd
func fire_heavy_shot() -> void:
    # 1. Create the config and override only what we need
    var config = ProjectileConfig.new()
    config.color = Color.RED
    config.damage = 50

    # 2. Pass the single config object to the Factory
    ProjectileFactory.spawn(config)
```

This bridges the gap. It keeps the actual `ProjectileFactory` simple and restricted to a single `spawn()` function, while giving you the flexible, optional customization capabilities that normally require a Builder. Use this approach for highly variable objects (like projectiles or particle effects), and reserve the true Builder Pattern for objects that require complex, multi-step structural assembly (like procedural dungeons or complex dialogue trees).

Ideally, keep in mind that if you need to make 100 of something right now, use a Factory Pattern. If you need to make 1 thing that requires 10 different steps to set up, use a Builder Pattern.

Summary

In this chapter, we tackled the growing pains of scaling a game by addressing the brittleness of scattered instantiation. By pulling creation logic out of individual gameplay scripts and centralizing it, we took a massive step toward a flexible, commercial-grade architecture.

We began by exploring the Factory Pattern. We built a universal **Spawner** component that completely hides the repetitive boilerplate of memory allocation, Scene Tree management, and deferred physics spawning. This decoupled our game managers, allowing them to focus purely on fun gameplay logic rather than the mechanics of object creation.

Then we moved on to the Builder Pattern. For objects too complex for a single-step Factory, we implemented a step-by-step Builder. By utilizing method chaining (the return self technique), we created a highly readable, programmatic way to generate dynamic UI elements on the fly.

Next, we combined our Factory with independent mathematical components (like the **RadialPositionRandomizer**) to prove that complex environments, like asteroid fields, can be generated procedurally through composition rather than massive, tangled scripts.

Finally, we focused on architectural decision-making. We established a clear rule of thumb for when to use each pattern: Factories are for the bulk creation of standardized clones (like a vending machine), while Builders are for the multi-step configuration of complex, unique objects (like a sandwich shop).

By adopting these creational patterns, you have transformed your rigid code into a highly automated, easily adjustable system. You can now spawn hundreds of entities or construct dynamic interfaces with a single line of clean, predictable code.

In the next chapter, we will take this step further. Now that we have decoupled how objects are created, we need to decouple how they act and access data. We will explore how to encapsulate player inputs into reusable commands (unlocking advanced features like input buffering and undo systems) and how to safely provide global access to core systems like audio and saving using services.

10

Applying Command and Service Patterns

When you first learn to program in Godot, the easiest way to make a character move is to write input checks directly into the character's script. You might write something like: If the *spacebar* is pressed, trigger the `shoot_laser()` function.

While this works perfectly for a prototype, it creates a tight, invisible knot between the *Invoker* (the keyboard) and the *Receiver* (the player ship).

But what happens when you want to let the player remap their controls? What if you want to implement an AI that controls the same ship? Or what if your player gets hit by a confusion probe, and you need to scramble their inputs temporarily? If your input logic is permanently glued to your movement logic, these features require writing messy, convoluted code.

This is where the *Command Pattern* comes in. The **Command Pattern** is a behavioral design pattern that takes a request, action, or behavior and encapsulates it into a standalone object.

In this chapter, you will learn how to break the invisible knots in your code by applying the Command and Service patterns to *Void Defenders*. In real-world game development, these patterns are essential for building robust, scalable systems. The **Command Pattern** treats actions as physical data objects rather than just fleeting function calls. This paradigm shift makes complex, highly requested features like custom input remapping, replay systems, and fully functioning undo/redo stacks simple to implement.

Meanwhile, the **Service Pattern** (often implemented as a **Service Locator**) provides a clean way to handle global, persistent systems, such as audio managers or save systems, without creating a tangled web of hardcoded dependencies. By decoupling the service provider from the scripts that use the service, you can seamlessly swap out core systems (like changing a local save file system to a cloud-based one) without having to rewrite a single line of your gameplay logic.

Ultimately, the goal of this chapter is to teach you how to separate what happens in your game from who triggers it, transforming rigid, hardcoded mechanics into flexible, modular systems. To achieve this, we will start by decoupling our player's input from the ship's movement, then tackle how to handle cross-cutting concerns, like audio and saving, without turning our project into a tangled web of global variables. Finally, we will put the Command Pattern to the ultimate test by building a fully functional, professional-grade undo/redo system from scratch.

This chapter will cover the following main topics:

- Using Command Pattern for input
- Creating reusable Command Objects
- The mechanics of Undo/Redo
- Applying the Service Pattern to cross-cutting systems
- Testing Command and Service patterns

By the end of this chapter, you will have crossed a major threshold in your development journey: transitioning from a scripter who hardcodes mechanics to an architect who designs flexible systems. You will possess the vocabulary and the technical skills to easily implement features that often stump intermediate developers, such as custom keybindings, action replay systems, and persistent save states, elevating your codebase to a truly commercial-grade standard.

Technical requirements

Readers should be familiar with basic Godot workflows, such as navigating the Godot editor, creating scenes, and scripting with GDScript.

You can download the example project and code for this book by following the instructions in the *Download the example code files* section in the *Preface* of this book.

This chapter's code files are included in the downloadable code bundle.

Understanding the Command Pattern

Before we dive into the GDScript implementation, it is crucial to understand what the Command Pattern is and why it exists. This pattern fundamentally changes how we think about executing logic in our games. Instead of treating an action, like jumping, firing a laser, or opening a menu, as an immediate, hardcoded function call, we encapsulate that action into its own standalone object. By taking the time to understand this conceptual shift first, the code we write later will feel like a natural, logical solution rather than a confusing, unnecessary layer of abstraction.

Let's break down the strict technical architecture of this pattern. It relies on four distinct roles:

- **The Client**: The system generating the request
- **The Invoker**: The system routing the request
- **The Command**: The encapsulated data object
- **The Receiver**: The object ultimately executing the action

In a standard, tightly coupled setup, your input script directly calls a function on your player character, such as `ship.fire_laser()`. In the Command Pattern, the input system (the *Invoker*) never touches the ship. Instead, it instantiates a `ShootCommand` object (the *Command*) and passes it along. The ship (the *Receiver*) eventually receives this object and executes the instructions inside. The ship doesn't care about who generated the command (the *Client*), whether it was a keyboard, a gamepad, an AI script, or a network packet from a multiplayer server.

Because the input system is completely blind to how the ship fires, and the ship is completely blind to which Controller Button triggered the action, the Command object serves as the strict, standardized contract connecting them.

By treating actions as lightweight, physical data objects (in Godot, extending `RefCounted`), you unlock several professional-grade mechanics that are otherwise difficult to program:

- **Decoupled AI**: You can build an AI brain that analyzes the battlefield and outputs the exact same Command objects that a player's keyboard would. This allows you to use the exact same character scripts to drive both players and enemies without duplicating code.
- **Parallel execution and queuing**: In an action game like *Void Defenders*, treating inputs as data packets allows you to cleanly process multiple actions simultaneously, such as executing a `MoveCommand` and a `ShootCommand` on the same frame, without tangling your movement physics with your weapon logic. In strategy games, it allows you to stack these objects in a list to queue up build orders.
- **Replays and macros**: If you want to show a kill cam or allow players to save a replay of a match, you don't need to record a massive video file. You simply record the stream of Command objects and play them back frame by frame.
- **Undo and Redo systems**: While rarely used in real-time shooters, puzzle and strategy games rely heavily on this. Because commands are just data objects, you can save them

in an array. If a player hits **Undo**, you grab the last command and tell it to run its exact process in reverse.

Now that we understand the core idea behind the Command Pattern and why it is useful in game development, let's apply it to a practical Godot workflow by decoupling player input from gameplay behavior.

Using Command Pattern for input

In most beginner Godot projects, input handling is hardcoded directly into the player character's physics or input functions. While this works for prototypes, it tightly couples the *intent* (pressing a button) with the *execution* (moving the ship).

We set up the player ship movement this way in *Void Defenders* by handling movement directly in the `_physics_process()` function. At the core of any game is an input handler. This system listens for physical actions from the user and translates those raw signals into meaningful mechanics within the game world. An illustrative implementation could look like this:

```
func handle_input() -> void:
    if Input.is_action_pressed("button_x"):
        jump()
    elif Input.is_action_pressed("button_y"):
        fire_weapon()
    elif Input.is_action_pressed("button_a"):
        swap_weapon()
```

Usually, the game loop calls the `handle_input()` function every single frame. This setup is perfectly adequate if you intend to permanently hard-wire specific buttons to specific game actions. However, most modern games allow players to customize their keybindings. To support remappable inputs, we need a way to easily swap out those direct calls to `jump()` and `fire_weapon()`. The best way to swap behaviors on the fly is to treat them like variables, which means we must convert our in-game actions into actual data objects. Hence, the Command Pattern.

Creating reusable Command Objects

To implement this pattern, we first define a base class that represents a triggerable game command. Because we want these commands to be lightweight data packets rather than heavy Scene Tree elements, we extend `RefCounted`. When you see a class with a single method (like `execute()`) that doesn't return anything, there is a very good chance it is utilizing the Command Pattern.

To make these commands truly reusable for a commercial game, they cannot assume global `jump()` or `fire_weapon()` functions magically exist, nor can they hunt the Scene Tree to find the player. If a command is hardcoded to find the player, it is completely useless for an enemy NPC. To solve this tight coupling, we pass the exact object we want to control (the *Receiver*) directly into the function:

```
class_name Command extends RefCounted

func execute(actor: Node) -> void:
    pass
```

Here, the actor represents any active game object in the world. We pass it into `execute()` so that the derived command can call methods on an entity of our choice. For example, a command to fire a weapon would look like this:

```
class_name ShootCommand extends Command

func execute(actor: Node) -> void:
    # Safely instruct the receiving actor to perform the action
    if actor.has_method("fire_blaster"):
        actor.fire_blaster()
```

Because of this decoupling, this single class can now make any character shoot.

What we need next is an **Invoker**, a middleman that listens to the player's inputs and generates the correct command. Rather than mapping commands to physical buttons like `button_x` or `button_y`, we leverage Godot's **InputMap** to listen for logical actions. Notice that this function does not execute the command; it simply creates the data object and returns it:

```
class_name PlayerInputHandler extends Node

func get_command() -> Command:
    if Input.is_action_pressed("fire_weapon"):
        return ShootCommand.new()
    elif Input.is_action_pressed("deploy_shield"):
        return ShieldCommand.new()

    return null
```

The input handler cannot execute the command right away because it doesn't know which actor to apply it to. However, because we have encapsulated the command as a data object, we can safely delay its execution until the target is ready.

To connect the instruction to the entity executing it, we wrap this logic inside the active game loop (such as `_process` or `_physics_process`) of our main `Player Controller` script:

```
class_name PlayerController extends Node

@export var player_actor: CharacterBody2D
@onready var input_handler: PlayerInputHandler = $PlayerInputHandler

func _physics_process(delta: float) -> void:
    # 1. Generate the command from the input stream
    var command: Command = input_handler.get_command()

    # 2. If a command was generated, execute it on our specific actor
    if command:
        command.execute(player_actor)
```

Here, assuming `player_actor` points to our ship, this setup successfully translates user inputs into on-screen action.

Introducing this intermediary step between the instruction and the entity unlocks a major structural benefit: the **command stream**. Because our actions are now discrete data objects rather than immediate function calls, they can be queued, routed, and treated as a continuous stream of instructions flowing into an actor.

The true power of this stream is that the receiver (the game entity) is completely blind to the source of the instructions. A `ShootCommand` looks the same whether it was generated by a physical keystroke, a network packet from a multiplayer server, or an AI-automated script.

Extending commands to AI systems

Until now, we have focused exclusively on the player. But how do we handle the rest of the entities in the game world? These are controlled by artificial intelligence (AI). Fortunately, we can utilize this identical command architecture to bridge the game's AI and its non-player characters. Rather than reacting to keyboard or controller inputs, the AI logic simply generates and dispatches Command objects directly into the entity's stream. Separating the *brain* that chooses the actions from the *body* that performs them offers tremendous versatility. It allows developers to seamlessly swap AI profiles to alter character behavior. Need an enemy that attacks relentlessly? Simply attach a more aggressive AI module that frequently outputs attack commands. You can even assign an AI controller to the Player, which is an excellent trick for creating automated testing modes or self-playing demo reels.

By converting character instructions into standalone objects, we eliminate the rigid dependency of direct function calls. It helps to visualize the system as a flowing pipeline: a *producer* (such as the player's input handler or an AI routine) creates commands and feeds them into a stream. On the other end, a *consumer* (the character or a centralized dispatcher) reads those commands and executes them.

By inserting this queue between the two ends, we have effectively isolated the system issuing the orders from the system carrying them out.

Building a Command Queue system

The Command Pattern encapsulates player actions into independent objects, allowing for easier input handling and action queuing. By decoupling the input from the execution, your code becomes much more maintainable and scalable.

First, we need a base class for all our commands. We will make our base command extend `RefCounted`. Commands should be lightweight data packets, not heavy Scene Tree elements. The framework for the base `Command` script looks like this:

```
class_name Command extends RefCounted

var command_name: String

# With 'await' inside derived commands, Godot treats this as a coroutine.
func execute(actor: Node) -> void:
	pass
```

Let's break down why this base class is structured this way:

- **Lightweight data (`RefCounted`)**: We explicitly avoid extending `Node` here. Generating a new `Node` for every single button press creates severe memory bloat. A Command is just an instruction; it doesn't need to exist in the Scene Tree.
- **The Actor (Receiver)**: As established earlier, we pass the actor into the `execute` function. If a `MoveCommand` needs to animate the ship, the command simply tells the actor to create a Tween. The actor handles the engine-level logic; the command just provides the directions.
- **Coroutines and the `await` keyword**: Notice that `execute()` returns void. So how does the queue know when an action is finished? In Godot 4, if you use the `await` keyword

inside a derived command's `execute()` function (for example, waiting for an animation signal to finish), Godot automatically turns that function into an asynchronous coroutine. This allows our queue manager to safely pause execution until the actor is done moving.

Now that we have a blueprint for our commands, we need a system to manage them. For this architecture, we are going to build a queue manager script that sits on our target receiver (the player's ship). Let's build this `CommandUnit` script piece by piece.

First, we set up the memory arrays:

```
class_name CommandUnit extends Node2D

var command_q: Array[Command] = []
var history_q: Array[Command] = []
var awaiting_execution: bool = false
const MAX_HISTORY: int = 50
```

We declare two separate arrays. The `command_q` (Queue) acts as a waiting room for actions the player wants to take. The `history_q` acts as a historical record (useful for replays or undo features). We also introduce a crucial Boolean variable: `awaiting_execution`. This acts as a lock, ensuring the unit finishes its current command before attempting to start the next one.

Next, we need a way to receive new commands from the input handler:

```
func add_command(c: Command) -> void:
    command_q.append(c)
    execute_next_command()
```

When the input handler generates a Command object, it passes it to this function. We append it to the waiting room and immediately tell the system to try to run the queue.

Executing and managing Commands sequentially

The final function is the beating heart of our Command Pattern. It processes the waiting room, awaits the animations, and logs the history safely:

```
func execute_next_command() -> void:
    # 1. The Guard Clause
    if awaiting_execution or command_q.is_empty():
        return

    awaiting_execution = true
```

```
    # 2. Grab and Execute
    var c: Command = command_q.front()

    # Safety Check: Ensure the actor still exists before commanding it
    if is_instance_valid(self):
        await c.execute(self)

    # 3. Clean up and Log History
    command_q.pop_front()
    history_q.push_front(c)

    # 4. Memory Management: Cap the history list
    if history_q.size() > MAX_HISTORY:
        history_q.pop_back()

    awaiting_execution = false

    # 5. Recursion (Keep going!)
    execute_next_command()
```

This function is a recursive loop (meaning it calls itself repeatedly) with five distinct steps:

- **The Guard clause**: If the queue is empty, or if we are already executing a command, we immediately return. Notice we use Godot's built-in `.is_empty()` for cleaner syntax.
- **Grab and execute**: We lock the system (`awaiting_execution = true`). We grab the very first command and await its execution. The script pauses on this exact line until the command's internal coroutine finishes.
- **Clean up and log history**: Once the command is 100% finished, we remove it from the waiting room (`pop_front`) and shove it into our history book (`push_front`).
- **Memory management**: We check if our history array has exceeded our `MAX_HISTORY` cap, deleting the oldest commands to prevent memory leaks.
- **Recursion**: We unlock the system and call the function again. It will loop back to the top, grab the next command in the queue, and repeat the process until the waiting room is completely empty.

Common pitfalls with Command Queues

While command queues are powerful, they introduce a new layer of time-based complexity. As highlighted in the code in the preceding section, watch out for these common traps:

- **Dangling references (State Desync)**: Because commands are delayed, the game state might change before a command executes. If you queue a `MoveCommand` for an enemy, but the player destroys that enemy before the command reaches the front of the queue, the game will crash. Always use `is_instance_valid()` before executing a command to ensure the receiver hasn't been deleted.
- **Infinite history lists (memory leaks)**: Pushing finished commands into a history array means that the array will grow continuously. If the player plays for hours, storing every input will consume massive amounts of RAM. Always enforce a cap on your history size (like our `MAX_HISTORY` constant) and discard the oldest entries (`pop_back()`).
- **Blocking the queue**: If a command is poorly written and never finishes its internal logic (for instance, waiting for a UI animation that was accidentally deleted), the `await` keyword in our queue loop will wait forever. The entire queue will jam, and the actor will freeze permanently. Always ensure your commands have a guaranteed exit condition.

Beyond simple execution, Command objects can also be stored and revisited. This makes them well-suited for implementing the Undo/Redo functionality, which we'll examine in the next section.

The mechanics of Undo/Redo

While an action game like *Void Defenders* relies on executing commands immediately, puzzle and strategy games treat the timeline as a malleable history. Architecturally, reversing a player's actions is notoriously difficult in tightly coupled code. If a player moves their ship using a direct `move_ship()` function call, reversing that action is practically impossible unless the game explicitly memorizes the exact previous coordinates.

This is exactly where the Command Pattern shines. Because every action is encapsulated into a discrete data object, we can design each command to not only know how to execute itself but also how to reverse itself.

Let's look at a concrete `MoveCommand`. Because it is a lightweight `RefCounted` object, we initialize it using `_init()` rather than `_ready()`. Notice how we explicitly cache the `initial_position` during the execution phase, ensuring the command always remembers exactly where it started:

```
class_name MoveCommand extends Command

var initial_position: Vector2
var target_position: Vector2

func _init(target: Vector2) -> void:
    command_name = "Move"
    target_position = target

func execute(actor: Node) -> void:
    # 1. Cache the starting state for an accurate undo
    initial_position = actor.global_position

    # 2. Command the actor to animate itself
    var tween: Tween = actor.create_tween()
    tween.tween_property(actor, "position", target_position, 0.5)

    await tween.finished

func undo(actor: Node) -> void:
    # 3. Animate the actor back to the cached starting state
    var tween: Tween = actor.create_tween()
    tween.tween_property(actor, "position", initial_position, 0.5)

    await tween.finished
```

> **Note**
>
> Because our command is not a Node, it cannot create Tweens itself. Instead, it explicitly commands the actor (our Receiver) to generate the Tween.

With the reversal logic safely isolated inside the object, building an undo/redo system simply becomes a matter of shifting these objects back and forth between two arrays. When the player presses an **Undo** button, your manager script performs three simple steps:

1. **Pop**: Remove the most recent command from the `history_q`.

2. **Undo**: Call `await command.undo(actor)`.
3. **Push**: Push that reversed command onto a `redo_q` stack so the player can reapply it later.

> Note
>
> **A note on time travel**
>
> In most games, if a player undoes three actions and then immediately performs a brand-new action, the original future timeline is permanently overwritten. To implement this, you simply clear the redo queue (`redo_q.clear()`) whenever a brand-new command is issued. This is purely a design choice depending on your game's mechanics, but it is the industry standard approach.

Action games: Parallel execution

While strict, awaiting queues are perfect for turn-based strategy or puzzle games, real-time action games operate differently. In *Void Defenders*, the player needs to fly their ship while simultaneously firing their lasers. If they had to wait for a movement animation to finish before the gun could fire, the game would feel broken.

The Command Pattern handles this elegantly. Because actions are decoupled data packets, you do not have to force them into a single blocking queue. You can execute them in parallel:

```
func _physics_process(delta: float) -> void:
    # 1. Handle continuous physics movement (No awaiting)
    var move_cmd = input_handler.get_move_command()
    if move_cmd:
        move_cmd.execute(player_actor, delta)

    # 2. Handle discrete combat actions simultaneously
    var shoot_cmd = input_handler.get_shoot_command()
    if shoot_cmd:
        shoot_cmd.execute(player_actor)
```

In this setup, the `MoveCommand` instantly applies math to the ship's velocity vector, while the `ShootCommand` instantly instantiates a laser. Because the weapon logic and the movement logic are trapped inside completely separate Command objects, they never tangle. You can safely trigger both on the exact same frame.

By applying the Command Pattern, we have successfully isolated how individual characters behave and respond to input. However, a commercial game is also filled with global systems, like audio management, achievement tracking, and saving user data, that live completely outside of any single character's control. We can now turn our attention to the final major architectural hurdle: establishing a clean macro-architecture to manage those game-wide systems.

Applying the Service Pattern to cross-cutting systems

Back in *Chapter 5*, we established the foundational mechanics of Autoloads and Singletons. Now, we are going to apply those concepts to solve a specific architectural problem: managing global game systems without creating a tangled mess. In any commercial game, there are certain features that almost every single object needs to communicate with. These are known as **cross-cutting concerns**. Examples include playing sound effects, saving the game state, or logging analytics.

Without a dedicated Service Pattern, developers typically resort to two messy extremes. They either attach redundant nodes to every single entity (for example, giving every single enemy its own **AudioStreamPlayer**), which bloats the Scene Tree and wastes memory, or they tightly couple their scripts to specific global variables, making the code rigid and fragile.

Furthermore, standard node attachment creates severe lifecycle bugs. For instance, if an enemy tells its personal `AudioStreamPlayer` to play an explosion sound, but the enemy is instantly removed from the game using `queue_free()`, the audio node is destroyed right alongside it. The explosion sound will instantly and jarringly cut off.

The Service Pattern solves this by decoupling the service provider (the audio system) from the client (the dying enemy). Instead of owning an audio player, the enemy simply broadcasts a request to a globally accessible Service. The Service handles the messy reality of allocating nodes and playing the sound independently. This allows the enemy to safely delete itself without interrupting the game's audio.

Before we build one, we must establish a professional best practice: *services should be as stateless as possible*. A service should perform a task (like playing a sound or writing to a file) without permanently hoarding game data. If your Autoload is storing player health, the current score, and inventory data all at once, you are building a spaghetti global, not a clean service. To understand the difference, look at this common beginner mistake:

```
# BAD: A Stateful Spaghetti Global
# This Autoload hoards data that belongs to other objects.
extends Node
```

```
var player_health: int = 100
var current_score: int = 0
var inventory: Array = []

func take_damage(amount: int) -> void:
    player_health -= amount
```

This is a nightmare to debug because any script in the game can change the player's health at any time. The global script is taking on responsibilities (like tracking damage) that should belong to the player's own code. Now, compare that to a properly designed, stateless service:

```
# GOOD: A Stateless Save Service
# This Autoload performs a specific job and immediately forgets the data.
extends Node

func save_game_state(health: int, score: int, inv: Array) -> void:
    var save_dict: Dictionary = {
        "health": health,
        "score": score,
        "inventory": inv
    }

    var file = FileAccess.open("user://save.dat", FileAccess.WRITE)
    file.store_string(JSON.stringify(save_dict))
    file.close()
```

Notice the difference? The `SaveService` does not store the player's health in a variable at the top of the script. Instead, the player passes their health into the function, the service writes it to the hard drive, and then the service completely forgets about it. It does its job and gets out of the way.

Let's build a centralized `AudioService` Autoload that any node can call to play a sound. It will use a pool of audio players so sounds aren't cut off when the original caller is destroyed. First, we need to set up the script and initialize our pool of reusable audio players:

```
# audio_service.gd (Set as an Autoload named 'Audio')
extends Node

var _audio_pool: Array[AudioStreamPlayer] = []
const POOL_SIZE: int = 10
```

```
func _ready() -> void:
    # Initialize our pool of audio players on startup
    for i in range(POOL_SIZE):
        var player: AudioStreamPlayer = AudioStreamPlayer.new()
        add_child(player)
        _audio_pool.append(player)
```

When the game boots up, this Autoload creates `10` `AudioStreamPlayer` nodes and attaches them to itself in the background. Because they live in the global scope rather than inside a specific enemy scene, they will never be accidentally deleted during gameplay.

Next, we need a function that our game objects can call to request a sound:

```
func play_sound(stream: AudioStream) -> void:
    # Find an available player that isn't currently outputting audio
    for player: AudioStreamPlayer in _audio_pool:
        if not player.playing:
            player.stream = stream
            player.play()
            return # Exit early once the sound is playing

    # If all 10 players are currently busy, let the developer know
    push_warning("Audio pool is full! Sound dropped.")
```

Whenever a node asks to play a sound, the service quickly loops through its pool. The moment it finds a player that is currently silent (`not player.playing`), it assigns the requested audio stream, plays it, and immediately ends the function.

Now, we can trigger this sound from our Kamikaze ship. However, as we discussed in earlier chapters regarding portability, directly hardcoding a global variable (like `Audio.play_sound()`) creates a strict dependency. If you copy this enemy into a brand new Godot project that doesn't have the Audio Autoload configured, the entire script will fail to compile.

To maintain strict decoupling and portability, we dynamically check the Scene Tree for the service before requesting the audio:

```
func die() -> void:
    # Safely fetch the service without creating a hard compilation dependency
    var audio_service: Node = get_node_or_null("/root/Audio")

    if audio_service and audio_service.has_method("play_sound"):
```

```
        audio_service.play_sound(explosion_sfx)

    queue_free()
```

By safely checking for the service's existence first, the sound is handed off to the global scope to play safely, allowing the enemy node to delete itself instantly without interrupting the audio, and, crucially, keeping the enemy script portable to other projects.

With our character actions neatly bundled into Commands and our cross-cutting systems cleanly centralized into Services, our game's architecture is finally decoupled from the Godot Scene Tree. This separation does more than just keep our codebase clean; it unlocks one of the most powerful advantages in professional software engineering: the ability to test our code in isolation.

Testing Command and Service patterns

One of the hidden superpowers of using Commands and Services is how testable they make your code. In a tightly coupled system where game logic is deeply entangled with the Scene Tree, testing is a nightmare. To verify that a ship moves at the correct speed, you would have to boot up the entire game engine, load the Level, wait for the player to spawn, simulate physics frames, and manually watch the screen. Because our patterns decouple the logic from the physical nodes, we can run automated tests in perfect isolation in a fraction of a second.

You can test a Command by creating a lightweight dummy (or mock) actor. For instance, to ensure your `MoveCommand` calculates its movement duration correctly, you don't need to load the complex `player_ship.tscn` file. You just need a blank node.

```
# A mock class just for testing
class_name MockShip extends Node2D

func test_duration_calculation() -> void:
    # 1. Setup the dummy ship
    var ship: MockShip = MockShip.new()
    ship.global_position = Vector2(0.0, 0.0)

    # 2. Setup the command
    var move_cmd: MoveCommand = MoveCommand.new()
    move_cmd.unit = ship
    move_cmd.speed = 100.0
    move_cmd.target_position = Vector2(500.0, 0.0)
```

```
    # 3. Run the command
    move_cmd.execute()

    # 4. Verify the math (500 distance / 100 speed = 5.0 seconds)
    if move_cmd.get_duration() == 5.0:
        print("Test Passed: Duration calculation is correct.")
    else:
        print("Test Failed.")
```

Here is exactly why this testing approach is so powerful:

- **Step 1 (set up dummy)**: We instantiate `MockShip` entirely in code. It doesn't need collisions, sprites, or cameras. It just needs a `global_position` property.
- **Step 2 (set up command)**: We explicitly configure the command with simple, predictable math (moving `500` pixels at a speed of `100`).
- **Step 3 (execute)**: We trigger the command's logic without needing a user to physically press a button.
- **Step 4 (verify)**: We mathematically verify the outcome. We know `500` divided by `100` is `5.0`. If `get_duration()` returns anything else, we instantly know our math is broken.

Testing failure scenarios

Decoupled architecture also allows us to safely test failure scenarios. For example, what happens if the player mashes the **Undo** button when the history queue is completely empty? In a coupled system, trying to access a non-existent array index might cause a hard crash. With our Command Pattern, we can test our guard clause safely:

```
func test_empty_undo_queue() -> void:
    var command_manager = CommandUnit.new()

    # Intentionally call undo with 0 commands in history
    command_manager.undo_last_command()

    if command_manager.awaiting_execution == false:
        print("Test Passed: Guard clause safely caught the empty queue.")
```

In this test, we instantiate a completely blank `CommandUnit`. Because no commands have been executed, its history stack is entirely empty. When we intentionally trigger `undo_last_command()`, the script should hit our guard clause and immediately abort. By asserting that the `awaiting_execution` lock remains false, we mathematically prove that the system successfully rejected the invalid request rather than attempting to process a non-existent command.

This simple test guarantees that no matter how aggressively a player mashes their input buttons, our underlying architecture remains completely stable.

Service maintainability and Silent Tests

You can apply this exact same methodology when testing Services. If you are writing a test suite to ensure your combat logic triggers an explosion effect, you generally don't want a hundred real explosion sounds blasting out of your speakers every time you run the test. Because our `AudioService` is a centralized Autoload, we can easily swap it out during the testing phase for a `MockAudioService`. This mock service doesn't actually interact with Godot's audio engine; it simply writes down a log that a sound would have played.

This massively improves the long-term maintainability of your code. If the real audio system breaks in the future due to an engine update, your combat tests using the `MockAudioService` will still pass. This instantly proves to you that your core gameplay logic is perfectly fine, and it isolates the bug purely to the audio implementation.

Summary

In this chapter, we took a massive leap forward in professional software architecture. We moved away from the beginner-friendly, but ultimately rigid, habit of hardcoding behaviors directly into our Godot nodes, and instead embraced structural patterns that will allow *Void Defenders* to scale infinitely without collapsing into a tangled mess of spaghetti code.

By separating the intent of an action from its execution, you have fundamentally changed how your game's logic operates. Specifically, you learned how to implement the Command Pattern: You learned how to encapsulate actions (like moving or spinning) into standalone objects. By placing a queue manager between the player's input and the ship's behavior, you successfully decoupled your systems, opening the door for remappable controls, AI integration, and action queuing.

You also learned how to build an Undo/Redo System. You leveraged the power of the Command Pattern to build a dual-queue history manager. By making your commands completely self-contained and strictly typing your variables, you created a system that can flawlessly reverse complex, time-based animations using the await keyword.

In addition, you explored how to centralize cross-cutting services. You explored the Service Pattern to manage global systems like audio. By building a stateless AudioService Autoload with a reusable node pool, you prevented scene bloat and solved the frustrating bug of sound effects cutting off when enemies are destroyed.

Finally, you learned how to test in isolation. You saw how decoupled architecture makes automated testing significantly easier by allowing commands and services to be validated independently of the full game scene. Using lightweight mock objects, you reliably tested gameplay logic without needing to boot up the entire project.

While our code architecture is now remarkably clean and scalable, the true power of this system is unleashed when you combine it with the tools you learned earlier in this book. By pairing these decoupled Commands and Services with Godot's powerful Resource system, you eliminate workflow bottlenecks entirely. You can treat gameplay behaviors and stats as pure data files, empowering yourself (and any game designers on your team) to create hundreds of unique enemies, weapons, and items, all without tangling your codebase or writing new scripts.

In the next chapter, we will shift our focus from writing rigid logic to building flexible systems, learning how to extract your game's behaviors and stats into pure data so you can infinitely scale your content without writing new code.

Get this book's PDF copy, code bundle, and more

11

Adopting Data-Driven Design

In previous chapters, we used Resources to store simple stats (like maximum health) and encapsulate specific logic (like our Weapon Strategies). While those techniques are useful, they barely scratch the surface of what is possible when you completely separate your game data from the codebase.

As a game scales, hardcoding variables or manually tweaking dozens of individual scenes becomes a massive bottleneck. If a game designer wants to balance enemy health, they shouldn't have to dig through complex GDScript files or ask a programmer for help. If you want to add 50 new weapons to your game, you shouldn't have to create 50 unique scenes.

In this chapter, we will adopt **Data-Driven Design** (**DDD**). We are going to build systems that treat your game engine not as a rigid set of rules, but as a blank canvas that reads external data and builds the game dynamically. We will explore advanced Resource management, learn to parse and validate external JSON files, and culminate by opening our game up to community modding.

In this chapter, we will see how all this works in more detail by covering the following main topics:

- Data-driven versus data-oriented design
- Separating Logic from Configuration
- Using Resources for data management
- Externalizing data with JSON
- Designing moddable systems

By the end of the chapter, you will understand how to completely decouple your game's data from its source code. You will be able to create custom Godot Resources to efficiently manage massive amounts of in-editor data, safely parse and validate external JSON files, and build an architecture flexible enough to support user-generated content and community modding.

Technical requirements

Readers should be familiar with basic Godot workflows, such as navigating the Godot editor, creating scenes, and scripting with GDScript.

You can download the example project and code for this book by following the instructions in the *Download the example code files* section in the *Preface* of this book.

This chapter's code files are included in the downloadable code bundle.

Data-driven versus data-oriented design

Game developers frequently confuse Data-Driven Design (DDD) with Data-Oriented Design (DOD). **Data-Driven Design (DDD)** is an architectural choice. It focuses on separating game logic (code) from game configuration (JSON, XML, Resources) so the game can be easily tweaked or modded. **Data-Oriented Design (DOD)** is a hardware-level optimization strategy. It focuses on how data is physically laid out in the computer's memory (RAM) to maximize CPU cache efficiency. Because GDScript is a high-level language that manages memory automatically, true DOD is generally reserved for Godot's lower-level C++ servers. This chapter focuses entirely on DDD.

To understand why Data-Driven Design is so powerful, we must look at how traditional Object-Oriented Programming (OOP) handles data. In strict OOP, source code is organized around *types*. If you want a flaming sword and an ice sword in your game, an object-oriented approach encourages you to create specific classes for them:

```
# Traditional OOP approach
class_name FireSword extends Weapon

var damage: int = 50
var element: String = "Fire"
```

In this setup, the data (`50, "Fire"`) is permanently trapped inside the logic (the `FireSword` script). If you want to change the damage, you must open the code, change the script, and recompile the game.

Data-Driven Design flips this relationship upside down. Instead of defining what an object is through a script, we write a single, generic `Weapon` script that acts as an empty vessel. We then feed data into that vessel from an external file:

```
{
  "weapon_id": "fire_sword",
  "damage": 50,
  "element": "Fire"
}
```

In DDD, the code dictates *how* the game works (for example, how to swing a sword), but the external data dictates *what* the game is (for example, how much damage it does). By drawing this hard line, your codebase stops growing every time you add content. You can add a thousand new weapons to your JSON file without writing a single new line of GDScript.

Understanding this distinction is only the first step. To apply Data-Driven Design effectively, we must learn how to separate the rules of our game from the data that defines its content.

Separating Logic from Configuration

One of the most common pitfalls in early game development is tightly coupling what a system does with the specific data it uses to do it. While having a dedicated script for every single item, weapon, or enemy type might work for a small game jam, it creates a rigid, bloated architecture that is impossible to maintain at scale. To solve this, we need to shift our mindset.

At its core, Data-Driven Design is about recognizing the difference between **Logic** (the rules of the game) and **Configuration** (the numbers, text, and assets that populate those rules). To understand why this separation is vital, we have to look at how games are actually made.

From a purely technological standpoint, programming a game is often equally as difficult as programming standard software. However, a perfectly functioning codebase does not guarantee a successful game. Most development time is spent tweaking content, adjusting enemy speed, balancing weapon damage, and altering spawn rates until the game finally feels fun. If your game data is trapped inside your code, you have created a massive bottleneck for this tweaking process.

Before we look at any code, it helps to understand why this separation matters by looking at how professional game studios operate. In a typical production environment, a development team is broadly split into disciplines with very different day-to-day goals, most notably, **Programmers** and **Designers**:

- **Programmers' domain**: Programmers are focused on building robust, performant, and bug-free systems. They care about architecture, memory management, and ensuring that when an entity attacks, the underlying math calculates correctly and triggers the right physics layers.

- **Designers' domain**: Designers are focused on crafting the player experience. They care about game feel, pacing, and balance. To do their jobs well, they need to rapidly iterate, testing whether a specific sword should deal `10` damage or `12`, or if an enemy needs to move just slightly faster to create the right level of tension.

When logic and configuration are tightly coupled, meaning the gameplay stats and text are hardcoded directly into the scripts, these two workflows inevitably collide. If a designer wants to tweak the attack speed of a boss, they are forced to open the source code, hunt down the specific variable, make the change, and save the script. This creates massive friction. It slows down the iteration process, risks accidental syntax errors that break the game, and forces programmers and designers to constantly step on each other's toes while trying to modify the same files.

A successful team workflow relies on establishing a clear boundary between these two domains. We achieve this by treating the *code* as the *engine* and the *configuration* as the *fuel*:

1. **Programmers build the framework:** They write the generalized logic that states, *"When this entity attacks, deal X amount of damage at Y speed."* The script does not need to know what *X* and *Y* are; it just needs to know how to process them when the time comes.
2. **Designers populate the content:** Using external data structures, such as JSON, CSV spreadsheets, or custom resources exposed directly in the **Inspector**, designers are free to define the specifics. They dictate that a Goblin has an **X** of `15` and a **Y** of `1.2`, while a Troll has an **X** of `40` and a **Y** of `0.5`.

By separating logic from configuration, you create an asynchronous pipeline. Programmers can confidently optimize and refactor the core systems without wiping out the designer's carefully balanced gameplay tweaks. Meanwhile, designers can freely experiment with the game's numbers, items, and pacing without ever needing to touch a single line of code. This *separation of concerns* is characteristic of professional architecture, allowing the whole team to work independently, safely, and efficiently.

Refactoring from hardcoded to Data-Driven

Let's look at a practical example. Imagine you are programming the movement speed for a new enemy in *Void Defenders*. A standard, beginner approach is to simply hardcode that variable directly into the enemy's script:

```
# The Hardcoded Approach (Avoid this!)
class_name BruiserEnemy extends CharacterBody2D
```

```
func _physics_process(delta: float) -> void:
    # The speed is permanently trapped inside this logic
    var speed: float = 150.0
    velocity = Vector2.RIGHT * speed
    move_and_slide()
```

While this works, it introduces a severe workflow problem. If a game designer plays the level and decides the enemy is slightly too slow, they must open the script, find the exact line of code, change the number, save the file, and restart the game to test it. Even if you move that variable to the top of the script as a constant, the designer still must dig through GDScript.

In a team environment, this means non-programmers cannot balance the game without risking breaking the code, and programmers are constantly distracted by requests to tweak minor values.

Hard architecture versus soft architecture

To solve this workflow bottleneck and eliminate the need for designers to edit source code, professional developers divide their games into two distinct layers: *hard architecture* and *soft architecture*, as explained below:

- **Hard architecture**: These are the low-level, universal systems that rarely change. In Godot, this includes the underlying physics engine (`move_and_slide`), the rendering server, and your core input handlers.
- **Soft architecture**: This is game-specific logic, such as how a power-up behaves or how the inventory works.

In DDD, your soft architecture should never contain hardcoded numbers. Instead, it should act as an empty vessel that relies entirely on an external data source (like a Godot Resource or a JSON file) to tell it what to do.

Instead of writing a specific `BruiserEnemy` script with a hardcoded speed, we write a generic system that simply asks for external data:

```
# The Data-Driven Approach
class_name EnemyController extends CharacterBody2D

# @export exposes this empty slot to the Godot Inspector
@export var stats: EnemyData

func _physics_process(delta: float) -> void:
    # The logic simply reads whatever data was injected into it
```

```
    velocity = Vector2.RIGHT * stats.speed
    move_and_slide()
```

Notice the crucial addition of the @export keyword. By exporting this custom EnemyData variable, Godot automatically creates a blank slot in the **Inspector** panel. This is the bridge between the programmer and the game designer. The programmer writes the underlying logic once, and the game designer can visually drag and drop different EnemyData files into that slot to instantly change the enemy's behavior without ever opening the script editor.

By drawing a hard line between the logic, `velocity = dir * speed`, and the configuration, `speed = 150.0`, you ensure that your code rarely needs to change. Designers can tweak thousands of external variables, add new levels, and balance the entire game without ever seeing a single line of GDScript.

Having established why we need to untangle our configuration data from our underlying code to create a healthy, scalable workflow, the next logical question is how we actually do it. While we could rely on external text files or spreadsheets to hold all these variables, the engine provides a natively integrated, highly optimized tool specifically designed for this exact purpose.

Using Resources for data management

Now that we understand the necessity of separating our soft architecture from our hard architecture, we need a reliable way to store and manage that external data. In Godot, the native tool for this job is the Resource. However, we are not just going to create a few scattered resources. We are going to adopt a professional architectural strategy known as the *Prototype Pattern*.

At its core, the **Prototype Pattern** is a technique where you create new objects by copying or referencing a pre-existing master object (the prototype), rather than building them from scratch every time.

In Godot, this means you can create a single data Resource containing the baseline stats for an entity, like a basic Drone. When you spawn that enemy in your game, the new instance simply reads its data from that shared prototype. You can even create sub-prototypes (like an Armored Drone that builds on the base Drone stats) to create variations without duplicating data.

To help visualize how this data flows from a single source down to the actual objects in your level, look at the following hierarchy:

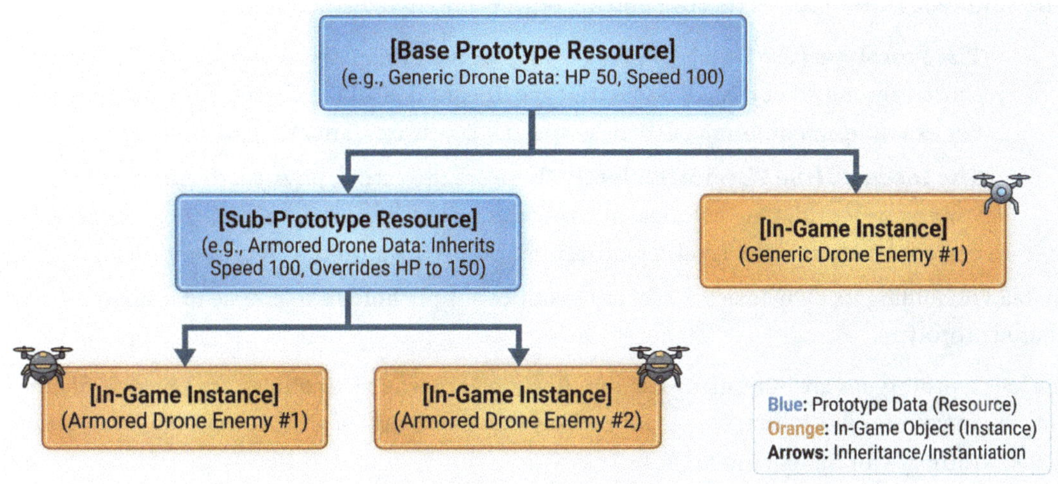

Figure 11.1 – Prototype hierarchy diagram

As illustrated in *Figure 11.1*, this data-driven hierarchy separates our blueprints from our active game objects.

At the top, the *blue* **Base Prototype Resource** acts as the master blueprint for a generic drone. Notice that we can either spawn an *orange* **In-Game Instance** directly from this blueprint, or we can use it to create a specialized **Sub-Prototype Resource**. The **Armored Drone** sub-prototype inherits the base speed (`100`) but overrides the health points (increasing them to `150`). From that single sub-prototype, we can spawn dozens of identical Armored Drone instances into the active scene.

This hierarchical approach means that if you ever decide to increase the base speed of all drones, you must only change the top-level **Base Prototype**, and the Armored Drones will automatically inherit the new speed without you having to manually update them.

In a typical game, you might have 50 scout enemies on screen at once. If every single one of those enemies stores its own `max_health`, `movement_speed`, `turn_rate`, and `sprite_texture` variables, you are wasting a tremendous amount of memory. Furthermore, if you want to tweak the Scout's speed, you must find a way to update all 50 scripts simultaneously.

The Prototype Pattern solves this by splitting objects into two distinct halves:

1. **The Prototype (the Data)**: This is a centralized template that describes the *basic traits* shared among all objects of a specific type. It contains all the shared, unchanging data. For example, maximum health, base speed, 2D textures, and AI aggressiveness.
2. **The Instance (the Physical Object)**: These are the actual, physical tokens that exist in your game world. The Instance only tracks data that is unique to itself. For example, its current location in the level, its current hit points, its current velocity, and so on.

Instead of holding its own base stats, every Instance simply holds a reference to a single, shared prototype.

In Godot, prototypes are built using Custom Resources. Because Resources are saved as files (`.tres`) in your project folder, they exist entirely independently of your Scene Tree. Let's create a base Prototype for our enemies:

```
# enemy_prototype.gd
class_name EnemyPrototype extends Resource

@export var prototype_id: String
@export var display_name: String
@export var base_health: int
@export var movement_speed: float
@export var sprite_texture: Texture2D
```

You can now right-click in your **FileSystem**, create a new `EnemyPrototype` Resource, name it `scout_prototype.tres`, and fill in the stats using the Godot **Inspector**. With this, you have created a piece of pure, tweakable data that your designers can adjust without touching any code.

Next, we build the Instance. This is a standard **CharacterBody2D** scene that acts as the physical manifestation of our enemy. Notice how lightweight this script becomes:

```
# enemy_instance.gd
class_name EnemyInstance extends CharacterBody2D

# 1. We inject the Prototype data into the Instance
@export var stats: EnemyPrototype

# 2. We track ONLY the data unique to this specific Instance
var current_health: int
```

```
@onready var sprite: Sprite2D = $Sprite2D

func _ready() -> void:
    # Initialize our physical state using the shared Prototype data
    current_health = stats.base_health
    sprite.texture = stats.sprite_texture

func take_damage(amount: int) -> void:
    # Subtract from the Instance's health pool, NOT the Prototype!
    current_health -= amount
    if current_health <= 0:
        queue_free()
```

If you spawn 50 **EnemyInstance** nodes and assign `scout_prototype.tres` to all of them, they will all share the same underlying data. If a designer changes the `movement_speed` in the `scout_prototype.tres` file, all `50` enemies instantly update.

However, this shared architecture requires you to make a critical distinction: *what data belongs to the prototype, and what data belongs to the specific instance?*

The prototype should only hold static, unchanging data, like base movement speed, maximum health, or damage output. The **EnemyInstance** node itself must hold its own unique, changing state, like its current health, its exact position in the world, or whether it is currently poisoned.

This distinction matters because Resources are shared references in memory. If you accidentally store a changing variable like Current Health inside the shared `scout_prototype.tres` file, a massive bug will occur: shooting one enemy will instantly drain the health of all 50 enemies on the screen, because they are all reading from that exact same health pool. Always keep static data in the Resource, and current state on the Node.

The true power of the **Prototype Pattern** reveals itself when you begin nesting this static data. You don't need to define every single property of an enemy in one massive prototype. Instead, prototypes can be composed of smaller sub-prototypes.

Let's say we want to give our enemies specific movement behaviors and weapons. Instead of hardcoding those variables into the `EnemyPrototype`, we can export variables that expect other Resources:

```
# enemy_prototype.gd
class_name EnemyPrototype extends Resource

@export var display_name: String
```

```
@export var base_health: int
@export var base_speed: float

# Mix and Match Sub-Prototypes!
@export var movement_logic: MovementPrototype
@export var weapon_loadout: WeaponPrototype
```

By structuring your data this way, you flatten your game's physical node hierarchy while building a rich, flexible data hierarchy. A designer can now create a `Bruiser` enemy and easily snap together a `slow_advance_movement.tres` sub-prototype and a `rocket_launcher.tres` sub-prototype in the **Inspector**. If they decide the `Bruiser` should aggressively ram the Player instead, they just drag and drop `kamikaze_movement.tres` into the slot.

But how exactly does a Resource store logic like movement, rather than just simple variables like health? The secret is treating the Resource like a stateless calculator. It holds a function that takes the current physical state of the enemy, calculates the math, and returns the result. First, you define the base logic `Resource`:

```
# movement_prototype.gd
class_name MovementPrototype extends Resource

# Virtual function expects to be overridden by specific movement types
func calculate_velocity(current_pos: Vector2, target_pos: Vector2, speed: float) -
> Vector2:
    return Vector2.ZERO
```

Next, you create a specific variation, such as our Kamikaze behavior. Notice that this script does not store the enemy's position; it simply processes the math it is handed:

```
# kamikaze_movement.gd
class_name KamikazeMovement extends MovementPrototype

func calculate_velocity(current_pos: Vector2, target_pos: Vector2, speed: float) -
> Vector2:
    # Logic: Calculate direction toward the target and multiply by speed
    var direction: Vector2 = (target_pos - current_pos).normalized()
    return direction * speed
```

Finally, you simply plug this logic into your physical `EnemyInstance`. Because the instance holds the prototype data (`stats`), it can call the nested logic function directly during its physics loop:

```
# Inside enemy_instance.gd...

func _physics_process(delta: float) -> void:
    # Safely ensure a movement logic resource is equipped
    if stats.movement_logic != null:

        # Pass physical state into Resource's logic function
        var new_velocity = stats.movement_logic.calculate_velocity(
            global_position,
            player.global_position,
            stats.base_speed
        )

        velocity = new_velocity
        move_and_slide()
```

No new scripts or complex class inheritance on the enemy itself; this is just pure, modular, data-driven design.

Up to this point, we have established a highly efficient workflow entirely within the comfort of the engine. For many projects, this is exactly where you want to be. But to fully embrace industry best practices for data management, we must recognize the boundaries of our current setup and explore formats that the rest of the software world uses.

Externalizing data with JSON

The Prototype Pattern we just built using Godot Resources (`.tres` files) is powerful. However, it still has one limitation: those files are tightly bound to the Godot editor. If you want a freelance level designer to balance the game's waves, or if you want to localize the game's dialogue into Spanish, you cannot expect those team members to download the Godot engine and learn its interface.

Moving data to a completely external source ensures that designers, writers, and programmers can all safely edit the game's configuration using the tools they are most comfortable with. To achieve this, we need to step outside of Godot's ecosystem and use a **universal data format**.

When externalizing data, developers must choose between plain text and binary formats. While binary files are smaller and faster for the computer to read, plain text is significantly easier for humans to debug, validate, and edit, particularly outside of the editor.

In modern game development, the undisputed king of plain text data is JSON (JavaScript Object Notation). It is lightweight and perfectly mimics the structure of Godot Dictionaries. A **Dictionary** is a built-in Godot data type that stores information in key-value pairs, allowing you to easily retrieve data by looking up a unique name (like `max_health: 100`) rather than using a numerical index. Because JSON perfectly mirrors this key-value structure, it is very easy to translate into your game, and it can be edited in any program, from a simple Notepad application to a massive Excel spreadsheet exported via a script.

Let's look at how we might format our wave spawning data in an external file called `level_1.json`:

```
{
  "level_name": "Asteroid Belt",
  "base_difficulty": 1.5,
  "waves": [
    { "enemy_id": "scout", "count": 5, "delay": 1.0 },
    { "enemy_id": "bruiser", "count": 2, "delay": 2.5 }
  ]
}
```

Because JSON files exist outside of your compiled game, you lose the safety nets of GDScript. A designer might accidentally type a string instead of an integer, or a player might corrupt the file. Therefore, when loading external data, you must adopt a *Zero-Trust policy*. Zero-Trust is a term borrowed directly from cybersecurity, and in the context of game development and software engineering, its core philosophy is simple: *Never trust, always verify*.

When your game reads its own compiled, internal GDScript, it operates on implicit trust. You wrote the code, the engine compiled it, and the engine trusts that health is an integer because you strictly typed `var health: int = 100`.

However, the moment your game opens a file from the outside world (like a JSON file sitting in the `user://mods/ folder`), that implicit trust is gone. A **Zero-Trust policy** means your code assumes that the external file is actively broken, corrupted, or trying to crash your game. If you blindly trust a JSON file and try to inject its contents straight into your game logic, you are exposing your game to three major hazards:

- **Human error (typos)**: A modder or designer might accidentally type `"health": "one hundred"` instead of `"health": 100`. If your code blindly forces that text string into an integer variable, the game crashes instantly.
- **Structural corruption (missing data)**: A user might accidentally delete a comma or delete an entire critical section, like the `"waves"` array. If your code assumes that the array exists and tries to loop through it, you get a fatal null reference error.
- **Malicious intent**: While less common in offline indie games, bad actors can intentionally format external files with massive numbers or unexpected structures to cause memory overflows or break the game's logic.

To enforce this policy, you must build a checkpoint system where the data has to prove its validity step-by-step before it is allowed to touch your game's actual logic. If the data fails at any step, the process is aborted safely.

Here is how we safely read, parse, and validate external JSON in Godot:

```
class_name LevelLoader extends Node

func load_level_data(file_path: String) -> Dictionary:
    # 1. Check if the file exists
    if not FileAccess.file_exists(file_path):
        push_error("Level file not found: ", file_path)
        return {}

    # 2. Open and read the plain text
    var file: FileAccess = FileAccess.open(
        file_path,
        FileAccess.READ
    )
    var json_text: String = file.get_as_text()

    # 3. Parse the JSON
    var json: JSON = JSON.new()
    var error: Error = json.parse(json_text)

    if error != OK:
        push_error(
            "JSON Parse Error at line ",
```

```
            json.get_error_line(),
            ": ",
            json.get_error_message()
        )
        return {}

    # 4. Type check the result
    var data = json.get_data()
    if typeof(data) != TYPE_DICTIONARY:
        push_error(
            "Invalid JSON format: Expected a base object/dictionary."
        )
        return {}

    # 5. Data Validation (Zero-Trust)
    if not data.has("waves") or typeof(data["waves"]) != TYPE_ARRAY:
        push_error("Level data is missing a valid 'waves' array.")
        return {}

    return data
```

If we look back at our Godot JSON parsing script, it illustrates a Zero-Trust pipeline. Let's see how:

1. **Existence check**: Does the file even exist on the hard drive? (*If no, abort*).
2. **Readability check**: Is the file locked or corrupted, preventing us from reading the raw text? (*If yes, abort*).
3. **Syntax check**: Is the text actually perfectly formatted JSON, or did the author forget a closing bracket? (*If the parser returns an error, abort*).
4. **Root structure check**: Did the JSON parse into a `Dictionary`, or is it just a random `Array` or a single string? (*If it's not a* `Dictionary`, *abort*).
5. **Key check**: Does the exact variable we need (for example, `"waves"`) actually exist inside this `Dictionary`? (*If* `data.has("waves")` *is false, abort*).
6. **Type check**: Is the `"waves"` variable actually an `Array`, or did someone incorrectly type `"waves": 5`? (*If* `typeof() != TYPE_ARRAY`, *abort*).

By the time the data reaches the end of this gauntlet, it has mathematically proven that it is safe to use. You can now inject it into your game with confidence.

Writing validation code this way feels slightly tedious at first, but it is the mark of a professional developer. A game with a strict Zero-Trust policy doesn't crash to the desktop when a modder makes a typo; it simply ignores the broken file, prints a polite warning in the console (for instance, **"JSON Parse Error: Expected an integer"**), and continues running gracefully. By validating the imported text, we ensure that our game fails gracefully, logging a helpful error to the console instead of silently crashing to the desktop.

Externalizing data prevents you from needing to recompile your code to test a minor variable change. But we can take this a massive step forward. If we must close and restart the game every time we change a value in our JSON file, we are still wasting valuable development time. Because JSON is read dynamically, we can build a system to reload game content on the fly while the game is running.

Imagine assigning a hotkey (like *F5*) in your `_input()` function that triggers the `load_level_data()` function we just wrote. With this implemented, your workflow looks like this:

1. You play the game and realize Wave 2 is too difficult.
2. You leave the game running, open `level_1.json` on your second monitor, and change the `"count"` from `2` to `1`.
3. You save the text file, switch back to the running game, and press *F5*. The game instantly reads the new text file, repopulates its internal data, and spawns the easier wave.

By pushing your data into external JSON files and allowing live reloading, you have transformed the tedious chore of balancing your game into a fluid, frictionless experience.

We have seen how moving from hardcoded scripts to externalized JSON files empowers your internal team, allowing designers to work independently of programmers. But what if we took this philosophy one step further? What if the team expanding your game could easily include the players themselves?

Designing moddable systems

The ultimate expression of DDD is exposing your game's systems to the community. Content generation, creating new ships, designing new levels, and balancing weapons is the most time-consuming bottleneck in game development.

However, because we have successfully separated our logic (hard architecture) from our configuration (soft architecture), we don't have to be the only ones generating that content. By opening our game to community modding, we can extend the lifespan of our game, *Void Defenders*, indefinitely.

Because our engine is now designed to act as a blank canvas that simply reads and executes JSON text, building a moddable system is surprisingly easy. One of the first things we need to do is bypass the `.pck` file. When you export a game in Godot, the engine bundles all your scenes, scripts, and resources into a single, compressed archive known as a Project Pack file (using the `.pck` extension). Because this file is a sealed archive, everyday players cannot easily open or modify the data inside.

To support user-generated content, we must instruct our game to look outside of this packed archive, searching for our JSON data directly in a standard, easily accessible folder on the player's hard drive instead.

When you export a game in Godot, it typically bundles all your scenes, scripts, and resources into a compressed `.pck` file. While Godot does offer an optional encryption feature in the export settings, by default, this file is simply an open archive. This is a closed system. However, Godot provides a special file path called `user://`, which points to a writable folder on the player's actual operating system (such as their `AppData` folder on Windows). If we instruct our game to look inside a `user://mods/` folder on startup, it can discover and load brand-new JSON files created by players.

Loading external assets

While JSON handles the mathematical stats of a mod, modders will inevitably want to add their own custom art. Godot's Image class allows us to load `.png` or `.jpg` files directly from the player's hard drive at runtime. An example of code that safely loads a player-created image and converts it into a texture the game can use is shown here:

```
func load_external_texture(path:String)-> ImageTexture:
    if not FileAccess.file_exists(path):
        push_warning("Mod asset missing: ", path)
        return null

    var image: Image = Image.new()
    var error: Error = image.load(path)

    if error != OK:
        push_warning("Failed to load mod image: ", path)
        return null

    # Convert the raw OS image data into an engine-ready Texture2D
    return ImageTexture.create_from_image(image)
```

To ensure our game doesn't crash when loading untrusted, external files, this function breaks the process into three safe steps:

- **Validation (`FileAccess`)**: Before attempting to load anything, we use `FileAccess.file_exists()` to verify that the file is actually sitting on the player's hard drive. If a modder makes a typo in their file path, this check catches it, pushes a helpful warning to the console, and safely returns null instead of crashing the game.
- **Loading raw data (`Image.new()`)**: We create a blank Image object and call its `load()` function. The `Image` class handles reading the raw pixel data directly from the operating system. We capture the result in an error variable and check it against Godot's built-in `OK` constant to ensure the image file isn't corrupted.
- **Texture conversion (`ImageTexture`)**: Raw Image data cannot be directly assigned to a **Sprite2D** or UI node. Godot's rendering nodes require a **Texture2D** resource. The final line uses `ImageTexture.create_from_image()` to translate the raw OS pixels into a format that the graphics card and the game engine can natively display.

Now that we can safely load both external data and custom assets, let's see how these individual systems work together as part of a complete Mod Loading Pipeline.

The Mod Loading Pipeline

Now we can combine everything we have learned in this chapter, prototypes, JSON parsing, Zero-Trust validation, and external asset loading, to create a complete **Mod Loading Pipeline**.

Let's say that a player creates a new enemy and places `dreadnought.json` and `dreadnought.png` into their `user://mods/` folder. When the game boots up, the pipeline executes the following steps:

1. **Discovery**: The game scans the `user://mods/` folder and finds the new files.
2. **Parsing and validation**: It reads `dreadnought.json`, putting the text through our strict Zero-Trust pipeline to ensure the modder didn't make any typos that would crash the game.
3. **Texture loading**: It uses our `load_external_texture()` function to pull the custom `.png` into the engine's memory.
4. **Dynamic prototype creation**: It creates a brand-new `EnemyPrototype` Resource entirely via code, populating it with the stats from the JSON and the newly loaded texture.
5. **Injection**: Finally, it pushes this new Prototype into a central Autoload so the rest of the game can find it.

This process is visualized in *Figure 11.2*, as follows:

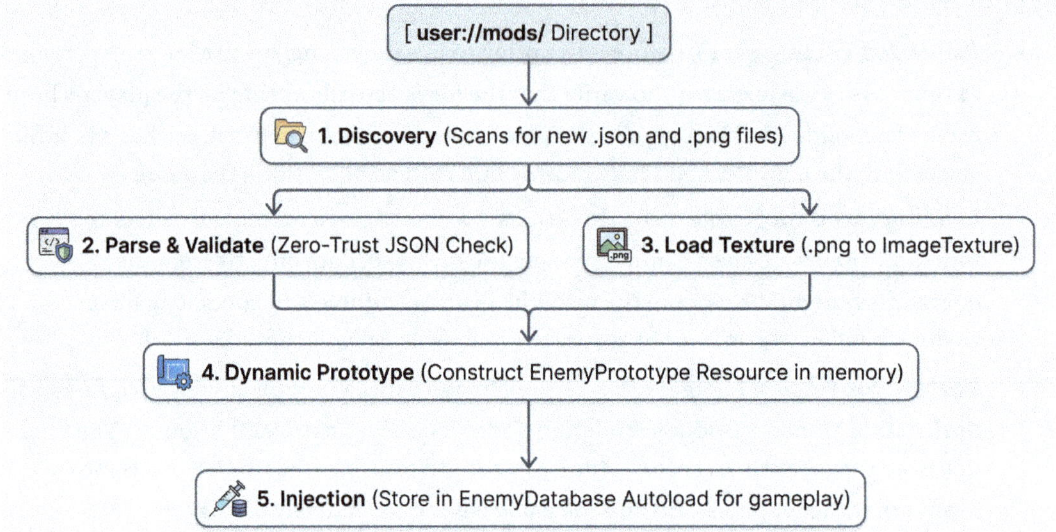

Figure 11.2 – The mod loading pipeline

While the diagram outlines the theory, the actual code execution for steps **4** and **5** is the final missing link. How exactly does a raw JSON dictionary become a Godot Resource?

Because Custom Resources are just objects, we can instantiate them directly in memory using the `.new()` method. We map our validated JSON data directly to the resource's variables, and then inject the finished object into a global Dictionary (our `EnemyDatabase` Autoload) so the rest of the game can access it:

```
# Assuming we have already parsed the JSON and loaded the PNG texture
func create_and_inject_mod(mod_id: String, parsed_json: Dictionary,
custom_texture: Texture2D) -> void:

    # STEP 4: Dynamic Prototype Creation
    # Instantiate a blank resource entirely in memory
    var new_prototype: EnemyPrototype = EnemyPrototype.new()

    # Map raw data from the JSON dictionary to the Resource properties
    new_prototype.display_name = parsed_json["display_name"]
    new_prototype.base_health = parsed_json["base_health"]
    new_prototype.base_speed = parsed_json["speed"]
    new_prototype.sprite_texture = custom_texture
```

```
    # STEP 5: Injection
    # Store the finished Resource in our global Autoload database
    if not EnemyDatabase.has_enemy(mod_id):
        EnemyDatabase.register_enemy(mod_id, new_prototype)
```

By storing the new resource in a central `EnemyDatabase` Autoload, the rest of your game logic doesn't need to know whether an enemy was built in by you or loaded externally via a mod. When the Wave Spawner randomly selects the `dreadnought` ID, it queries the database, and the game runs perfectly. The `EnemyInstance` script simply reads the injected Prototype and flies the ship across the screen, utilizing an enemy that did not exist when you originally compiled the code.

By adopting Data-Driven Design, you transform your game from a closed, rigid application into a flexible, scalable engine. You remove the bottlenecks of hardcoded logic, empower your designers to iterate rapidly, and ultimately invite your players to help build the universe of your game.

Summary

In this chapter, we executed a fundamental paradigm shift in how we architect games. We moved away from the rigid, hardcoded constraints of traditional Object-Oriented Programming and fully embraced Data-Driven Design (DDD). By recognizing the critical difference between the rules of the game (hard architecture) and the content that populates it (soft architecture), we transformed *Void Defenders* from a closed application into a highly scalable, flexible engine.

We began by solving the iteration bottleneck. Instead of forcing game designers to dig through GDScript to tweak a ship's speed, we implemented the Prototype Pattern. With Godot's native Resources, we created centralized, modular databases where all base stats could be adjusted in the **Inspector** without touching a single line of code. We then learned how to nest these Resources to create a rich mix-and-match data hierarchy, allowing us to snap different movement styles and weapons onto enemies instantly.

To decouple our data, we then stepped outside the Godot editor. We learned how to read universal JSON files, ensuring that writers, designers, and translators can tweak the game using plain text. Crucially, we established a strict Zero-Trust policy, building a gauntlet of validation checks to ensure that typos or corrupted files would be caught gracefully without crashing the game.

Finally, we took this philosophy to its logical conclusion by designing a Mod Loading Pipeline. By pointing our engine to the OS `user://` directory, we built a system capable of discovering external JSON files, loading custom `.png` images from the player's hard drive, and injecting them into the game at runtime. We proved that with a truly soft architecture, you can empower your community to build new content for your game indefinitely.

Now that we have successfully separated our data from our code and built a flexible foundation, it is time to look at how we orchestrate the actual moment-to-moment flow of our game in the next chapter.

Get this book's PDF copy, code bundle, and more

Scan the QR code (or go to `packtpub.com/unlock`). Search for this book by name, confirm the edition, and then follow the steps on the page.

UNLOCK NOW

Note: Have your invoice handy. Purchases made directly from the Packt website don't require an invoice.

12

Structuring Gameplay Logic

Every game developer knows the rush of building a prototype. When you are just trying to figure out if a core mechanic is fun, you are not thinking about long-term architecture. You throw scripts together, tightly coupling user input, physics calculations, and UI updates into a single file to get the game running as quickly as possible. In the short term, this works perfectly. However, as a project scales, developers eventually pay the price for that initial velocity.

If you ignore architectural best practices to get things done quickly, you end up solving complex problems with tangled, one-off solutions. This rapid-fire approach inevitably breeds God classes, monstrous, monolithic scripts that try to manage everything from player movement and health points to scoring, saving, and sound effects.

As we have seen throughout this book, when every system is hard-wired into every other system, your codebase becomes fragile and unstable. A simple tweak to your main menu could inexplicably break your enemy spawning logic. Eventually, it becomes agonizingly difficult to add new features, fix bugs, or even remember how your own systems work.

To transition a project from a messy prototype to a robust, commercial-grade codebase, we must fundamentally rethink how we structure our logic. In this chapter, we will learn how to untangle these chaotic dependencies by enforcing a strict *Separation of Concerns*. At its core, **Separation of Concerns** is a fundamental software engineering principle that dictates dividing a program into distinct, isolated sections. In game development, a concern is simply a specific job or responsibility, such as calculating physics, playing audio, updating the UI, or saving player data.

Instead of writing a massive, `monolithic player.gd` script that tries to manage all of these jobs at the same time, we separate them. The `movement` script only cares about movement; the `health` script only cares about taking damage. By strictly separating these responsibilities, your code becomes modular, much easier to isolate and debug when things go wrong, and highly reusable across your entire project.

We will break down monolithic scripts and reorganize our gameplay logic into clean, distinct, and isolated layers.

- **The Presentation Layer:** This comprises the "dumb" systems responsible only for rendering visuals, managing animations, and playing audio. It is the physical manifestation of your game in the Scene Tree.
- **The Domain Layer:** This layer is the pure mathematical and systematic heart of your game, where the actual rules, state machines, and mechanics live independently of the visual engine.
- **The Persistence Layer:** This comprises the secure data structures responsible for saving and loading game states without interfering with active gameplay.

By isolating these responsibilities, you will ensure your code remains readable, highly testable, and infinitely scalable. You will no longer just be writing scripts to force things to happen on screen; you will be architecting a professional game.

We will learn how to do this by focusing on the following main topics in this chapter:

- Studying the architecture roadmap
- Identifying God classes in Godot
- Separating Presentation from Logic
- Introducing Pure Data, Contexts, and Persistence
- Refactoring a monolithic script

By the end of the chapter, you will possess the tools to dismantle massive, unwieldy scripts into clean, independent layers. You will understand how to safely save and load player data without polluting your gameplay code, and how to permanently banish God classes from your projects. More importantly, as this is the final chapter of our journey, these advanced techniques will serve as your graduation. You will close this book not just knowing how to write Godot scripts, but possessing the architectural mindset required to design, scale, and release professional-grade games.

Technical requirements

Readers should be familiar with basic Godot workflows, such as navigating the Godot editor, creating scenes, and scripting with GDScript.

You can download the example project and code for this book by following the instructions in the *Download the example code files* section in the *Preface* of this book.

This chapter's code files are included in the downloadable code bundle.

Studying the architecture roadmap

Before we write code or dive deeply into the topics for this chapter, we need to map out how all of these advanced concepts interact. It is easy to get lost in the weeds of Dependency Injection and Contexts, so whenever you feel overwhelmed in this chapter, refer to this diagram:

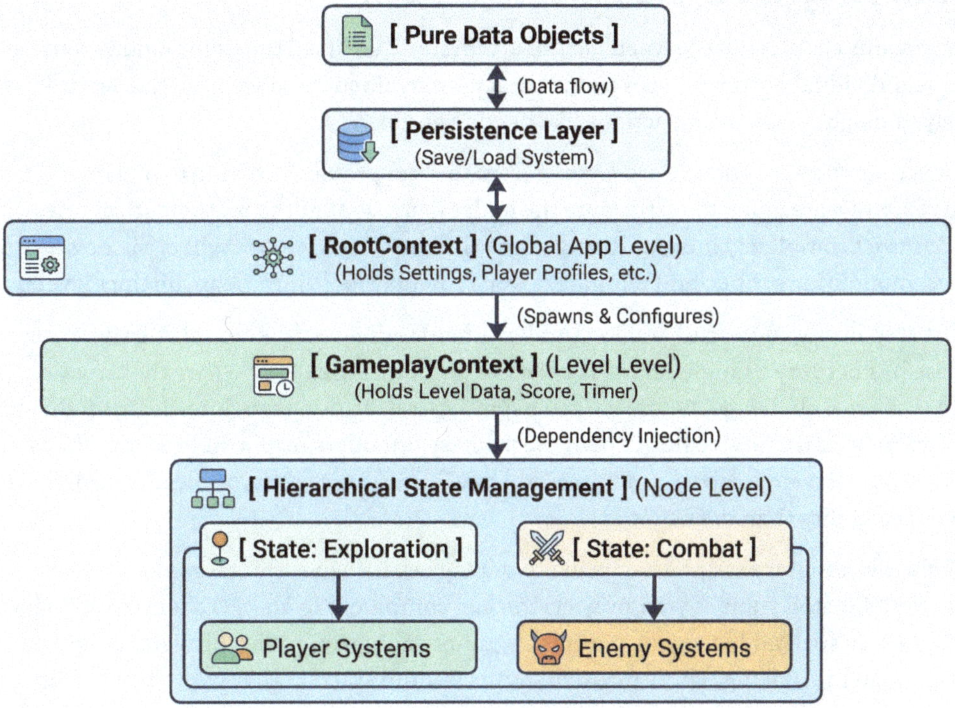

Figure 12.1 – The Architecture Roadmap

To bridge the gap between theory and practice, notice how our three conceptual layers map directly onto this chart:

1. **The Persistence Layer**: This lives at the very top of the diagram, handling the secure flow of **Pure Data Objects** in and out of the hard drive.
2. **The Domain Layer**: This makes up the bulk of the diagram. The Contexts (**Root** and **Gameplay**) and the **Hierarchical State Management** blocks represent the pure logic that dictates the rules of the game.
3. **The Presentation Layer**: While not explicitly drawn as its own macro-box, this layer is the ultimate recipient of the waterfall. The **Player Systems** and **Enemy Systems** at the

very bottom push the final mathematical results from the Domain Layer into Godot's visual nodes (like moving a **Sprite2D** or playing an **AudioStreamPlayer**).

Think of this architecture as a waterfall: pure data is stored at the very top, translated into mathematical rules in the middle, and flows downward to physically move the graphics at the bottom exactly when required.

Identifying God classes in Godot

In the previous chapters, we learned *tactical architecture*. We used the Command Pattern to decouple individual button presses from character movement, and we used the Service Pattern to safely manage cross-cutting actions like playing audio.

Now, it is time to zoom out. We are moving from tactical problem-solving to macro-architecture. We are going to restructure the entire game so that the mathematical rules of *Void Defenders* exist completely independently of the Godot Scene Tree. We will break down massive, monolithic scripts, and reorganize our gameplay logic into clean, distinct layers.

The first step in any successful architectural overhaul is diagnosis. Recognizing that your codebase has become a tangled mess is easy, but pinpointing exactly where the structural rot started is the real challenge. Before we can begin separating our game into clean, modular layers, we must learn how to hunt down the primary offenders responsible for the chaos. In the world of Godot development, no architectural flaw is more notorious or more destructive to a project's scalability than the God class.

A **God class** is a solitary script attempting to manage every aspect of the game, the omnipotent, bloated giant of your project. You can compare it to an RPG character who has mastered every spell and weapon: it seems awesome in theory, but in software design, it is a catastrophe in the making. These massive scripts seldom start off that way. They usually begin with good intentions, maybe just a basic script to handle the game state. But lured by the promise of rapid development, programmers keep piling new tasks into this one file to meet deadlines. In the early stages of *Void Defenders*, you might have drafted a `LevelManager.gd` or `player_ship.gd` that single-handedly manages:

- Processing raw player inputs
- Animating and moving the ship sprites
- Computing physics and laser impacts
- Tracking the score and active enemy waves
- Triggering audio for explosions

When a single script hoards dependencies from across the entire game, it becomes tightly coupled. It is physically unable to run without its web of interconnected systems. Centralizing all these functions into a single class comes with many hidden costs, and the early speed boost you got from writing one giant script eventually turns into a massive roadblock. Relying so heavily on a single class creates deep structural vulnerabilities:

- **The blast radius of updates**: Introducing new mechanics becomes a terrifying prospect. Because the code is so tangled, adjusting the player's velocity might somehow break the enemy AI. Making changes feels like dismantling an explosive, where the fallout from a single error is massive.
- **A nightmare to debug**: When things inevitably break, tracking down the exact cause within a gigantic, tightly knit script is like searching for a specific drop of water in an ocean.
- **Teamwork bottlenecks**: If *Void Defenders* grows to include a development team, a God class forces every programmer to edit the same file. Collaborating on such a class is like trying to share a steering wheel; it guarantees daily merge conflicts and makes training new team members virtually impossible.

In the Godot engine, this all-encompassing anti-pattern tends to manifest in a few distinct ways. If you are unsure whether a script has bloated into a God class, run it against this diagnostic checklist. If your script checks multiple boxes, it is time to refactor:

- **It exceeds a manageable size**: While there is no strict rule, if a single script stretches for many hundreds or thousands of lines, it is almost certainly handling too many responsibilities.
- **It manages multiple domains simultaneously**: A true God class refuses to delegate. It directly calculates enemy damage (gameplay logic), updates the player's health bar (UI), and writes the new high score to the hard drive (persistence), all inside the exact same script.
- **It owns massive lists of node references**: If the top of your script is a graveyard of a dozen `@onready var` statements pointing to completely unrelated nodes across the Scene Tree, the script is trying to control too much of the game world.
- **It acts as a universal hub**: It routes every signal in your project or stores global game state via an Autoload, forcing every other object in the game, from the main menu to a background asteroid, to rely directly on it.

Now that we have identified the symptoms of tight coupling, it is time to start performing surgery on our codebase. Dismantling a God class is not about arbitrarily chopping a massive script into smaller, equally tangled pieces; it is about drawing strict architectural boundaries based on responsibility. The single most important boundary you can draw in Godot, and the first step in untangling our *Void Defenders* prototype, is severing the mathematical rules of the game from the physical nodes that display them.

Separating Presentation from Logic

When building complex systems, the visual representation of your game should be completely ignorant of the underlying mathematical rules. In this section, we will learn how to split our game into two distinct halves: the *Presentation Layer* and the *Domain Layer*. You will discover how to extract your core game logic away from Godot's visual nodes, ensuring that your mechanics remain intact and testable even if you completely redesign the game's graphics or user interface.

To fix a tightly coupled architecture, our first step is to decouple what the game is doing (the logic) from how the game looks (the presentation). In Godot, it is incredibly tempting to let the Scene Tree dictate your game logic. You might check a laser Sprite's `global_position` to determine if it has left the screen or use a **Timer** node attached to an enemy to track its attack cooldown.

However, mixing these concerns creates fragile code. For example, if your player's health points are calculated and stored directly inside the value property of a **ProgressBar** UI node, what happens when a designer decides to delete that health bar and replace it with a text Label? Because the mathematical logic was tethered to a visual node, the game immediately crashes with a null reference error. Your core mechanics just broke because of a cosmetic UI change.

As mentioned earlier, the **Presentation Layer** is the outer shell of your game. It is strictly responsible for rendering visual assets, managing animations, and playing audio tracks. A `HUDManager.gd` script operating in this layer should not know how to calculate a score multiplier or determine if the player is dead; it should only know how to take a final integer and draw it on the screen.

The Presentation Layer

Now that we have established what this layer does, we need to enforce its boundaries in our code. The golden rule of the Presentation Layer is that it must remain entirely *dumb*. It acts purely as a two-way translator between the human player and the game's internal math. When a player presses a button, the Presentation Layer blindly passes that input down to the underlying logic systems without trying to process it. Conversely, when the logic systems update the score, they hand a raw number back up, and the Presentation Layer simply updates the font text.

Isolating the Presentation Layer protects your core game logic from cosmetic changes. If you decide to swap your 2D pixel-art ships in *Void Defenders* for high-fidelity 3D models, or if you completely redesign the layout of your user interface, your underlying math, scoring, and wave-spawning systems remain perfectly intact. By stripping all the logical decision-making out of your visual nodes, you guarantee that a simple tweak to a particle effect or an animation will never accidentally break your gameplay.

The Domain Logic Layer

If the *Presentation Layer* is the skin of your game, the *Domain Layer* is the brain. It is the pure mathematical and systematic core of *Void Defenders*. Crucially, scripts operating in this layer are completely blind to Godot's Scene Tree. They know absolutely nothing about `Sprite2D` nodes, `Tweens`, or `AudioStreamPlayers`. Instead, the Domain Layer deals exclusively with raw data: arrays of active enemies, integers representing the player's hull integrity, and state machines dictating AI behavior. A `wave_controller.gd` script in this layer doesn't know what a computer monitor is; it simply calculates that `10` seconds have passed and dispatches a set of spawning coordinates.

Extracting your rules into a pure Domain Layer unlocks one of the most powerful benefits of professional software architecture: testability and predictability. Because your domain logic does not rely on rendering loops, visual animations, or Godot's physical frames, it cannot be broken by graphical lag or missing visual assets. You can write an automated test that instantly verifies if your laser damage calculations are mathematically correct without ever loading a level or physically clicking a mouse. By keeping your rules completely abstract, you ensure your gameplay is governed by strict, unbreakable logic rather than the unpredictable timing of visual effects.

Our powerful mantra, **Call Down, Signal Up** (which we explored in detail in *Chapter 6*), is a perfect fit here. A parent node (the controller) should call methods directly on its children to update the presentation, while the children (the visual nodes) should only emit signals upward to notify the parent that an animation finished or an input occurred. The child should never know who its parent is.

Refactoring: Decoupling by example

To illustrate this in practical terms, let's look at a simplified example of score calculation. Here is the beginner approach, where the Presentation and Domain layers are dangerously tangled:

```
# The Bad Approach (Avoid this!)
# hud.gd
extends CanvasLayer

var current_score: int = 0
@onready var score_label = $ScoreLabel

func _on_enemy_defeated(base_points: int, combo_multiplier: float) -> void:
    # BAD: The visual UI script is calculating gameplay math!
```

```
    current_score += (base_points * combo_multiplier)
    score_label.text = "Score: " + str(current_score)
```

In this bad example, the HUD is responsible for the rules of the game. If we want to change how combos work, or if we want to calculate the score in a headless server environment without UI, the game breaks. Here is the refactored, decoupled approach. Notice how we introduce a third script to act as the glue between the math and the visuals:

```
# The Good Approach: Strict Separation

# 1. score_manager.gd (Domain Layer - No visuals)
extends Node

var current_score: int = 0
signal score_changed(new_score: int)

func add_points(base_points: int, combo_multiplier: float) -> void:
    # The dedicated controller handles the math and remembers the state
    current_score += (base_points * combo_multiplier)
    score_changed.emit(current_score)

# 2. hud.gd (Presentation Layer - No math)
extends CanvasLayer
@onready var score_label = $ScoreLabel

# The HUD is a translator that only updates when commanded
func update_score_display(new_score: int) -> void:
    score_label.text = "Score: " + str(new_score)

# 3. gameplay_context.gd (The Glue - Wires them together)
extends Node

@export var score_manager: Node
@export var hud: CanvasLayer

func _ready() -> void:
    # Context safely connects Domain's output to Presentation's input
    score_manager.score_changed.connect(hud.update_score_display)
```

By moving the calculation into a dedicated controller (`score_manager.gd`), the HUD is reduced to a simple visual component that just takes a finished number and puts it on the screen. The `gameplay_context.gd` script acts as our invisible manager, quietly piping the data from the brain to the skin without letting them directly touch.

With our visuals stripped of their decision-making power and our mathematical rules safely isolated in the Domain Layer, we face a final, crucial question: *where does the game store its memory?* If the HUD is no longer holding the player's score, and the `WaveController` is strictly focused on processing spawn timers, the raw data itself needs a safe, permanent home. Furthermore, as *Void Defenders* grows, we need a way to ensure that the logic managing the Main Menu doesn't accidentally overwrite the player's health data during a match. We need secure borders and reliable memory. This brings us to the final pillars of our macro-architecture.

Introducing Pure Data, Contexts, and Persistence

Once we separate the visuals from the mechanics, we need to organize our remaining logic into specific, purposeful layers. This requires a major shift in how intermediate developers use Godot. One of the worst habits in game development is storing critical game data inside physical Scene Tree nodes, for example, storing the player's score inside a **Label** node, or relying on a global `Node` Autoload to hold all your variables. Instead, we must separate long-term state data from functional logic by creating **Pure Data Objects**.

By extending `RefCounted` or `Resource` rather than `Node`, these scripts float completely free of the Scene Tree. They act as simple structs that contain your variables, but no functional code. Your active gameplay scripts can safely mutate this state without ever worrying about physics frames, pausing, or `queue_free()` lifecycle bugs. This pure data approach is also the safest way to handle complex data types like enumerations (for instance, tracking if a level is in a day or night state). You simply convert the enumerator into an integer to store it cleanly in your data object, and when loading, you can safely cast it back by referencing the enumerator's `.values()` array.

Extracting our game state into Pure Data Objects solves the problem of Scene Tree dependency, but it immediately introduces a new dilemma: *if this data is no longer attached to a physical node, where does it live while the game is running?*

The beginner instinct is to stuff this pure data into a global Autoload so every script can easily reach it. However, giving your **Main Menu** global access to the player's in-match health data is a recipe for disaster. If any script can access the data, any script can accidentally break it. To protect our game logic, we need to establish secure borders and strict chains of command. This brings us to our second macro-architectural pillar.

Context-based hierarchical architecture

In the previous chapter, we built global Services (like an `AudioService`) that every part of the game could access. However, for gameplay logic and state management, global access is dangerous. We do not want a `Main Menu` script to accidentally trigger a game-over sequence, nor do we want to rely on a massive global Singleton (like a `GlobalVars` Autoload) to arbitrate our save data across every scene.

To solve this, we divide our game into *Contexts*. A **Context** represents a major state of your game that has secure boundaries and distinct rules. These contexts sit under a `RootContext` (your main scene). The `RootContext` is responsible for managing global systems. Beneath it, you might have a `MainMenuContext` and a `GameplayContext`. The `GameplayContext` is strictly responsible for building and managing the level, the wave controllers, and the UI. It securely holds the Pure Data Object for that specific match, ensuring no outside scripts can tamper with it.

We have successfully extracted our game state into Pure Data Objects and built secure Contexts to protect them while the game is running. But what happens when a player defeats a brutal wave of enemies in *Void Defenders* and wants to close the game for the night? The moment the `GameplayContext` is unloaded from the Scene Tree, all of its secure data vanishes with it. To make our game truly functional, we need a way to safely transport this data from temporary memory to permanent storage, without tangling it back up in the Godot engine's node hierarchy. This brings us to the final piece of our macro-architecture.

The Persistence Layer

The Persistence Layer handles data that must survive between game sessions. By isolating our state into pure data objects and utilizing a strict Context hierarchy, saving the game becomes simple.

You do not need to hunt through the Scene Tree to find the player's health, nor do you have to save fragile Scene Tree node paths that will break if you reorganize your project. You simply ask the `GameplayContext` for its data object and hand it to the Persistence Layer.

Before we write the code, let's look at the big picture. Here is the complete pipeline for how data travels from an on-screen action all the way to the player's hard drive:

1. **Gameplay**: The player performs an action in the game world (for example, defeats a boss and receives a new laser weapon).
2. **LevelState**: The active node hierarchy registers this event and updates its temporary, local state (the player's inventory array).

3. **GameplayContext**: Following our signal up mantra, the `LevelState` emits a signal containing the updated inventory. The `GameplayContext` catches this signal and securely holds the updated data for the current level.
4. **Persistence Manager**: When a save is triggered (either manually or via a scene transition), the `GameplayContext` hands its pure data over to our dedicated file management system.
5. **JSON file**: The Persistence Manager translates that data and writes it safely to a plain text `.json` file on the physical disk.

We could create such a system in *Void Defenders* by using a persistence manager Autoload. While we established that gameplay state should not be global, the file manager is a perfect candidate for a global Service, as it simply provides read/write utilities to the rest of the game.

First, we establish our global Autoload (`PersistenceManager.gd`). It is responsible for exactly two things: ensuring the save folder exists and writing the data it is handed:

```
extends Node
# PersistenceManager.gd

# Signal used to warn Contexts that a scene transition is imminent.
signal pre_save_path_changed

const BASE_SAVE_DIR: String = "user://game_saves/"
const MASTER_FILE_NAME: String = "void_defenders_save.json"

func _ready() -> void:
    # DirAccess allows us to interact with the OS file system safely.
    if not DirAccess.dir_exists_absolute(BASE_SAVE_DIR):
        # ensures parent folders are also created if missing
        DirAccess.make_dir_recursive_absolute(BASE_SAVE_DIR)

# The Context hands its data here to be saved to the hard drive
func write_save_data(save_dict: Dictionary) -> void:
    var file_path: String = BASE_SAVE_DIR + MASTER_FILE_NAME
    var file = FileAccess.open(file_path, FileAccess.WRITE)
    if file:
        file.store_string(JSON.stringify(save_dict))
        file.close()
```

By explicitly checking if the directory exists using `DirAccess.dir_exists_absolute()`, we guarantee the game will never crash when trying to write files on a brand-new installation. Notice how the actual file writing is handled. The manager takes the Dictionary, converts it into a text string using Godot's built-in `JSON.stringify()`, and uses `FileAccess.open()` to write that text directly into the `.json` file.

But how does the manager get that Dictionary in the first place? We use the `pre_save_path_changed` signal.

By emitting this signal whenever the player quits to the main menu, the `PersistenceManager` acts as an alarm bell. It alerts the `GameplayContext` to instantly pack up its Pure Data Object and serialize it before the current level is unloaded, guaranteeing zero data loss. Because we decoupled our pure data (`LevelState`) from our Godot nodes, saving is straightforward. The `GameplayContext` simply listens for the alarm, grabs the Pure Data Object, formats it, and hands it off to be serialized:

```
class_name GameplayContext extends Node
# GameplayContext.gd

var level_state: LevelState

func _ready() -> void:
    level_state = LevelState.new()

    # Connect to our Persistence Manager's global signal
    PersistenceManager.pre_save_path_changed.connect(_on_pre_save_path_changed)

func _on_pre_save_path_changed() -> void:
    # Triggered automatically right before the player quits

    print("Saving Void Defenders game state...")

    # Convert the pure data object into a JSON-friendly Dictionary
    var save_dict: Dictionary = {
        "score": level_state.current_score,
        "wave": level_state.current_wave,
        "health": level_state.player_health
    }
```

```
    # Hand the formatted dictionary off to the global manager
    PersistenceManager.write_save_data(save_dict)
```

So far, we have established the theoretical foundation of our new macro-architecture. By extracting our game state into Pure Data Objects, we permanently severed our mathematical logic from the Godot Scene Tree. Through establishing Contexts, we built secure borders to protect that data from outside interference while it lives in active memory. Finally, by designing a dedicated Persistence Layer, we created a robust, automated system for safely writing that data to the hard drive without data loss.

At this point, you might be wondering if every single Godot project requires these strict layers. The short answer is **no**. In game development, there is a constant trade-off between simplicity and scalability. If you are building a weekend game jam project, a simple mobile puzzle game, or a small prototype, implementing pure data objects, Context hierarchies, and a dedicated Persistence Layer is massive overkill. In those scenarios, tightly coupling your mechanics directly to your Scene Tree using quick `@onready` variables is perfectly acceptable, as the project will never grow large enough for structural rot to set in.

However, if you are building a commercial title, a data-heavy RPG, or a codebase that an entire team of developers will need to maintain for years, this architecture becomes mandatory. The extra time spent building these systems upfront acts as an insurance policy, ensuring your codebase remains flexible, testable, and robust as it scales into a massive project.

Understanding these concepts in a vacuum is one thing; applying them to a tangled codebase is another. It is time to roll up our sleeves and perform the surgery. In the next section, we will look at a messy, monolithic prototype script from *Void Defenders* and refactor it step by step into these clean, distinct architectural layers.

Refactoring a monolithic script

Let's put this layered macro-architecture into practice. Imagine we have a messy, prototypical `LevelManager.gd` in *Void Defenders* that handles scoring, wave progression, updating the UI, and checking if the player is dead all at once. We will refactor this into cleanly separated layers.

To understand how to layer our architecture, we first need to look at what we are trying to fix. Below is a classic example of a monolithic God class. If you were rapidly prototyping *Void Defenders*, your `LevelManager.gd` script could end up looking like this:

```
class_name LevelManager extends Node
# BAD: A Monolithic God Class

# 1. PRESENTATION: Tightly coupled to specific Scene Tree UI nodes
```

```
@onready var score_label = $HUD/MarginContainer/ScoreLabel
@onready var wave_label = $HUD/MarginContainer/WaveLabel
@onready var game_over_screen = $HUD/GameOverScreen
@onready var explosion_audio = $ExplosionPlayer

# 2. PURE DATA: State variables are trapped inside a functional Node
var current_score = 0
var current_wave = 1
var player_health = 100
var is_game_over = false

func _ready():
    # 3. GLOBAL DEPENDENCY: Relying Autoload for all communication
    Events.enemy_died.connect(_on_enemy_died)
    Events.player_hit.connect(_on_player_hit)
    update_ui()

func _on_enemy_died(point_value):
    if is_game_over:
        return

    # DOMAIN LOGIC: Mutating the game math
    current_score += point_value

    if current_score > current_wave * 1000:
        current_wave += 1

    # PRESENTATION: Forcing logic script to handle audio and visuals
    explosion_audio.play()
    update_ui()

func _on_player_hit(amount):
    # DOMAIN LOGIC: Mutating health
    player_health -= amount

    if player_health <= 0:
        is_game_over = true

        # PRESENTATION: Directly manipulating the UI upon death
        game_over_screen.visible = true
        Events.play_music.emit("game_over_theme")
```

```
func update_ui():
    # PRESENTATION:Formatting mixed directly with domain variables
    score_label.text = "SCORE: %d" % current_score
    wave_label.text = "WAVE: %d" % current_wave
```

While the comments highlight the individual issues, walking through the two main methods reveals exactly how deeply tangled these responsibilities have become:

- **Inside** `_on_enemy_died()`: The script starts by acting as the game's core rulebook (**Domain Logic**). It takes a point value, adds it to the score, and calculates if the math crosses a new wave threshold. However, immediately after doing this math, it abruptly shifts jobs to act as an audio controller and a UI renderer (**Presentation Logic**).
  If a designer deletes the `ExplosionPlayer` node from the scene, the `explosion_audio.play()` line will throw a fatal null reference error. Because Godot halts a function's execution the moment it hits an error like this, the script will crash right before it ever reaches the `update_ui()` call. Because the logic is tangled, the game will literally fail to update the player's score on the screen just because a sound effect was missing.
- **Inside** `_on_player_hit()`: This function begins by subtracting damage to calculate the player's health (**Domain Logic**). But when the health drops to zero, the script does not simply update the state and wait for the rest of the game to react. Instead, it reaches directly into the Scene Tree to force a Game Over screen to become visible (**Presentation Logic**), and then blasts a signal out to a global Autoload to change the background music (**Global Communication**).

Because these concerns are completely tangled together, this script is impossible to test or scale. You cannot test if the wave calculation math works without also forcing the engine to load the UI menus and audio players into memory. In the next section, we will begin extracting these pieces into their own dedicated layers.

If we look closer, we can see even more major problems with this approach. Firstly, there are no boundaries. The math (Domain Logic) is executing directly alongside the audio triggers and UI updates (Presentation). If you delete the `$ExplosionPlayer` node in the editor, this entire script crashes, breaking your scoring system.

Also, the data is trapped. The `current_score` and `player_health` variables are locked inside this physical `Node`. To save the game, your save system would have to hunt down this specific node in the active Scene Tree.

Finally, the script relies on global magic. It listens to an `Events` Autoload. This means an enemy dying in a completely different level, or even a test scene, could accidentally trigger the score to go up here.

To fix this, we need to shatter this monolith into our three distinct layers: *Pure Data*, *Domain Logic*, and *Presentation*. But first, we must enforce Static Typing. Before refactoring, we must convert our GDScript to use strict Static Typing:

```
# BAD: Untyped and vague
var score = 0
func add_points(amount):
    score += amount

# GOOD: Statically typed
var score: int = 0
func add_points(amount: int) -> void:
    score += amount
```

When you rip a massive script apart and move functions into entirely different files, it is easy to accidentally pass the wrong data between your newly separated layers. If your code is untyped, Godot will blindly accept these mistakes, and the game will simply crash later at runtime.

By enforcing strict Static Typing before you begin refactoring, you activate the Godot editor's built-in safety net. The moment you wire a new Domain controller to a Presentation script incorrectly, the editor will instantly flag the mistake with a red error line. Static typing clarifies exactly what data is flowing through your systems, preventing you from introducing silent, untraceable bugs while moving code around.

Step two is to extract the *Game State (the Pure Data Layer)*. We should create a pure data script to hold the state of the level. Notice that this extends `RefCounted`. It will not be attached to any object in the Godot editor:

```
class_name LevelState extends RefCounted

var current_score: int = 0
var current_wave: int = 1
var player_health: int = 100
var is_game_over: bool = false
```

This script contains zero logic; there are no functions, no signals, and no math. It is a pure, passive container. By isolating these variables into this lightweight container, you make saving your game easy. Instead of hunting through the Scene Tree to find a UI `Label` that holds the `score`, and then searching for a **Player** Node to find the `health`, your save system only needs to grab this single `LevelState` object and write it to the hard drive.

The third step is to create the *Controller (Domain Logic Layer)*. The controller dictates the rules of the level. It mutates the state but does not handle any visuals. It relies strictly on the `LevelState` provided to it:

```
class_name LevelController extends Node

signal score_changed(new_score: int)
signal game_over

var state: LevelState

func _init(initial_state: LevelState) -> void:
    state = initial_state

func enemy_destroyed(point_value: int) -> void:
    if state.is_game_over:
        return

    state.current_score += point_value
    score_changed.emit(state.current_score)

func player_took_damage(amount: int) -> void:
    state.player_health -= amount
    if state.player_health <= 0:
        state.is_game_over = true
        game_over.emit()
```

The `LevelController` script acts as the active brain of the Domain Logic layer, responsible for enforcing the mathematical rules of the level. When initialized, it receives the `LevelState` Pure Data Object via Dependency Injection and safely mutates its variables whenever key gameplay events occur, such as an enemy dying or the player taking damage.

Crucially, this script never touches the Scene Tree or the UI directly; instead, it strictly performs the underlying calculations and broadcasts signals (`score_changed`, `game_over`) upwards, allowing the Presentation Layer to independently listen and update the graphics without tangling the game's core rules with its visual nodes.

Step four is to create the *Renderer (the Presentation Layer)*. The renderer (our HUD) does not actively listen for signals or monitor the game's state. Instead, it acts as a purely passive helper class. Following our call down architecture, the `GameplayContext` directly calls functions on the HUD, handing it the final data and commanding it to update the screen:

```
class_name HUDManager extends CanvasLayer

@onready var score_label: Label = $MarginContainer/ScoreLabel
@onready var game_over_screen: Control = $GameOverScreen

func update_score_display(new_score: int) -> void:
    score_label.text = "SCORE: %d" % new_score

func show_game_over() -> void:
    game_over_screen.visible = true
```

Compared to our original monolithic script, this refactored Presentation Layer has three critical improvements:

- **No game math**: The `update_score_display()` function accepts a pre-calculated `new_score` integer. It no longer knows or cares how many points an enemy is worth or what the current combo multiplier is.
- **No state checking**: The `show_game_over()` function doesn't check if the player's health has dropped to zero. It blindly trusts the Domain Layer to make that calculation, simply revealing the game-over screen exactly when commanded.
- **No global dependencies**: Notice the complete lack of global Autoload connections (like `Events.enemy_died.connect`). The HUD is no longer tangled in a global web of signals; it sits completely isolated, waiting for a direct command from its parent controller.

The fifth step is to *bind the Services via Dependency Injection*. In our `GameplayContext` (the secure parent node managing the level), we orchestrate these pieces. Instead of relying on a tangled web of Autoloads to find the player's score, we instantiate our data object and explicitly pass it to the scripts that need it. This is a highly stable, macro-level form of Dependency Injection:

```
class_name GameplayContext extends Node

@onready var hud_manager: HUDManager = $HUDManager
var level_controller: LevelController
var level_state: LevelState
```

```
func _ready() -> void:
    # 1. Initialize the Pure Data State (Load from Persistence)
    var saved_data: Dictionary = PersistenceManager.read_save_data()

    level_state = LevelState.new()

    if not saved_data.is_empty():
        print("Loading saved game state...")
        level_state.current_score = saved_data.get("score", 0)
        level_state.current_wave = saved_data.get("wave", 1)
        level_state.player_health = saved_data.get("health", 100)
    else:
        print("Starting a new game...")

    # 2. Inject state into the Domain Logic
    level_controller = LevelController.new(level_state)
    add_child(level_controller)

    # 3. Connect the Logic to the Presentation (Call down, signal up)
    level_controller.score_changed.connect(
        hud_manager.update_score_display
    )

    level_controller.game_over.connect(
        hud_manager.show_game_over
    )
```

This `GameplayContext` script acts as the orchestrator for the level, demonstrating our three-layer architecture in action:

1. **Step 1 (Pure Data)**: We create a brand-new instance of our `LevelState`. This lightweight object holds the memory for the level (`score`, `health`, `wave`) but exists entirely outside the visual Scene Tree.
2. **Step 2 (Dependency Injection)**: We create the `LevelController` and pass the `level_state` directly into its constructor. This is the heart of Dependency Injection. The controller doesn't need to hunt the Scene Tree or ping a global Autoload to find the player's score; it is handed exactly what it needs the moment it is created.
3. **Step 3 (Connecting Presentation)**: Finally, we wire the Domain Layer to the Presentation Layer. This single interaction is the crux of our entire macro-architecture.

Notice that the `LevelController` (the brain) and the `HUDManager` (the skin) never actually know about each other. The Context acts as the invisible glue, securely passing the mathematical output from the logic directly down to the Presentation Layer so the HUD is instantly commanded to draw it.

By refactoring this monolith script into Presentation, Domain, and Persistence layers, our *Void Defenders* code is now loosely coupled and highly secure. Just like we saw when testing the Command Pattern in the previous chapter, we can now write an automated test for the `LevelController` by passing it a fake `LevelState`, without ever needing to load the `HUDManager` or boot up the graphics engine. We have completely separated the math from the visual representation.

To fully appreciate the transformation our codebase has undergone, look at this side-by-side comparison of where we started versus where we are now in *Table 12.1*:

Feature	Problem (God class)	Solution (layered architecture)
Responsibilities	A single script calculates game math, updates UI text, and triggers audio.	Separated completely into Presentation nodes and purely mathematical Domain controllers.
Data storage	Variables like `current_score` are permanently trapped inside logic scripts.	State is isolated into Pure Data Objects (`LevelState`) that can be easily serialized.
Data flow	Scripts rely on global Autoloads to communicate, hiding dependencies.	A parent Context uses Dependency Injection to explicitly hand data only to the scripts that need it.
Testability	Testing requires booting the entire Scene Tree, UI, and graphics engine.	Controllers can be tested headlessly in complete isolation by passing them fake data.
File organization	Files are arbitrarily sorted by type (for example, throwing everything into `/Scripts`).	Files are grouped intelligently by feature (for example, `/Features/LevelManagement/`).

Table 12.1 – Architectural improvements achieved through refactoring

By breaking our God class into these distinct pieces, a purely mathematical `LevelController`, a purely visual **HUDManager**, and a secure `GameplayContext` to glue them together, we have eliminated the structural rot. If a designer changes the UI, the math survives. If a programmer tweaks the scoring formula, the visuals remain intact. This is the ultimate power of Separation of Concerns.

Summary

Over the course of this chapter, we tackled the hidden dangers of rapid prototyping. We identified how tight coupling and God classes eventually cripple a project's scalability. We moved beyond the tactical solutions of previous chapters and completely overhauled our macro-architecture.

By cleanly separating our game into a Presentation Layer and a pure, data-driven Domain Layer (using `RefCounted` objects), we protected our core logic from visual and structural changes in the Scene Tree. We established a secure Context-based architecture, utilizing Dependency Injection to tie our `LevelState`, `LevelController`, and `HUDManager` together without relying on fragile global Autoloads.

When your code is isolated, explicit, and fully encapsulated, your project can scale indefinitely. You are no longer just writing scripts to make ships move; you are architecting a professional, commercial-grade game.

Congratulations on reaching the end of this journey. Building a game from scratch is no small feat, and mastering the architecture required to make that codebase robust, scalable, and professional is a monumental achievement. The patterns and practices you have learned, from decoupling your presentation to injecting your dependencies, are the same principles used by veteran developers to ship successful commercial titles in Godot 4.

As you close this book and open your next project, remember that software architecture is a constantly evolving discipline. Trust the clean habits you have built, do not be afraid to refactor when things get tangled, and most importantly, keep creating. You now possess the blueprint; it is time to go build your masterpiece!

Get this book's PDF copy, code bundle, and more

Scan the QR code (or go to `packtpub.com/unlock`). Search for this book by name, confirm the edition, and then follow the steps on the page.

UNLOCK NOW

Note: Have your invoice handy. Purchases made directly from the Packt website don't require an invoice.

13

Unlock Access to the Code Bundle and the PDF Version

Your copy of this book includes the following exclusive benefits:

Complete Code Bundle

Download the full source code for this book's examples and projects.

DRM-Free PDF Version

Download DRM-free PDF and ePub copies of this book.

7-Day Packt Library Access

Get 7-day unlimited access to 8,000+ books and videos. No credit card required.

Available for first-time Packt+ trial users only.

Next-Gen Reader Access

Read this book on Packt Reader with progress sync, dark mode and note-taking.

Follow this guide to unlock them. The process takes only a few minutes and only needs to be completed once.

Unlock this book's free benefits in three easy steps

Step 1

Have your purchase invoice ready for *step 3*. If you have a physical copy, scan it using your phone and save it as a PDF, JPG, or PNG.

For more help on finding your invoice, visit `https://www.packtpub.com/unlock-benefits/help`.

> **Note**
>
> If you bought this book directly from the Packt website, no invoice is required. After *step 2*, you can access your exclusive content right away.

Step 2

Scan the QR code or go to `packtpub.com/unlock`.

On the page that opens (similar to *Figure 13.1* on desktop), search for this book by name and select the correct edition.

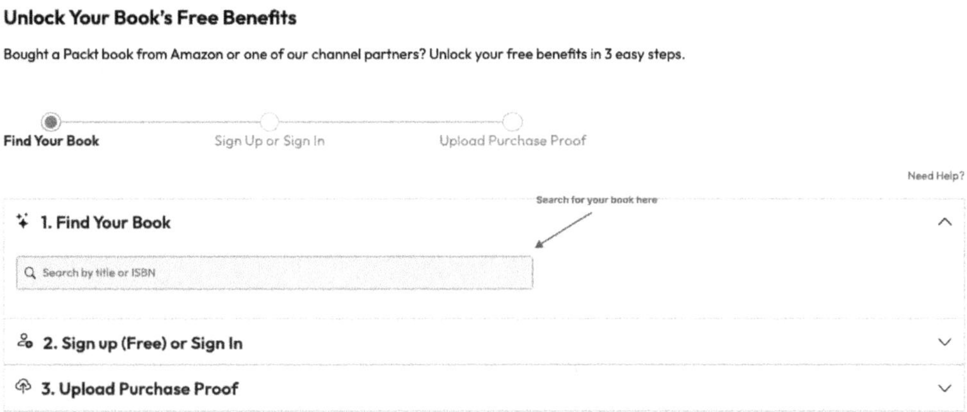

Figure 13.1 – Packt unlock landing page on desktop

Step 3

After selecting the book, sign in to your Packt account or create one for free. Then, upload your invoice (PDF, PNG, or JPG, up to 10 MB). Follow the on-screen instructions to finish the process.

Need help?

If you get stuck and need help, visit `https://www.packtpub.com/unlock-benefits/help` for a detailed FAQ on how to find your invoice and more. This QR code will take you to the help page.

> **Note**
>
> If you are still facing issues, reach out to `customercare@packt.com`.

Other Books You May Enjoy

If you enjoyed this book, you may be interested in these other books by Packt:

Godot 4 for Beginners

Robert Henning

ISBN: 978-1-83620-309-4

- Navigate and master the Godot 4 interface effectively
- Utilize nodes and scenes for structured game development
- Create dynamic 2D and immersive 3D game environments
- Manipulate lighting to enhance game visuals
- Script game mechanics using GDScript
- Implement key elements such as players, enemies, and collectibles
- Design engaging levels and manage game states

Game Development Patterns with Godot 4

Henrique Campos

ISBN: 978-1-83588-029-6

- Create reusable and scalable code that follows SOLID principles
- Identify common game development issues and apply industry-standard solutions
- Understand feature requests and how to turn them into concrete solutions leveraging design patterns
- Analyze game development pathologies to figure out underlying issues
- Architect reliable systems that are understandable, intuitive, and scalable
- Structure professional, collaborative game systems that are easy to maintain

Packt is searching for authors like you

If you're interested in becoming an author for Packt, please visit `authors.packt.com` and apply today. We have worked with thousands of developers and tech professionals, just like you, to help them share their insight with the global tech community. You can make a general application, apply for a specific hot topic that we are recruiting an author for, or submit your own idea.

Share your thoughts

Now that you've finished *Godot 4 Best Practices*, we'd love to hear your thoughts! Scan the QR code below to go straight to the Amazon review page for this book and share your feedback or leave a review on the site that you purchased it from.

https://packt.link/r/1835465110

Your review is important to us and the tech community and will help us make sure we're delivering excellent quality content.

Index

Y

Z

www.ingramcontent.com/pod-product-compliance
Lightning Source LLC
LaVergne TN
LVHW060026210926
848481LV00013B/3792
* 9 7 8 1 8 3 5 4 6 5 1 1 0 *